Implementing Rural Development Projects

Lessons from AID and World Bank Experiences

edited by Elliott R. Morss
and David D. Gow

Westview Press / Boulder and London

A Westview Replica Edition

Copyright © 1985 by Westview Press, Inc.

Published in 1985 in the United States of America by
    Westview Press, Inc.
    5500 Central Avenue
    Boulder, Colorado 80301
    Frederick A. Praeger, Publisher

Library of Congress Catalog Card Number: 83-3555
ISBN: 0-86531-942-1

Printed and bound in the United States of America

10 9 8 7 6 5 4 3 2 1

About the Book and Editors

Implementing Rural Development Projects:
Lessons from AID and World Bank Experiences
edited by Elliott R. Morss and David D. Gow

With the enactment of the "New Directions" legislation of the 1970s, the focus of U.S. foreign aid
shifted from nationwide planning and broad, programmatic
efforts to the implementation of specific assistance
projects. Reflecting the new emphasis in development
strategy, this book analyzes critical problems encountered at the level of project implementation. Each of
the nine chapters offers a synthesis of research findings related to a specific problem, documents the
sources and significance of the problem, and identifies
solutions and future research needs. The book is the
result of a three-year, government-sponsored study
incorporating World Bank and AID project evaluations,
interviews with professional project administrators, and
reports from the authors' own field research.

Elliott R. Morss, formerly director of research
for Development Alternatives, Inc., is coauthor, with
Victoria Morss, of *U.S. Foreign Aid: An Assessment of New and
Traditional Development Strategies* (Westview, 1982), and has
researched and written on a wide range of development
subjects. David D. Gow is currently managing a large
rural development project in North Shaba, Zaire.

Contents

Tables and Figures

Figures

Preface

BACKGROUND

This book deals with problems frequently encountered by agencies, managers, and technicians who try
to implement large-scale development projects.
Specifically, it focuses on the implementation
problems associated with projects sponsored by the
U.S. Agency for International Development (AID) and
the World Bank in developing countries. Some
historical background on how implementation problems
became a focus of concern is presented below.

Development assistance on a significant scale
started with Marshall Plan aid to reconstruct Western
Europe following World War II.[1] In that case, the
donor (the United States) asked not to be part of the
process that determined how the money was to be spent.
Instead, the United States asked the West European
countries to establish their own priorities for
assistance (which they did after a considerable amount
of inter-country negotiation).

In the early 1960s, the United States launched
the first significant foreign aid programs to
developing countries. In this case, it insisted on
more participation in decisions about how the aid
monies were spent, but the recipient countries
retained considerable latitude of choice.

Until that time, development thought had focused
on macro-development models designed to address the
problems of inadequate resources and technical
knowledge; foreign aid's role was to provide these
resources and this knowledge. Since development
assistance was new, little thought had been given to
questions of detail--exactly what was needed and how
it should be provided. As a result, most development
assistance offered through the mid-1960s was of a
general program nature.

Project-specific assistance was initiated in the
mid-1960s and has continued to gain in popularity.

Today, development assistance--which now comes from a
large variety of bilateral and multilateral donors--is
almost entirely of the project type. The switch to
project assistance was significant:

> The development project is a special kind of
> investment. The term connotes purposefulness,
> some minimum size, a specific location, the
> introduction of something qualitatively new, and
> the expectation that a sequence of further
> development moves will be set in motion.[2]

In short, the project era has introduced greater
concern for the details of what development monies are
intended to do and how these goals are to be achieved.
Unlike the earlier days of program support, the
project era has set the stage for detailed evaluative
work. Did the project follow the steps outlined in
the planning documents, and has it achieved its stated
objectives? Many evaluations have now been carried
out, and they all point to a similar conclusion:
regardless of their degree of success, almost all
projects encountered serious problems during implementation.
    This finding says nothing about whether a
project-specific approach is better than the more
general program strategy. There are two reasons for
this. First, donors have only recently started to
spend significant amounts of money on evaluations, and
most of these monies have been spent on examining
projects and not programs. Second, projects, because
of their more specific statement of what is to be done
and how, are easier to evaluate. It is simpler to
analyze a problem that arises in attempting to achieve
a specific objective with a specific approach than it
is to identify implementation problems associated with
more general program assistance.
    This current emphasis on the problems of project
implementation may be exaggerated: many of the
so-called problems may really be the unavoidable
results of unreasonably ambitious project designs.
Whatever the reality, concern about the difficulties
of implementation now overshadows the debate on the
choice among development strategies that characterized
the 1950s, 1960s, and 1970s.[3] This book responds to
the growing awareness that smooth and successful
implementation cannot be taken for granted and that it
is the exception, rather than the rule, in large-scale
projects. But the book's purpose is not to provide a
catalogue of failures; the analysis aims at resolving
--or when feasible, avoiding--the most critical and
common problems.

GENESIS OF THIS STUDY

In 1978, the Development Support Bureau[4] of AID
contracted with Development Alternatives, Inc.
(DAI)[5] to study problems related to the organization
and administration of integrated rural development
projects and to provide assistance to field missions
in dealing with these problems. Subsequently, 24
projects in 19 countries of Africa, Asia, Latin
America, the Caribbean, and the Near East received
field assistance under this contract. The reports
produced for each field visit and the working papers
written under this contract provided much of the
information base for this study.

The essays in this book, however, expand on the
mandate provided in the contract. The authors
concluded that:

- The problems regularly encountered in field
  work usually went far beyond those that could
  be classified as organizational and administrative; and

- The problems that were encountered applied not
  just to integrated rural development projects,
  but more broadly to all large-scale
  development projects.

Although no attempt was made to document these
statements rigorously, the accumulation of evidence
confirming them led to the development of a distinct
research track to identify and study the most
pervasive implementation problems.[6]

RESEARCH METHODOLOGY

At the outset, the authors decided to identify
and focus on those problems that most seriously
impeded progress in large-scale development projects.
Early discussions made it clear that the problems were
interrelated and that there was no satisfactory documentation to rank them in terms of their seriousness
or their incidence. Nonetheless, it was concluded
that the study would be most valuable if it treated a
limited number of these problems in considerable
detail.

In the first phase of the research, the authors
reviewed the literature, undertook the field work
called for in the contract, talked with major donor
agencies and firms that provide technicians and other
forms of support to projects in developing countries,
and debated the composition of the problem agenda.
This ultimately led to the selection of nine problem

areas, which were intensively studied. Each problem area is discussed in a separate chapter. These are not the only serious difficulties faced by large-scale development projects, nor do they affect all projects equally. However, the authors encountered them frequently and have found that they consistently impede the progress of implementation.

ESSAY STRUCTURE

Each essay follows a four-part outline:

- Problem definition;

- Problem manifestation;

- Reasons for problem; and

- Alleviation of problem.

These problems have received varying amounts of attention. Thus, one essay may be devoted to defining and documenting the existence of a problem, whereas another may focus on what can be done to alleviate it. The emphasis depends on the current state of the art with regard to the examination of that issue.

No checklists or handbook-like instructions appear in the essays. This is because these problems are complex, requiring solutions specific to the settings in which they are encountered. The authors believe that a book of essays can be most useful by providing development practitioners with ideas on how to anticipate and understand the reasons for the problems they are likely to encounter. Practitioners themselves are in the best position to develop appropriate remedies.

THE PROBLEMS

Chapters 1, 2, and 3 deal with broad constraints to project success that are encountered in developing countries. Chapter 1 focuses on macroeconomic and political policies that impede development, such as low prices paid to farmers for their produce. Chapter 2 examines institutional inadequacies--from poor management to destructive bureaucratic dynamics. Chapter 3 looks at a wide range of human resource problems, ranging from shortages of skilled personnel to the reluctance of available staff to spend much time in rural areas.

Chapters 4 through 7 deal with more narrow problems that plague large-scale development projects. Chapter 4 discusses the frequently observed failure of projects to make effective use of foreign technicians.

Chapter 5 deals with difficulties in implementing two concepts consistently correlated with project success: decentralization and participation. Although much has been written about these topics, this chapter focuses on an aspect that has received little attention: the importance of coordination efforts. Chapter 6, in contrast, highlights the importance of timing issues--a set of problems that has been largely overlooked in the literature on development.

In the 1970s, monitoring and evaluation systems were seen as at least a partial answer to the difficulties of implementing development projects. Chapter 7 looks at why these information systems have not lived up to expectations and makes recommendations for the future.

Chapter 8, which deals with the differing agendas of all the important actors in development projects, reflects problems discussed in the preceding chapters. The existence of these differing agendas is at least a partial explanation of why these problems occur.

The final chapter, Chapter 9, is devoted to the most fundamental problem of all donor-supported projects--sustainability: the likelihood that when outside aid terminates, project benefits will cease. This frequently occurs as a result of one or more of the implementation problems discussed above.

NOTES

1. For a detailed discussion of the history of foreign assistance, see Elliott R. Morss and Victoria A. Morss, U.S. Foreign Aid: An Assessment of New and Traditional Strategies (Boulder, Colo.: Westview Press, 1982).

2. Albert O. Hirschman, Development Projects Observed (Washington, D.C.: Brookings Institution, 1967).

3. For examples, see Judith Tendler, Inside Foreign AID (Baltimore, Md.: Johns Hopkins Press, 1975); Marcus D. Ingle, "Implementing Development Programs: A State-of-the-Art Review" (Paper prepared for the Office of Rural Development and Development Administration, Development Support Bureau, Agency for International Development, Washington, D.C., March 1979); William J. Siffin, "Administrative Problems and Integrated Rural Development," (A PASITAM Design Study, Bloomington, Ind., 1979); Merilee S. Grindle, ed., Politics and Policy Implementation in the Third World (Princeton, N.J.: Princeton University Press, 1980); Coralie Bryant and Louise G. White, Managing Development in the Third World (Boulder, Colo.: Westview Press, 1982); Jon R. Moris, Managing Induced Rural Development (Bloomington, Ind., Indiana

University, International Development Institute,
1981); Goran Hyden, <u>No Shortcuts to Progress: African
Development Management in Perspective</u> (Berkeley:
University of California Press, 1983); and Victoria A.
Morss, "The Special Problems of Projects with
Significant Implementation Problems: An Examination
of Evaluation Findings and Lessons" (Washington, D.C.:
Office of Evaluation, Bureau for Program and Policy
Coordination, Agency for International Development,
April 1982).

    4. Now the Science and Technology Bureau.

    5. The Research Triangle Institute (RTI) provided
services under a subcontract to DAI.

    6. The rationale for this track and the research
strategy to be followed are set forth in Elliott R.
Morss and David D. Gow, <u>Integrated Rural Development:
Nine Critical Implementation Problems</u>, IRD Research
Note no. 1 (Washington, D.C.: Development
Alternatives, Inc., 1981).

Elliott R. Morss
David D. Gow

1
Coping with Political, Economic, Environmental, and Institutional Constraints

Jerry Van Sant and Paul R. Crawford

INTRODUCTION

Experienced project managers are usually aware of their own limitations, and most have a reasonable understanding of the constraints that impede their implementation efforts. Correctly, they classify certain constraints as environmental because these constraints reflect pre-existing conditions in which the project must operate but which are not susceptible to direct management control. The constraints on any given project include a mix of national political and economic policies, adverse conditions affecting the area and population served by the project, and institutional weaknesses and rivalries.

Although these constraints may be largely beyond the control of project managers, recognizing them and developing strategies to deal with them are appropriate management tasks. Unfortunately, these constraints tend to be inadequately addressed in both the design and implementation of projects. The results are inappropriate strategies and severe implementation problems:

- The objectives of a development project may be at odds with prevailing political priorities. Assisting the rural poor is probably one of a number of competing government priorities. The low priority accorded rural development in routine decisions may lead to neglible administrative support for, and poor coordination of, project activities.

- Sometimes governments address economic problems such as balance of payments deficits, unemployment, and high inflation in ways that adversely affect the implementation of development projects. For example, domestic price

1

ceilings imposed to improve exports may lower
incentives for farmers to adopt agricultural
innovations, or restrictive monetary policies
may limit the access of small-scale farmers to
credit.

● Factors in the immediate project environment
such as polarization within the community,
past unfavorable experience with government
services, seasonal labor patterns, and ecology
of the project area may lead to unexpected
responses to project initiatives.

● Institutional factors such as roles of local
elites, incentives for civil servants in
important support roles, and decision-making
patterns in the project management structure
may significantly influence the degree to
which project managers are able to achieve
performance targets.

Dealing with these constraints is an important
and necessary step in project implementation. For
various reasons, however, managers and staff in many
development projects adopt a fatalistic approach: they
carry on with those functional activities that they
can control and avoid the environmental factors, even
when these factors pose a serious threat to the
project's success.

The thesis of this chapter, and others in this
book, is that simply accepting these problems with
resignation is unacceptable. Although they appear in
a wide variety of forms, the problems are generic to
the process of rural development and have caused many
projects to suffer precisely because they have not
been addressed. Thus, the argument begins by
examining the nature and causes of the environmental
constraints that typically arise in complex development projects and then describes techniques that may
be used to alleviate them.

DEFINING THE PROBLEMS

There are four categories of problems that
project designers and implementers should address:
national politics, macroeconomic policies, the local
environment, and institutional factors. Each category
is discussed below.

National Politics

The pursuit of broad political objectives can
easily override efforts to initiate development.
Typically, government priorities include:

- Achieving self-sufficiency in the production of critical goods such as food, agricultural inputs, and certain consumer items;

- Maintaining low food prices in urban areas to limit discontent and reduce the attractiveness of imported foodstuffs;

- Pursuing international goals, such as increased national stature; and

- Winning or maintaining the support of certain ethnic or political groups within the country.

The contradictions between these political priorities and development goals have been manifested in many ways. For example, the Government of Mali's drive to achieve self-sufficiency in basic food grains and agricultural inputs had an adverse impact on Operation Mils Mopti, a project aimed primarily at increasing millet and sorghum production. To maintain low domestic food prices for urban consumers--a political imperative--the government set the official prices of these grains at only 60-70 percent of production costs.

In response, a parallel market for food crops developed and thrived, involving substantial illegal exports to neighboring Sahelian countries where prices were as much as 100 percent higher. However, it was chiefly the large-scale farmers who were able to export their grain and profit from this opportunity. Small-scale farmers continued to sell most of their surplus to the Malian government at low prices to meet production quotas imposed upon them.[1]

Sources of Pressure. In general, political pressure to keep food prices low comes from two sources: urban workers, and employers who, when their workers are faced with rising food costs, are forced to pay higher wages. Since governments themselves are major employers, and frequently sponsors of industry as well, they tend to side with urban consumers, workers, and industry in seeking ways to restrain price increases for basic foodstuffs.[2]

The principal exception occurs when an elite group engages in the production of a particular food item. In these cases, usually involving export crops, the government is unlikely to depress prices.[3] This favoritism, of course, rarely benefits the rural poor, who are usually on the short side of discriminatory policies.

The basis for discrimination is not always urban-rural. It may reflect the political domination of one ethnic or cultural group in a society. Groups in remote geographic areas with atypical ecological features may miss the benefits of government services oriented toward the majority. In Indonesia, for example, dryland areas such as Timor and Madura receive little attention in national agricultural research and extension programs, which are oriented toward rice-producing irrigated areas.

These problems are compounded by the risk that resources allocated to achieve program goals will be reallocated to serve pressing political purposes:

> Although individual officials may have the best of intentions, political realities may dictate that redistributive policies are implemented effectively only when they do not threaten interests whose support is essential to the regime. It is, moreover, unlikely that many redistributive policies would meet this criterion.[4]

Conflicting Objectives. Political influences are often subtle. High-level government support for a donor-assisted project may mask the real objective--increasing to a maximum degree foreign exchange inflows to the economy. A related problem may arise in projects working through the decentralized management of a ministry or national planning body. National support for decentralization may reflect a genuine belief that local decision making is responsive to beneficiary interests. Or, paradoxically, decentralization may be spurred by a desire to increase central political control. Since decentralized authority is rarely accompanied by real local control over resources, decentralized projects can be used to augment a centrally directed bureaucratic presence at the grassroots. At the opposite extreme, decentralization in a context of fragmented political power may increase political conflict and paralyze implementation.[5]

Political support can cause other problems if it is expressed as pressure for quick results. Governments may press for rapid, expensive service delivery systems that cannot be sustained with local resources. This happened in Jamaica, where the Second Integrated Rural Development Project (IRDP II) employed a soil conservation technology whose costs were out of proportion to its total budget. Only 4,000 farm families lived in the area, and total project expenditures (including cash subsidies to attract farmer participation) averaged $6,500 per family. To replicate this technology for all of Jamaica's estimated 150,000 farm

families working in similar hillside conditions would
have cost more than $900 million.[6]
    Strong, visible political support for development
projects may undermine project implementation through:

- Articulation of multiple or ambiguous goals;

- Emphasis on short-run, measurable results;

- Inhibition of normal processes of feedback and
  learning;

- Pressure to spend money without critical self-
  examination; and

- Insulation of projects from external
  criticism.[7]

    IRDP II in Jamaica illustrates the additional
hazard posed when a change in government transforms
political visibility into a liability, especially in a
politically charged atmosphere. After the change of
government in late 1980, several key staff, including
the director, were transferred from the project, while
many new, superfluous junior staff were added to the
rolls.[8] This sort of political tampering causes
disruption, insecurity, and reduced morale. The
project is usually the victim.

Macroeconomic Policies

    Developing countries have historically been faced
with serious economic problems. Resource constraints,
coupled with fluctuating terms of trade, have led to
balance-of-payments problems, exacerbated by policies
that maintain officially overvalued exchange rates.
Resource constraints have also slowed domestic
economic activity, resulting in unemployment, inflation, and an excess of demand over supply. Often
governments choose, or are forced, to address these
problems in ways that adversely affect the implementation of development programs.[9]
    Macroeconomic policies can affect development
projects in many ways, for example:

- Domestic price ceilings imposed to promote
  exports may kill the incentive for farmers to
  adopt agricultural innovations;

- Import tariffs or quotas, designed to foster
  domestic production of fertilizers, chemicals,
  and farm implements, may increase production
  costs and lower incentives to produce;

- Restrictive monetary policies may limit the access of small farmers to credit; and

- Tight budget restrictions may reduce the government's ability to assume critical recurrent costs.

Pricing Policies. The price ceilings imposed by governments for political reasons may have a variety of economic consequences that work against the rural sector:

- Agricultural production and investment may be curtailed;

- Food imports may be increased;

- Black market trade, both domestic and foreign, may be encouraged; and

- Patterns of urban modernization and rural stagnation may be extended, thereby accelerating the rate of migration to urban areas.[10]

However, price floors are sometimes imposed to insulate the farmer from short-term market fluctuations and to provide an incentive to increase agricultural output or adopt new production practices. Although guaranteed prices can play a positive role, they must be well planned and administered, and coordinated with other subsidies; if they are not, they create additional problems. For example:

Ad hoc price policies which are often adopted by specific projects or programs as a reaction to unanticipated crises are usually dysfunctional, causing, among other problems, considerable income discrepancies among food and non-food crop producers, even within program areas.[11]

Inconsistencies between national pricing policy and project-specific pricing arrangements also tend to limit the adoption of new technologies and divert scarce administrative resources into dealing with the problems of marketing agricultural surpluses.

Import-Export Policies. Policies intended to promote exports or restrict imports, although possibly beneficial to the manufacturing sector, can worsen the terms of trade for subsistence farmers. At the least, the demands of international trade may focus disproportionate attention on progressive farmers who

produce cash crops for export, at the expense of those
who produce staples for home consumption.[12]

In Sudan, the deteriorating balance of payments
has led the government, with the encouragement of
international donors, to concentrate its human and
financial resources on the export-oriented agricultural sector, particularly irrigated cotton production. This has decreased the resources available for
small-scale farmer development projects in the
country's rainfed areas.

In Mali, an attempt to boost production under
Operation Mils Mopti was seriously hampered by the
government's ban on the import of a light plow.
Although light plows had been imported and were in
great demand among farmers in the Mopti region, the
government agency with control of agricultural inputs
tried vainly to substitute a heavier model. As a
result, farmers did not gain access to a known
technology that would have helped achieve the
project's main objective.[13]

Sometimes import restrictions emerge from other
economic circumstances and limit the availability of
necessary inputs. For example, the North Shaba Rural
Development Project in Zaire was seriously affected by
the country's deteriorating macroeconomic situation.
The economic decline increased budgetary and balance-
of-payments deficits and fueled inflation. Zaire's
volume of imports between 1974 and 1978 declined 50
percent. As a result, critical shortages of fuel and
cement hindered the project's construction and
transportation activities. The difficulty in
obtaining trucks, spare parts, fuel, and sacks also
adversely affected the project's maize-marketing
effort.[14]

    <u>Economic Incentives</u>. Typical incentives that
economic policy makers use include direct subsidies,
preferential foreign exchange rates, subsidized
credit, foreign aid, and marketing inputs. Although
sometimes clearly warranted to encourage the adoption
of new farming methods, these incentives must be
coordinated with other macroeconomic policies or they
may cause unwelcome imbalances. The combination of
direct subsidies, overvalued domestic currencies, and
foreign assistance, for example, can cause the
domestic price of inputs--labor, credit, capital,
fertilizer, seed, and foreign aid--to fall below their
real market value, encouraging farmers to use an input
package that is not sustainable in the long run.[15]
These policies may also hurt domestic small-scale
enterprise.

In Bolivia, a national policy of subsidized
interest rates has principally benefited large-scale
farmers and limited the supply of capital for

small-scale farmer credit programs. Subsidies for
agricultural equipment purchases have led to the use
of capital-intensive techniques that decrease
employment of the poor. In this case, as in most
cases of economic policy making, incentives to help
one group may produce severe problems for another,
often the rural poor.

The Local Project Environment

Physical and sociocultural factors in the project
environment affect the use of goods and services by
the local population and the capacity of communities
to generate organized responses to perceived problems
and opportunities. Thus:

- Historical factors, including ethnic origins,
  patterns of collective action and past
  experience with development efforts, may
  influence reactions to new development ideas.

- Demographic factors, such as seasonal employment and migration patterns, may affect the
  willingness of local people to contribute
  labor to project activities.

- Sociocultural factors, such as religion,
  language, sex roles, kinship networks, and
  communication patterns may affect how well
  administrative behavior follows the cooperative patterns that are required in complex
  development efforts.[16]

- The physical environment of the project area
  may place severe constraints on the
  feasibility of a particular development
  scheme.

The performance of extension services, for
example, is likely to be strongly influenced by the
local setting in which they have to operate:

When a village (or county) is divided by class,
religion, caste, linguistic, or factional cleavages, exchange of farming information between
groups is very limited. Formal extension
programs could have a major impact in such a
situation but, in practice, such a village is
likely to receive less extension contact because
the internal cleavages create a situation in
which extension agents find it less comfortable
to work.[17]

A different problem results when the local socio-political structure is so strongly cohesive that few people will deviate from the norm and try something new. An innovator may risk becoming socially isolated, and even be accused of witchcraft.[18]

The Abyei Development Project in Sudan illustrates the combined impact of several of these factors. This project was initiated in a remote area on Sudan's north-south boundary, one year after violent clashes took place between two ethnic groups, the Messirya Humr, Arabic-speaking pastoralists, and the less politically advantaged Ngok Dinka, a Nilotic group whose economy combines settled agriculture and pastoralism. Although the violence declined between 1977 and mid-1978, it increased later with the southward advance of the Messirya in search of pasture and water. The conflict was aggravated by strong political differences about Abyei's future political status, specifically, the proposed transfer of Ngok Dinka territory from the northern region of Kordofan to the then Southern Region. This conflict placed three major constraints on the project:

- Staff mobility and commitment to extension activities were restricted. Ngok Dinka staff were generally unwilling to travel in areas where the Messirya were present;

- Settlement patterns were disrupted, which impeded access to the project beneficiaries; and

- Delivery of services, such as water and grain storage facilities at sites where both groups claimed traditional rights, became a potential source of conflict.[19]

Constraints of Location. Implementation of the Abyei project was also hindered by its physical location, remote even by Sudanese standards. The region is virtually inaccessible during the rainy season, which lasts from mid-May to mid-November. Even during the dry season, transportation by air is erratic and travel from the capital by land takes days. An evaluation of the project noted the effects of its geographic isolation, stating that "delays or failure in project outputs can be attributed to delay in the delivery of health supplies, construction materials, tools and hardware, agricultural implements, and staff with technical expertise."[20]

This is not an unusual problem. Development projects, because they often are a means of reaching disadvantaged groups, are increasingly targeted on remote areas. In these places, development strategies run a high risk of failure--a risk that is compounded when crucial environmental features are either unwittingly or deliberately ignored.

A different problem can occur when projects are situated in marginal ecological zones, where expectations may be unrealistic or even inappropriate. The proposed Mandara Area Development Project in northern Cameroon, for example, was to improve the social and economic welfare of a poor, remote mountain region.

Initially, AID and the government of Cameroon hoped to transform the subsistence economy of this area, which is characterized by shallow soils, a short but intense rainy season, rugged terrain, and high erosion. Mandara farmers had developed a sophisticated system of terracing, and their production practices reflected an ecologically successful adaptation to difficult conditions. A series of base-line studies, commissioned as part of the project design process, identified no opportunities for major innovation in this system; instead, the studies suggested the need for a less glamorous (but still essential) program emphasizing natural resource conservation and human resource development. AID concluded that the chances of dramatically increasing economic welfare in the area were slight, and declined to fund the alternative version of the project.[21]

Manmade Constraints. Many of the environmental constraints on agricultural productivity are not subject to human control, including those imposed by rainfall, temperature, availability of water, length of growing season, and type of soil. However, some limitations are manmade--such as soil exhaustion and erosion. Because these are often a direct result of increasing population, the ratio of people to land is important. There is mounting evidence that the immediate impact of improved health, education, and nutrition is to increase the rate of population growth. Thus, the productive results of some development efforts exacerbate a problem that constrains others.[22]

Seasonal Factors. Seasonality is a particular dimension of rural life that development managers often ignore, with serious consequences. This is a matter not only of climate; it also concerns economics, culture, and psychology. Since most visits by outsiders to project areas take place when access is relatively easy, a bias toward the dry season often produces distortions in project planning and management. It is in the dry season, when disease diminishes, the harvest is in, stocks of food are adequate, body weights rise, ceremonies take place,

and people are least deprived, that rural people
become most visible. In contrast, in the season of
greatest deprivation, the rural poor remain largely
unseen.[23] Even when efforts are made to observe
rural life in the wet season, disciplinary
specialization (usually agricultural) makes it
unlikely that detailed analysis of the project area
will be carried out in the village or at the family
level.[24]

An example of a long-established relationship
between religion and seasonality occurs in parts of
Bali, where rice planting is keyed to a cycle of
temple ceremonies that differs by village. One
outcome is the sequential use of irrigation water from
a common source; while some fields are flooded for
planting, others are drained for harvest. Occasional
attempts by outside experts to rationalize the process
have run afoul of the power of religion in Balinese
life and the rational system of water sharing the
temple cycles have fostered. It is encouraging to
realize that cultural constraints may bring bad development schemes to grief just as easily as good ones.

Institutional Factors

The institutional context in which development
activities take place, whether by local or outside
initiative, is a major determinant of project success.
Variations in institutional capability are a frequent
cause of failure when attempts are made to replicate
successful pilot projects. A design appropriate in
one context may not work elsewhere, even if the
technical package is sound.

Institutional factors of greatest importance
include:

- Administrative capacity, especially local
  organizational competence to support decentralized projects;

- Selection of agencies responsible for project
  management and oversight;

- Access to resources by jurisdictions or
  agencies responsible for development; and

- Structures that support effective information
  flow, horizontally between line and technical
  agencies, and vertically between beneficiaries, local government, and higher jurisdictions.

The Provincial Area Development Program (PDP) in Indonesia illustrates the importance of administrative capacity. Credit is a major element in many of the subprojects funded by PDP. Where existing credit structures are relatively strong, such as in the provinces of Central and East Java, the PDP strategy of extending credit access to small local traders has had a beneficial impact. Although the existing credit system in the two provinces differed, in each case the credit facilities were made more accessible, the process of loan application was simplified, and the supervision of outstanding loans was strengthened.

Credit is also a major component of the PDP strategy in Bengkulu; it represented over 60 percent of the total PDP budget for that province in fiscal year 1981. In this case, however, virtually no credit infrastructure existed before PDP, and the new system did not take hold. As a result, credit delays seriously affected the plans of technical agencies responsible for individual subprojects. This was particularly true for agricultural initiatives where seasonal factors are of great importance and even short delays can cost a whole cropping cycle. Also, government staff often began work with local people in an atmosphere in which trust was lacking: credit delays and failed expectations reinforced that wariness. In view of this, the heavy concentration of credit programs in the Bengkulu PDP may be considered an unnecessary risk in a program that requires a relatively sophisticated and mature organizational base.[25]

In Jamaica, administrative constraints led to a number of problems for IRDP II, including delays in filling staff positions and slow release of funds from the Ministry of Agriculture. Project plans, such as the purchase of steep hillside land for conversion to forest to prevent erosion, were significantly delayed. On paper, IRDP II commanded the resources necessary to achieve its objectives; in reality, however, the project was seriously handicapped by its bureaucratic environment. The government agencies on which it depended for critical support operated on a business-as-usual basis, with no particular concern for project goals or deadlines.[26]

Dependence on funding allocations and disbursements by central government authorities is a chronic source of difficulty for development projects. The timely release of funds and the availability of the full amount committed to a project in the government's budgeting process are the exception, not the rule. When delays and shortfalls occur during project implementation, the results can be highly disruptive. In the North Shaba project, for example, funding cuts in the government of Zaire's budget in late 1979 caused the layoff of more than 400 project employees, drastically reduced expenditures for fuel and vehicle maintenance, and eliminated overnight allowances for supervisory staff. As a result, all project activities suffered in the 1979-1980 agricultural season.[27]

These examples are typical of centrally designed programs that often do not adapt well to local institutional realities. The consequences are reduced incentives for local involvement and greater reliance on central authority, thus compounding problems of misunderstanding and mistrust. Even when development projects are locally managed, they still depend on support services provided by institutions outside the project area--institutions that provide information, credit, technical inputs, and marketing and transport services.[28]

REASONS FOR THE PROBLEMS

The problems described above exemplify the ways in which contextual factors, often beyond direct managment control, may affect the success of development projects. Their impact is greatest, of course, when failure to recognize them leads to inappropriate strategies and a lack of attention to possible compensating forces.

Project designers and implementers generally fail to address these constraints because:

- They do not understand or they fail to take seriously the importance of factors that are beyond their direct control;

- They operate on the assumption that certain constraints must be accepted, regardless of how seriously these may reduce the chance of project success;

- They are bound by rigid project designs that do not provide for later adjustment to external realities;

- They are reluctant to interfere with host government policies for fear of being accused of political meddling; and

- They are driven by political imperatives to ignore potential constraints.

These problems can be grouped into two categories: failure to anticipate and failure to act. These failures are discussed below.

Failure to Anticipate

As a result of political considerations and short budget cycles, there frequently is pressure to implement development projects quickly. Design work and even so-called feasibility studies are often performed within boundaries defined by earlier decisions to proceed with a particular project in a particular area. With their field of inquiry thus limited, project designers often fail to observe potential constraints in the project environment. This problem is sometimes compounded by the preference for use of technical specialists whose very choice for design or feasibility work implies preselection of certain disciplines as relevant. In the process, this preselection may widen gaps in understanding of unexpected constraints.

Clearly, donor investment in expensive cost-benefit studies and social impact analyses has not solved the problem. In fact, it has been argued that "there is no project which cannot be justified. Much depends on who wants the project, who is going to finance it, and who has been hired to appraise it."[29]

A review of projects in Sudan, Kenya, and Tanzania found that many proceeded without an intensive analysis of the planning and administrative functions that needed to be delegated or of the capacity of lower levels to absorb new functions. Moreover, little consideration was given to the significance of changing capabilities over time.[30] Failure to anticipate these institutional factors renders difficult the implementation of technical strategies, however sound they may be.

In IRDP II in Jamaica, two noncontiguous watersheds were selected for a project originally designed for one. Evidently social aspects (number of poor families), conservation needs (severity of soil erosion), and political considerations took precedence over the original intent to create a model for replication elsewhere. The selection of two watersheds could be rationalized as an attempt to compare different implementation approaches, but no such intent was evident in the project design. In fact, this selection became a permanent constraint to the development and testing of a model that could reasonably be replicated:

● Management and technical staff based at head-quarters could not adequately support the distant watershed program because of the three-hour round-trip drive involved.

- Substantial project funds were used to provide vehicles, drivers, maintenance staff, and facilities just to serve the distant watershed.

- Rising gasoline costs resulted in steady budgetary pressure to reduce the services provided.[31]

Project design documents yield no evidence that these problems of physical distance were anticipated or compensated for in the project strategy. The designers made an even more serious error in following a development strategy that had been tried twice in the area without notable success. The concept of paying subsidies to farmers for their participation in soil conservation schemes had been the basis of earlier programs that failed on two counts: they did not encourage farmers to maintain the subsidized soil conservation works, and they did little to increase production and income on the hill farms. Yet experiences of these earlier programs were not analyzed in the IRDP II documents.

In another case, the project paper for Thaba Bosiu, a large agricultural project in Lesotho, did not mention the employment of project beneficiaries in South African mines, nor did it evaluate the importance of this critical factor to the viability of the project.[32] As it turned out, the opportunity to work in South African mines reduced the agricultural labor force in Lesotho below the anticipated level. Extension information had to be timed and packaged to get to the mine workers, who usually made the families' agricultural production decisions, even though they were absent most of the year.

The constraints cited in these examples are neither unique nor necessarily intractable. They became problems because they were not anticipated in the design phase, greatly increasing their detrimental impact. Nonetheless, unanticipated constraints continue to plague most development projects.

Failure to Act

Recognizing possible constraints in the environment is not enough. Appropriate action must be taken to cope with them. In broad terms, there are three options:

- Accept the constraints, and design the project to avoid them. For example, designers can use a project management unit to avoid control-oriented government bureaucracies that are unsympathetic to the target group, select project sites where accessibility is not a serious problem, and concentrate on areas in which resource distribution or other local socioeconomic issues are not major barriers.

- Recognize the constraints and attempt to change them. For example, political or economic leverage may be applied to cause a change in government policies that are seen as counterproductive, or special training programs can be used to alleviate institutional deficiencies.

- Determine that the recognized constraints are not amenable to change, and decide to abandon the proposed project.

Choosing among these options is difficult. In fact, the choice is most often forced by circumstances after problems emerge. Rarely do project designs reflect a conscious, rational selection of strategies to respond to constraints, even when they are recognized in advance. Most often, implementers are left to cope with crippling constraints that emerge after the project is well under way. Their ability to cope with these constraints is increased if the design is flexible. But even if the design encourages adaptation to newly understood circumstances, it may be too late. For politically popular projects, the increased visibility of the implementing agency may cause it to ignore adverse signals.

The option of attempting to change recognized constraints is rarely chosen. Some constraints—particularly those in the local project environment—cannot or should not be interfered with. Physical factors, such as weather, do not lend themselves to manipulation. Sociocultural or other behavioral factors must be dealt with cautiously, especially by outsiders. Although most development projects seek to elicit some sort of behavioral response from beneficiaries, there usually is reluctance to interfere with traditional norms.

Policy constraints are generally left alone for political reasons, or are beyond the influence of project designers and implementers. Leverage, of course, varies among donors. Multinational agencies such as the World Bank and the International Monetary Fund have exercised considerable influence over the

policies of some developing countries. Bilateral
influence on policy, however, generally has been less
significant and is declining. A Department of State
cable to AID/Indonesia addressed this issue:

> Because of the relatively small size of the U.S.
> assistance program, there is no expectation of
> using the program for major policy leverage.
> There [is], however, concern that GOI
> macroeconomic policies could have significant
> implications on the relative success or failure
> of various U.S. projects.[33]

Even when policy leverage is slight, information
may be gathered to document the deleterious impact of
policies on project performance. Although this is a
time-consuming process that may be overshadowed by
short-term implementation imperatives, it can still
benefit future activities.

The third option--abandoning the project--is even
more rarely chosen. The decision to proceed is often
made before the design team is in the field. If not,
the design team itself may have a vested interest in
later implementation, however serious the recognized
constraints may be. All too often, the result is a
project doomed to fail before it begins.

Failure to address environmental constraints
during implementation is generally the result of a
project design that either is too rigid or is
perceived to be so. In IRDP II in Jamaica, project
management recognized the design flaws, but was
reluctant to change a clearly inappropriate strategy
for fear of alienating donor support for this high-
cost project, which was dependent on external
resources.

Another example of a failure to act is reported
from the Sahel, where control of resources by elite
groups is "interfering with the execution of
development projects and indeed threatens to turn many
of them into environmental hazards."[34] In Gao,
Mali, for example, unequal access to land and the
existence of commercial networks for grains indicate
the potential development of a landed, commercial
elite, encouraged, in part, by AID-financed cereal
production projects. AID's response to this situation
could be characterized as benign neglect:

> A project officer in Mali stated: 'We don't get
> involved in the land problem: that is purely the
> business of the governor and his staff. This
> project is strictly technical.'[35]

Through failure to anticipate or to act, many development projects are severely constrained by external factors that are addressed ineffectively or not at all.

ALLEVIATING THE PROBLEMS

Although these problems are complex, they are not totally intractable. Possible solutions for coping with these political, economic, environmental, and institutional constraints may be grouped under three headings:

- Anticipating design requirements;

- Acting on design requirements; and

- Adjusting implementation strategy.

Each is discussed in detail below.

Anticipating Design Requirements

Thus, effective development planning requires an awareness of the policy environment combined with a sensitive and detailed knowledge of local conditions, practices, and needs. Indigenous social and economic arrangements survive because they perform necessary traditional functions and satisfy local needs.

An understanding of how farmers perceive project risks, therefore, is part of assessing local needs and providing the target group with the opportunity to participate in the process of addressing those needs. Behavior and attitudes that seem irrational to project planners may be quite rational from the farmers' perspective. Local perceptions are an essential element in development planning.[36]

One study has suggested three categories of local data essential for projects targeted at small-scale farmers; similar requirements would apply to projects for other groups. These categories are:[37]

- Data to understand and overcome the constraints imposed on farmers by the local environment;

- Data to ensure that project components are adequate or to determine alternative ways of providing the needed services and knowledge; and

- Data to determine project focus and organizational capabilities within an area so that
  farmers receive the benefits of project
  activities.

Collection and analysis of good micro-level data
should also be complemented by a fourth category,
comprising the macroeconomic policies and conditions
affecting development potential in the project area.
This point is underscored by experience with a number
of recent projects--the Arusha Planning and Village
Development Project in Tanzania, for example--in which
macro-level factors were underestimated at the project
design stage.[38]

Sophisticated feasibility studies or area
profiles, usually developed by foreign specialists at
considerable cost, do not anticipate design requirements. The constraints that can upset project plans
are unpredictable and dynamic. Traditionally, project
design teams have banked too heavily on academic
specialists who are limited by static, predetermined
categories of inquiry. What is needed is a broader
view, with greater weight placed on implementation
experience and local knowledge. In particular, the
design process should emphasize the use of key local
informants and the participation of beneficiaries.
Outsiders can provide needed technical skills, but
those skills must be applied with a knowledge of the
local setting.

Rapid reconnaissance methods of information
gathering have particular value for sensing potential
constraints. These methods generally use proxy
indicators to assess factors whose direct measurement
may be complex, expensive, or time consuming. For
example, in measuring the relative strength of
different government ministries, one possible
indicator is the relationship between the annual
budget of the ministry and its budget request. The
higher the percentage obtained, the stronger the
organization, since a declining or insecure agency
will feel a need to request large increases to obtain
small ones.[39]

Rapid reconnaissance techniques, which are
impressionistic, should be used with care. Designers
must weigh the advantages of timeliness, low cost, and
flexibility against the difficulty of estimating the
degree of confidence that can be placed in the data,
and of judging the quality of the investigator's performance.[40] These difficulties can be reduced
through the use of multiple indicators in a particular
situation, by checking the results of the reconnaissance against local perceptions or by using impressionistic data to complement quantitative survey data.

Multiple information sources also help assess the conjunction of adverse factors in rural life, especially at certain seasons of the year. Rural planning should have seasonal analysis as the central concern, with particular attention given to what happens at the worst times of the year.[41]

Secondary information sources can supplement direct information collection. World Bank or International Monetary Fund reports contain useful economic data, and informed journalists may have helpful perspectives on potential economic, political, or institutional constraints. Local researchers are often familiar with local history and culture.

Design data should be used to anticipate what is likely to go wrong and how to deal with it. There is a connection here with the important assumptions included in the Logframe annex of AID project documentation. These assumptions, rarely given the attention they deserve, are supposed to identify "an event or action which must take place, or a condition which must exist, if a project is to succeed, but, over which the project team has little or no control."[42] Typically, these assumptions take the following form:

- "Conditions of political stability will continue";

- "National-level support [exists] for the [project]"; or

- "No unusual natural calamities [will occur]."[43]

These assumptions are characteristic in their vagueness and in the implication that project management need not worry about them. Since the Logframe (or the equivalent for other donors) is usually part of a document aimed at securing funding approval, potentially difficult assumptions are generally avoided in the design process and the opportunity to anticipate real problems is lost.

Acting on Design Requirements

The purpose of anticipating problems caused by environmental constraints is to provide a basis for appropriate action in the design phase. One possible action is to abandon the project idea altogether.

Abandoning the proposed project requires not only the technical competence to recognize fatal constraints, but also the freedom to recommend against implementing a project. But abandoning a project is not easy, particularly if a political or bureaucratic

commitment has already been made. Unfortunately, most
development schemes are generated by persons with more
interest in getting projects started than in seeing
them successfully finished. In both donor and host
government bureaucracies, rewards are skewed toward
obtaining funding for proposals or moving money.
Until incentives are more effectively linked to the
end results of the activity, it is unlikely that the
option of abandoning an ill-conceived project will be
attractive.[44]

   Design Adjustments. One obvious way to improve
the design-implementation linkage is to include
implementation personnel on the design team. For one
rural development project in Panama, for example, the
design team included Ministry of Agriculture technicians from the project area. The main benefit was
that foreign specialists on the design team were
exposed to local knowledge while designing the
project's technical package. The principal disad-
vantage was that the Panamanian technicians had their
own special interest groups in the project area, in
this case, land reform beneficiaries.[45]
   The decision to attack a constraint directly or
to design around it is always situational, depending
on the timing, cultural sensitivity, politics, and
nature of the constraint. One study calls this
problem the "dilemma of design":

      If the project is planned, built, and operated on
      the basis of certain negative attributes of the
      status quo, taking them for granted as inevitable
      and unchangeable, it may miss important oppor-
      tunities for effecting positive changes in these
      attributes. On the contrary, it may even confirm
      and strengthen them . . . . If, on the other
      hand, success in the construction and operation
      of the project is made to hinge on a prior or
      concurrent or subsequent change in some of the
      attributes of backwardness, then the project's
      fate becomes a wager; if the wager is lost, so
      that the needed change does not occur and the
      project's success is thereby jeopardized, the
      project planners will be accused of ignoring
      local circumstances, traditions, and
      sociopolitical structure.[46]

   The art of project design consists of escaping
this dilemma, often by using the two strategies
jointly. For example, high-cost marketing monopolies
or hastily developed farmer marketing organizations
are common strategies, which often fail for lack of
administrative capacity. It has been suggested that,
as a design alternative, marketing services could

emphasize improving the bargaining position of the
farmer through the construction of public facilities
for seasonal storage, improvement of records and market information systems, and standardization of
weights and measures.[47] Concurrently, training and
organizational development activities could be used to
build capacity in farmer marketing organizations as a
long-term strategy.

   Capacity Building. Capacity building is one way
to address institutional constraints. The problem of
human resource development is recognized in most project proposals. The common response is to enroll
selected community leaders and government staff in
training programs. Although these programs may teach
basic skills and provide useful information, they are
limited. First, they tend to segregate the people
chosen for training from the rest of the community,
making the development of a broad leadership base more
difficult. Second, they may remove key people from
local project management while they attend training,
leaving major gaps. Finally, and most important, they
tend to divorce learning from doing. Therefore, although special training programs have their role,
greater emphasis should be placed on on-the-job training and organizational development activities that are
rooted in the institutional context of the project.

   Institutional Reform. Institutional development
takes time, even if there is commitment and the necessary decisions are made. Frequently, the time required for institutional development, or the changes
in the distribution of political and administrative
power that this development implies, deters policy
makers from taking the necessary steps, despite the
attention that institutional reform may receive in
policy pronouncements.[48] Thus, there is a need to
ensure strong commitment to institutional change
before investing in activities expected to generate
it.
   In their attempts to alleviate policy constraints
to rural development, project designers should build a
planning and evaluation component into projects that
can document how external constraints interfere with
goal achievement. Although the results may be uncertain, introducing this component is preferable to
simply hoping that obstacles to development will
someday dissolve. Although powerful interests may
block one aspect of development, they may support
another--especially if they perceive it to be in their
own interest to do so.[49]
   Projects can sometimes also be designed to
circumvent macro-level constraints. In the Upper Lofa
County Rural Development Project in Liberia, a project

management unit was used to avoid many of the
difficulties entailed in following regular government
channels, including archaic salary disbursement
procedures and an authoritarian management structure.
As with any placement strategy, use of a project
management unit involves tradeoffs that must be
carefully considered. The most prominent concern is
sustainability.[50] Past experience with project
management units suggests that they are no substitute
for institutional reform.

Some constraints are inherent in the conflicting
policy objectives built into many rural development
projects. The Abyei project in Sudan, for example,
was to be for all the people of Abyei, including the
relatively better off Messirya Humr group. Yet the
project was to address primarily the needs of the
poorest and most disadvantaged elements of the
population, the majority of whom were Dinka. This
conflict in the design reflected an effort to respond
both to Sudanese political realities and to those of
the U.S. Congress, embodied in the New Directions
Mandate.

Primarily because of tension between the two
groups, the project during implementation more or less
excluded the Messirya, in spite of the stated goal to
the contrary. No Messirya, for example, were on the
project staff, although it did include other Arabic
speakers (including the project director), nor were
services extended to Messirya areas. Hiring Messirya
staff members and providing at least token assistance
to the Messirya group might have mitigated subsequent
political criticism of the project.[51]

Funding Leverage. Sometimes conditions precedent
to the release of funds can be used to apply donor
leverage on a host government, to push the government
to address or at least investigate political
constraints. The effectiveness of this tool depends
on the type of constraint and the capacity of the host
government to act on it. One example is the INVIERNO
project in Nicaragua. To attack the land reform issue
raised with respect to the project, AID required that
the Nicaraguan government undertake interim measures
to protect small-scale farmers and tenants until final
landlord-tenant regulations could be enacted.[52]

Similarly, as a condition for the disbursement of
funds for the final two years of Operation Mils Mopti,
AID required that the Government of Mali, through a
private contractor, conduct a study of peanut production and marketing in the Mopti region. The study was
to determine what effect, if any, increased peanut
production would have on farmers' net revenue, soil
fertility, and millet production and whether the
marketing of peanuts would increase the project's

financial viability. Furthermore, if the study
recommended that Operation Mils Mopti should market
peanuts, the government was to give the project that
authority prior to the disbursement of funds for the
second project year. Finally, although AID concluded
that solving the grain-pricing policy of Mali was
beyond the scope of the project, it did require that
the government not increase the grain quota for the
region. This ensured that small-scale farmers would
not have to sell surplus output at the official price.
Instead, any increased production could be sold on the
parallel market, thus providing a greater incentive to
produce a surplus.[53]

In circumstances in which national resources are
extremely scarce, posing conditions precedent to the
release of funds may be unrealistic or may engender
donor competition. In this case, examining possibilities for mobilizing local resources may be more
appropriate.

Building Local Support. Many projects must begin
without a strong constituency committed to innovation
and change. Often, project staff are not equipped
with a proven package of recommended practices,
inputs, or technological improvements. In these
cases, the project design must permit sufficient time
and activities to build local interest and confidence.
This can often be accomplished through cooperative
solutions to specific problems to develop a base for
broader responses. As one study noted, there are many
situations in which actors commit themselves to a
specific technical innovation without realizing the
extent to which this commitment slowly and subtly, but
irresistibly, induces additional, unanticipated
changes in behavior.[54]

When the influence of local leaders is a
constraint, projects can assist in transfering
responsibility and authority to local organizations of
private citizens. These organizations can stimulate
widespread enthusiasm and develop the political power
of small-scale farmers to offset that of entrenched
elites.[55] In these cases, specification of these
participating organizations in the project plan will
help protect them from the demands of powerful local
interests, particularly if the plan has important
political backing.

Adjusting Implementation Strategy

If a constraint is not addressed in the project
design, it usually is confronted during implementation, if and when project managers see the link
between the constraint and the success of the project.
This will involve costs to the project in terms of

staff time and resources. In deciding whether to address a given constraint, project managers should:

- Estimate the probability that the project will succeed even if the constraint is ignored;

- Estimate the probability that addressing the constraint will improve the chances of project success;

- Estimate the costs involved in trying to avoid, eliminate, or lessen the impact of the constraint; and

- Estimate the probability of succeeding.

Project managers and staff work in a state of imperfect knowledge when making these estimates. In addition, they may see personal obstacles to action. They may wish to avoid being accused of political meddling, they may be locked into rigid project designs that limit their options, or they may feel more comfortable addressing only technical questions.
A project manager facing constraints that were not adequately anticipated in the design of the project has several options:

- Change the project strategy to respond to the constraint, that is, change target groups, geographic areas of concentration, or project components;

- Divert project resources to address the problem, including using staff time to expedite resource deliveries or political decisions, using project funds to pay the extra costs brought about by the constraints, and taking on additional activities or responsibilities not planned for in the project design;

- Wait for the evaluation process to point out the problem and then hope that it will be resolved at higher policy-making levels;

- Document the problem in preparation for subsequent project funding negotiations; or

- Accept the constraint and warn donor agencies and the host government to expect slower progress and lower target-level achievements.

Project resources were successfully diverted in Colombia, for example, where an integrated rural

development project sponsored by the Save the Children
Federation covered three distinct areas. In two
areas, the project effectively gained beneficiary
support and met its objectives. In the third,
beneficiary participation was almost nonexistent, a
result of historical factors and low population
density. Faced with a dearth of tangible results, the
third project area was terminated early and the funds
reallocated to the other two areas.[56]

Sometimes project management is forced to divert
resources to cover unplanned costs resulting from
constraints over which it has no control. Because of
high-level political problems in Upper Volta, the
government was unable to make its financial
contribution to the Eastern ORD Integrated Rural
Development Project. Consequently, the project
director used money that had been set aside for a
revolving credit fund to cover the project's recurrent
costs, mainly salaries. Although this transfer was to
be a temporary loan to be repaid after recurrent
budget funds were received, those funds did not arrive
and the accounts were never reconciled. The viability
of the credit fund was undercut by this ad hoc
technique, even though no formal decision had been
made to shift priorities within the project.[57]

Thus, diversion of resources is a risky procedure
unless it is part of a change in strategy. Before
deciding to shift resources to deal with unexpected
constraints, managers must carefully assess the
possible costs.

Sometimes external issues can be addressed and
corrected through the evaluation process. The issue
of the availability of light plows in Operation Mils
Mopti originally emerged during a routine evaluation.
AID then asked officials in Mali to consider making
them available to the project. By the time the final
evaluation report came out seven months later, the
government of Mali had authorized the project to
import the lighter plows.[58]

Pointing out the adverse effects of government
practices may not be enough. In the case of a project
in which serious construction delays occurred as a
result of the lengthy and redundant contract review
process, an AID evaluation proposed several options,
including:

- Granting more authority to the project to
  negotiate and sign contracts, regardless of
  amount;

- Exempting contracts executed under the loan
  agreement with AID from the presidential
  directive requiring approval by the
  presidential review committee; or

- Combining sequential checks into a single, simultaneous review.[59]

In this case, however, these contract reviews were believed to be a source of graft for high-level officials. If this is true, one could expect significant resistance at the national level to streamlining the contract review process.

Nevertheless, experience from the North Shaba project in Zaire indicates that addressing macro constraints during implementation can be effective. An amendment to the project budget included several conditions precedent to deal with constraints. One condition was the creation of a high-level project liaison committee to review the project's budget and ensure that the funds would be disbursed in a timely manner. A second condition authorized the use of counterpart fund advances to cover project operating costs when scheduled budget releases were delayed. Finally, two conditions were included to thwart the attempts of a powerful regional politician to create a sanctioned marketing monopoly in the project area.[60]

The ability to address external constraints during project implementation depends on the quality of information available to project managers. Relevant, timely information is crucial to the success of any intervention; otherwise, flexibility is valueless.[61] With this information, competent central planners can combine indigenous knowledge and practice at the local level with the insight required to carry out effective project negotiations.

CONCLUSION

In development practice, many strategies fail because the planning process does not fully consider implementation requirements. First, there is a failure to anticipate potential implementation constraints that occur outside the immediate project system. Second, there is a failure to act, even when constraints are identified and strategies are formulated. The cost of these failures is high. Implementers face unexpected difficulties that they are ill equipped to address; they are locked into designs that are fundamentally unsound; and they are given inadequate leeway and time to redirect strategies found to be inappropriate.

Alleviating the problem is a design issue. Although designers cannot realistically anticipate every external constraint, they should be expected to recognize the fallibility of their initial assumptions. By taking uncertainty more seriously, project designers could facilitate the application of what is

learned during implementation. At a minimum, key
categories of potential learning could be identified
and possible options anticipated.

The project paper for the Local Resource
Management Project in the Philippines, for example,
emphasized systems development and institutional
learning within existing government structures,
"requiring continual experimentation, incremental
adjustment, and evaluation of approaches and process
for replicability and sustainability across different
localities."[62] Consistent with this emphasis, AID
funding for the project was programmed in phases, so
as not to lock either AID or the government of the
Philippines into specific long-term funding expectations or implementation arrangements.

Many failures stem from treating design as a
discrete activity, divorced from implementation and
conducted by foreign specialists. Design products are
then judged as research products or technical
analyses, more than as guides for implementation. The
tendency of donors to procure design services sep-
arately from implementation assistance compounds the
problem. Designers are rarely held accountable for
the results of their work.

Ongoing planning and evaluation should be treated
as part of the task of management, the basis for defining strategies and organizing resources to achieve
explicit goals. This planning will be served by a
blend of local knowledge and technical expertise, and
by the recognition of political, economic, and bureaucratic realities that may affect project implementation. This awareness, if followed by appropriate
design and implementation choices, will go far to help
development practitioners cope with external
constraints.

NOTES

1. "Operation Mils Mopti, Phase II Project Paper"
(Washington, D.C.: Agency for International
Development, July 12, 1979), p. 3.
2. Robert H. Bates, Markets and States in Tropical
Africa: The Political Basis of Agricultural Policies
(Berkeley: University of California Press, 1981),
chapter 2.
3. Ibid.
4. Merilee S. Grindle, "Policy Content and Context
in Implementation," Politics and Policy Implementation
in the Third World, ed. Merilee S. Grindle (Princeton,
N.J.: Princeton University Press, 1980), pp. 31-32.
5. Irene F. Rothenberg, "Administrative
Decentralization and the Implementation of Housing
Policy in Colombia," Politics and Policy
Implementation in the Third World, ed. Merilee S.

Grindle (Princeton, N.J.: Princeton University Press, 1980), pp. 145-169.

6. Jerry Van Sant et al., <u>Management Support to the Jamaica Ministry of Agriculture Second Integrated Rural Development Project</u>, IRD Field Report no. 13 (Washington, D.C.: Development Alternatives, Inc., April 1981), p. 25.

7. Stephen A. Quick, "The Paradox of Popularity: 'Ideological' Program Implementation in Zambia," <u>Politics and Policy Implementation in the Third World</u>, ed. Merilee S. Grindle (Princeton, N.J.: Princeton University Press, 1980), pp. 40-63.

8. Jerry Van Sant et al., <u>Management Support</u>, p. 26.

9. Vernon W. Ruttan, "Integrated Rural Development: A Skeptical Perspective," <u>International Development Review</u> 17:4 (1975): 9-16.

10. George H. Honadle et al., <u>Integrated Rural Development: Making It Work? Executive Summary</u> (Washington, D.C.: Development Alternatives, Inc., July 1980), pp. 112-113.

11. Uma Lele, <u>The Design of Rural Development: Lessons from Africa</u> (Baltimore, Md.: The Johns Hopkins University Press, 1975), p. 181.

12. Ibid., p. 184.

13. "Evaluation Report of Operation Mils Mopti, Project Evaluation Summary (79-2)" (Washington, D.C., Agency for International Development, January 1979), p. 5.

14. <u>Internal Evaluation of Project North Shaba</u> (Washington, D.C.: Development Alternatives, Inc., 1980), pp. 15-30.

15. Honadle et al., <u>Integrated Rural Development</u>, pp. 114-115.

16. Abraham Waldenstein, "Comments on DS/RAD Draft Strategy Paper," Unpublished correspondence in <u>Management Development Strategy Paper: AID's Response to the Implementation Needs of 1980's</u> (Washington, D.C.: Office of Rural Development and Development Administration, Agency for International Development, June 1981), p. 9.

17. Ben Stavis, <u>Agricultural Extension for the Rural Poor</u> (East Lansing: Michigan State University, Department of Agricultural Economics, January 1979), p. 13.

18. Lele, <u>Design of Rural Development</u>, p. 76.

19. A.H. Barclay, Jr. et al., <u>Evaluation of the Abyei Development Project, Sudan: Final Report</u> (Washington, D.C.: Development Alternatives, Inc., April 1981), pp. 7-8.

20. Ibid., p. I-8.

21. Albert H. Barclay, Jr. and Gary Eilerts, Institutional Options for the Mandara Area Development Project, IRD Field Report no. 11 (Washington, D.C.: Development Alternatives, Inc. 1980), pp. 2-5.

22. Research Triangle Institute and Southeast Consortium for International Development, "Rural Development Programs and Their Impact on Fertility: State of the Art" (Paper prepared for the Agency for International Development, Washington, D.C., June 1979.)

23. Robert Chambers, Rural Poverty Unperceived: Problems and Remedies (Washington, D.C.: The World Bank, July 1980), pp. 21-23.

24. Robert Chambers et al., Seasonal Dimensions to Rural Poverty: Analysis and Practical Implications (Brighton, England: Institute of Development Studies, February 1979), p. 6.

25. Jerry Van Sant et al., Supporting Capacity-Building in the Indonesian Provincial Development Program, IRD Field Report no. 12 (Washington, D.C.: Development Alternatives, Inc., February 1981), pp. 16-17.

26. Van Sant et al., Management Support, pp. 28-29.

27. Development Alternatives, Inc., Internal Evaluation of Project North Shaba, pp. 26-27.

28. Montague Yudelman, "Integrated Rural Development Projects: The Bank's Experience," Finance and Development 14:1 (1977): 17.

29. R. P. Misra, "A Critical Analysis of the Traditional Cost Benefit Approach to Economic Development," Development 3/4 (1981): 51.

30. Dennis A. Rondinelli, Administrative Decentralization and Area Development Planning in East Africa: Implications for United States Aid Policy, Regional Planning and Area Development Project Occasional Paper no. 1 (Madison: University of Wisconsin, 1980), p. 98.

31. Van Sant et al., Management Support, p. 25.

32. "Project Evaluation Summary: Thaba Bosiu Rural Development Project (80-4)" (Washington, D.C., Agency for International Development, April 1980).

33. UNCLAS State 60016, U.S. Department of State cable to U.S. Embassy, Jakarta, April 1981.

34. Richard W. Franke and Barbra H. Chasin, Seeds of Famine (Montclair, N.J.: Allanheld and Osmun, 1980), p. 203.

35. Ibid., p. 207.

36. Jerry Van Sant, "Local Needs and the Planning Process for Rural Service Delivery" (Paper prepared for the Rural Project Organization and Management Course, Economic Development Institute of The World Bank, Washington, D.C., October 26, 1981), p. 4.

37. Elliott R. Morss et al., Strategies for Small Farmer Development: An Empirical Study of Rural Development Projects, 2 vols. (Washington, D.C.: Development Alternatives, Inc., May 1975), 1:26.

38. Donald R. Mickelwait, Elliott R. Morss, and Jerry M. Silverman, A Formative Evalluation of the Arusha Planning and Village Development Project, (Washington, D.C.: Development Alternatives, Inc., April 1980).

39. Naomi Caiden and Aaron Wildavsky, Planning and Budgeting in Poor Countries (New York: Wiley Interscience, 1974).

40. George H. Honadle, "Rapid Reconnaissance Approaches to Organizational Analysis for Development Administration," World Development, 10:8 (1982):633-649.

41. Chambers et al., Seasonal Dimensions, pp. 16-17.

42. Project Evaluation Guidelines, Third Edition (M.O. 1026), Supplement I (Washington, D.C.: Agency for International Development, 1974), p. 35.

43. "Indonesia--Provincial Area Development I Project Paper" (Washington, D.C., Agency for International Development, September 2, 1977), pp. C1-C2.

44. Donald R. Mickelwait et al., New Directions in Development: A Study of USAID (Boulder, Co.: Westview Press, 1979), pp. 225-231.

45. David D. Gow et al., Differing Agendas: The Politics of IRD Project Design in Panama, IRD Field Report no. 17 (Washington, D.C.: Development Alternatives, Inc., July 1981), pp. 3, 42.

46. Albert O. Hirschman, Development Projects Observed (Washington, D.C.: The Brookings Institution, 1967), pp. 130-131.

47. Lele, Design of Rural Development, p. 191.

48. Ibid., p. 187.

49. Ben Stavis, Dilemmas in Strategies for Equitable Rural Development (East Lansing: Michigan State University, Department of Agricultural Economics, February 1979), pp. 39-46.

50. Honadle et al., Integrated Rural Development, pp. 48-51.

51. Barclay et al., Evaluation of the Abyei Development Project.

52. "Nicaragua-Rural Development Sector Loan, AID-DLC/p-2091, Capital Assistance Paper" (Washington, D.C., Agency for International Development), p. 5.

53. Agency for International Development, "Operation Mils Mopti," p. 105.

54. Hirschman, Development Projects, p. 151.

55. Ralph W. Cummings, Jr., Land Tenure and Agricultural Development, LTC No. 117 (Madison: University of Wisconsin, Land Tenure Center, July 1978).

56. "Save the Children--Colombia Operational Program Grant (Project No. 514-240), Project Evaluation Summary" (Washington, D.C., Agency for International Development, September 1978).

57. "Review of Selected AID-Financed Activities in Upper Volta," Audit Report No. 81-44 (Washington, D.C.: Agency for International Development, February 13, 1981), pp. 3-5.

58. Agency for International Development, "Operation Mils Mopti," p. 5.

59. "Evaluation: Bula Integrated Area Development Project (Project No. 492-0310) Camarines Sur Province, Philippines" (Washington, D.C., Agency for International Development, June 23, 1979), pp. 9-10.

60. "North Shaba Rural Development Project Authorization Amendment" (Washington, D.C., Agency for International Development, July 30, 1980).

61. David D. Gow and Jerry Van Sant, "Beyond the Rhetoric of Rural Development Participation: How Can It Be Done?," World Development 11:8 (1983): 435-436.

62. "Local Resource Management Project Paper," USAID Discussion Draft (Washington, D.C., Agency for International Development, April 30, 1982), p. 2.

2
Dealing with Institutional and Organizational Realities

George H. Honadle, S. Tjip Walker, and Jerry M. Silverman

INTRODUCTION

When development projects emphasize production at the expense of strengthening institutions, the result is an inability to sustain those production gains over the long run: roads are built, but not maintained; new technologies are implanted, but not supported; people are trained in new techniques, but are unable to apply them within their organizations. Thus, to have a long-term effect, projects should be equipped to strengthen weak organizations.

Implementers are constantly confronted with performance constraints that have organizational roots. This fact is demonstrated by three field experiences.

- Nearly twenty individuals--project staff, line ministry staff, regional planning staff, and people sent down from the capital city--spent half a day in a closed room. The subject of their attention was an organization chart. The focus of the argument was whether a dotted line or a solid line should connect two boxes on the chart, exactly what people belonged in which box, and what it should be called. The underlying themes were whether a coordinating committee was advisory or policy making and which line ministry was going to have its model triumph. Organizational interests clashed with project interests and raised conflict during implementation. This happened in the Philippines.

- A project was designed so that an autonomous management unit would replace ministry activity in a geographic area, bypass local merchants, and build the capacity of farmer cooperatives to perform public and private sector functions. As the project staff received training, however, they decided that, since their capacity was superior to that of the cooperatives, they rather than the cooperatives should continue to provide the services. Group interests were at odds with project plans, and self-reliance was not built. This happened in Liberia.

- In a project intended to provide training in villages, the vehicles were in excellent condition because they were seldom driven off the pavement. This situation stemmed from reimbursement procedures that encouraged efforts to keep vehicle maintenance costs at a minimum, since the person in charge of the vehicle was allowed to keep the difference between the fixed vehicle allowance and the actual maintenance costs. Predictably, the village training required for the project to achieve its goals did not take place. This happened in Indonesia.

These examples illustrate a common implementation problem: when the stated objectives of a project and its formal authority structure are inconsistent with either the real goals of the actors or the real patterns of local decision making, conflict and poor performance result. This chapter explores why this is the case and what measures might be taken to change the situation.

THE NATURE OF THE PROBLEM

The prevalence of organizational problems during implementation results from the following tendencies that appear during the project design process:

- The organizational dimension is treated as peripheral;

- Overly formalistic analyses take the place of understanding local circumstances;

- Contradictions inherent to the development process are avoided; and

- Organization is seen as a static choice of project placement, rather than a dynamic set of human interactions.

Each tendency is discussed below.

Avoidance

The notion that institutions matter and that they
have an impact on implementation is integral to
official AID thinking:

> A critical element in development projects is the
> organization (or organizations) which will be
> responsible for implementing project activities.
> AID experience indicates that erroneous
> assumptions about project organizations and
> management/administrative factors have been a
> major cause of failure or lack of complete
> success of many development projects.[1]

This presentation not only embraces the idea that
institutions matter, but also states that institutional capacity is sufficiently critical to project
sustainability. The absence of institutional capacity
is grounds for abandoning the project. The indications are that many projects suffer from institutional
inadequacies. Clearly, something is amiss if project
designs are not leading to projects that raise local
organizational capacities.

Organizational analysts have offered a wide range
of possible antidotes. One analyst has called for
more precise organizational analysis, and another
thinks that simpler designs are the answer. Some have
called for increased coordination between organizational actors and have sought methods to accomplish
this goal. Still others have emphasized strategies
for institutional change, from organization development to bureaucratic reorientation.[2]

But instead of recognizing the importance of
institutional issues, the conventional response of
project designers is to see the problem as trivial, to
reduce it to fatuous statements about coordination
between various organizational black boxes or
perfunctory observations about how the various boxes
on the organizational chart will interact with one
another to achieve project aims. Alternatively,
project designers see the problem as one of getting
the right people. The search begins for a knight in
shining armor, with the assumption that if only this
great leader is found, all institutional barriers will
crumble before the onslaught. This also diminishes in
importance organizational factors by implying that
only when incompetents are in change does organization
become a key issue.

The result of this approach is a focus on the
more easily measured and attainable production
targets. This focus reinforces the problem. Since
institutional issues are seen as trivial, they receive
little attention or analysis during design. Since

organization is treated as a secondary, nontechnical
issue, project reviewers give it little weight. Since
design teams know that institutional issues are not
considered significant during reviews, they perpetuate
the problem by virtually ignoring it. Finally, since
designers seldom implement projects, they remain
unmoved by the recurrence of organizational problems
and the treatment of these issues remains superficial.
Thus, the circle is closed and the problems are pushed
onto the shoulders of implementers.

Formalism

A quest for certainty combined with an optimizing
mentality invariably results in some type of formalism. Internal rates of return and PERT charts are
symptoms of this phenomenon, and they play important
political roles in the project approval process.
The organizational equivalent of these formalistic methods has been the organization chart.
Donors developed a preoccupation with formal
government or government-created organizations, such
as project management offices or cooperatives. This
is understandable, in part, because:

- Donor agency and host country officials
  require accountability and control, which are
  easier to exercise over formal rather than
  informal institutions;

- The project orientation reinforces the need
  for an identifiable outside agent of change,
  such as a formal organization;

- There is an ingrained professional bias toward
  formalism on the part of those experts
  generally called on to address organizational
  issues;

- There is a historical bias: host country
  elites and donors often perceive traditional
  institutions to be backward and argue that
  they have to be replaced by modern ones; and

- The attempt to use traditional organizations
  is likely to be more administratively
  intensive and costly in the short run than
  establishing new organizations to bypass the
  existing ones.

The political clout of formal methods reinforces
this situation--an internal rate of return, with its
standard procedures and quantifiable results, carries

more weight than a social or managerial soundness
analysis, with its varying format and impressionistic
product. This is made worse when no one believes the
formal depiction. After all, who really expects an
organization chart to represent power relationships
and organizational dynamics?

An obsession with formalistic views misses most
of the relevant dynamics. An examination of the legal
basis for an agricultural extension service, for
example, would not include the fact that in Zaire the
service was often used to extract food and taxes from
rural areas rather than to support the efforts of
farmers to grow more food. Numerous other cases have
been cited in which it was necessary to go beyond
formal depiction of the way organizations function.[3]

Another aspect of the over-concentration on
formalism is the misguided belief that coordination
can be imposed from outside. There have been numerous
efforts to induce coordination, but like information
exchange, coordination is largely an informal process.
Coordination has to occur for a reason; it cannot be
mandated.

Narrow views also slight indigenous organizations: cooperatives registered with the government
are perceived to be real, whereas local work groups or
savings societies are not. However, many studies
suggest that most embedded institutions grew out of
felt needs rather than government decrees.[4]   In
fact, local organizations introduced by projects are
often the weakest in the vicinity.[5]

Contradictions

Transforming development resources into welfare
gains is not simple. Even in its simplest form, the
process requires four steps. First, resources,
including skilled personnel, money, and equipment, are
channeled into an area that did not previously have
them. Second, these resources are managed to produce
goods and services, such as roads, farmer training
programs, and health clinics. Third, local people
respond by using these goods and services; they travel
on new roads, grow crops using new methods, or adopt
new patterns of preventative or curative health
behavior. Fourth, these responses improve well-being
in such ways as reducing travel times between villages
and markets, increasing income received from higher
crop yields, and reducing the incidence of disease.
This sequence is shown in Figure 2.1.

FIGURE 2.1
Sequential Effects of Program Interventions

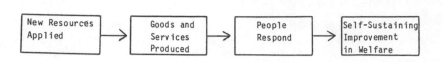

Although this sequence can be depicted as linear,
achieving one stage does not necessarily lead to
achievement of the next. Impinging on the arrows
between the boxes are a variety of differing
constraints and factors. This refutes the perception
shared by many donor agency personnel that the timely
release of resources, or the absence of a backlog in
the provision of resources, should be equated with
project success. Similarly misguided is the belief
that the completion of infrastructure or the provision
of a set of technical services is equivalent to
welfare gains. Even prompting local response is no
guarantee of increasing welfare. Development
literature is rife with examples of initiatives that
left the beneficiaries worse off than before the
project started.[6]
     It therefore follows that, as long as the
delivery of goods and services is all important, a
strategy that is modeled after an engineering project
is entirely appropriate, down to its project
blueprints and procurement techniques. However, if
positive local response is the aim, and welfare is a
concern, then the intervention strategy must be
responsive to local initiatives and attitudes. Thus,
a single organizational mechanism may not be the most
appropriate way to oversee each of the four steps in
the process of transforming resources into welfare.
Yet that is often what happens in practice. An
organizational configuration appropriate to manage one
stage may be entirely inappropriate, and even
contradictory, during another stage.
     For example, independent project management units
that concentrate authority and command an independent
but temporary resource base have often been successful
at building roads, dams, and ports. However, they are
by their very nature incapable of covering recurrent
costs. Thus, an organizational placement designed to
ensure long-term maintenance and capacity building
would probably utilize a permanent institution rather
than a project management unit. One contradiction,
then, is that both temporary and permanent
institutions may be desirable to achieve different
objectives in a single project.

A second contradiction is also widespread. Concentrated authority is good for building roads, clinics, and other facilities, but if the delivery of services is part of this process--for example, introducing new crop production technologies--a more decentralized configuration that incorporates farmers into decision making is a better option for achieving the desired response. Generally, installing infrastructure is handled better by the concentrated authority of temporary organizations. Local response, however, is enhanced by diffused authority, which is shared with villagers. Thus, another contradiction is the need for both concentrated and shared authority.

No single organizational option is capable of reconciling these contradictions. This fact is highlighted by Table 2.1, which notes the strengths and weaknesses of using new versus existing organizations. Overcoming contradictions requires going beyond a static view.

Static View

The combination of emphasizing formal factors and avoiding contradictory strategies reinforces a static perspective on organizations. Contradictions emerge only as changes over time cause opposing factors to collide. Nevertheless, the tendency in project designs is to find a host for a project and then consider the organizational design completed. Thus, the need for an organization to evolve is ignored.

The static approach greatly effects the way development is perceived, practiced, and measured. A static view reinforces a definition emphasizing production levels, gross domestic product, and other quantitative measures. This approach slights the institutional dimension by emphasizing a census mentality at the expense of a process mentality. It also supports the blueprint approach to project design and implementation.[7]

An alternative view of development accepts the sustainability imperative and places the institutional dimension in the forefront. From this vantage point, the essence of development is seen as being institutional learning rather than the attainment of temporary targets. A central tenet of this school is that the capacity to mobilize resources and achieve objectives must be embodied in local institutions for development to be self-sustaining, and only when projects contribute to a capacity-building process can they be considered truly developmental.[8]

In short, experience suggests that failure to understand the importance of evolutionary, learning-oriented, institution-targeted strategies is a major cause of poor project performance.[9]

TABLE 2.1
Advantages and Disadvantages of Using Existing Versus
Creating New Organizations

Advantages	
Existing Organizations	New Organizations
Patterns of leadership are already established	Can incorporate adequate management and technical skills
Linkages in place	Can define functions to cover project aims
Traditional functions and roles well established	Can introduce new group boundaries to expand participation
Culturally consistent and acceptable to people	Can incorporate specific incentives for linkages
Legitimacy established through governmental support	Can introduce accounta-bility specifically for project goals
Traditional access to resources and information	Creates a new channel for interaction between elites and nonelites
More aware of local needs	
May not require legal or statutory action to incor-porate project	Simplifies funding process and reinforces donor control

TABLE 2.1 (continued)

Disadvantages

Existing Organizations	New Organizations
May be unrepresentative of target population	May be perceived as illegitimate (outside of community norms)
Jurisdictional boundaries may not relate to project functions	Can be seen as competitor for scarce resources
	Access to information or resources may be restricted
May lack problem-solving skills and technical capabilities	Must establish linkages
Traditional structure may be unable to accept innovation	Initially not familiar with local cultural norms and needs
May be identified with previous undesirable actions (i.e., colonial heritage)	Can be viewed as a means of bypassing local leaders
Will usually require re--structuring and capacity building to carry out activities	May be perceived as being manipulated by outsiders (i.e., donors)
	May require high-level intervention or statute to establish

ATTACKING THE PROBLEM

The causes of each problem must be confronted
directly: institutional factors must be in the
forefront, a preoccupation with formalistic views must
be abandoned, contradictions must be embraced, and
change must be harnessed.

Understanding Institutional Cues

Interdisciplinary perspectives (including anthro-
pology, economics, public administration, psychology,
political science, and sociology) can all be utilized
to depict institutions as entities arising from
collective action intended to influence individual
behavior. This broad definition of institutions
includes relationships ranging from formal laws to
customs and taboos, from bureaucratic structures to
traditional lineage and authority patterns, and from
economic institutions such as markets and firms to
traditional relationships between landlords and
tenants.

Yet at the heart of each institution is a similar
intent--to provide information to individuals so that
they can make decisions. The information that institutions provide is a cue. A cue does not compel an
individual to act in one way as opposed to another.
Instead, it simply helps the individual make
decisions.

Consider, for example, the market and its cues--
prices. To the individual consumer, the price gives
sufficient information to determine whether to buy.
If a market cannot yield a price, or if the price is
meaningless (as in controlled economies), the formal
market ceases to provide essential information and
will cease to influence decisions. Its function will
be performed by an informal parallel market. Laws,
customs, and internal bureaucratic regulations all
work on the same principle. Designers should understand and conform to the system of cues that pervades
the project environment; the organizational shadow
price must be identified and used to good advantage.

Job design also influences cues. When agricultural extension agents are expected to communicate
information and to collect credit payments, for
example, mixed cues are sent to the farmer, that is,
delinquent debtors may avoid contact when the agent is
providing critical information. Thus, the behaviorial
effects of role assignments should be carefully
identified and appropriate ones chosen.

Spotlighting Institutional Development

An increase in agricultural production can provide rural people with surplus produce. But marketing institutions are needed so the people can transform this surplus into cash. Additional institutions, such as banks and stores, are necessary to provide incentives to accumulate cash income. Consider the Maasai of Tanzania, for example. Could they be expected to increase the offtake of cattle from their herds when beer remained the only year-round commodity that could be purchased in the area? Without institutions capable of responding to their marketing needs, the Maasai have no incentive to change their behavior.[10]

Many failures in development are not failures of production or technology. Instead, they are institutional failures. This is often partially recognized in large development projects. Rice-growing schemes in the Bicol area of the Philippines, for example, commonly include institutional and agriculture divisions alongside engineering divisions. However, the budget, attention, and talent are skewed toward physical infrastructure, with institutional development relegated to secondary status. By the time the importance of institutional development is realized, usually late in implementation, it may be too late.

To rectify this situation, project designers must give institutional development objectives an increased priority. This reorientation requires three basic changes in project design. First, primary emphasis must be switched from production increases to performance improvements. Second, potential side effects on local institutional capacity must be carefully scrutinized. Third, designs must reflect a deeper understanding of the existing institutional landscape. Each of these changes deserves further discussion.

Emphasizing performance improvements does not mean substituting one production target for another, for example, participants trained rather than tons grown. Instead, it requires focusing on organizational processes and human behavior. Such activities as meeting deadlines, collecting fees, recruiting volunteers, identifying needs, achieving broad-based participation, approximating time requirements to do a job, analyzing constraints, delivering goods or services, and keeping records become important indicators of effectiveness. Bringing about these improvements in ways that do not require outside assistance for their continuation becomes the central concern. When this happens, building resource bases and incentives to sustain performance becomes a key priority.

The need for sustainability also demands that
serious attention be given to side effects. A
project's most important results may be related less
to production increases than to the strengthening or
weakening of organizations. A large rural development
project in Liberia, for example, may have contributed
to the dismal history of the development of
cooperatives. When the project bypassed the informal
marketing system of Mandingo and Lebanese traders, the
project may have increased organizational conflict
without improving efficiency. Even if crop production
increases temporarily, the dispersion of limited
institutional capacity may hinder development in the
long run.

The cues received by different actors will have
more influence than documents proclaiming project
objectives. The problem, however, is that donors
typically use quick visits by foreign specialists to
design a project, forming the basis for a formal
agreement between donor and recipient.[11] Meanwhile,
both parties, through their normal operating procedures, send cues to other actors in the project
environment that negate the formal agreement. To
avoid or at least reduce to a minimum this situation,
the design process must be changed to include an in-
depth probing of the system of cues that controls
response to the local institutional setting. If this
is done, it then becomes possible to explore
alternative implementation mechanisms and their fit
with the local situation.

Using Informal Processes

Some managers are adept at using informal
decision-making methods. Dinner meetings at village
festivals, for example, may be more appropriate places
to settle interministerial disputes than official
meetings in government offices. Similarly, managers
who use informal conversations rather than formal
meetings or memoranda to discuss policy directions are
likely to encounter less resistance in the
implementation of these policies.[12]

Although undue emphasis is placed on formal
arrangements, the importance of the informal dimension
is also recognized. One analyst thinks that informal
practices should provide the pattern for management
behavior.[13] Other commentators see these practices
as reflecting the basic values of traditional
societies and responding to the fact that bureaucratic
norms are often at odds with these values:[14]

When social status is determined by the extent of
one's positive social relations, as is true in
most African societies, only with great

trepidation can a bureaucrat risk the application
of universalistic standards when these are in
conflict with particularistic expectations.[15]

Project expectations about organizational
behavior may be at variance with socially sanctioned
behavior. As a result, staff actions may succumb to
forces at odds with project objectives.

An obsession with values does not allow designers
much freedom, but if cues are redefined to be the
result of historical and political processes that are
in flux, the question is how to identify potentially
supportive cues and to build on them. Values and
attitudes then become less important, and behavior
assumes priority.

This has two major implications. First, project
interventions should rely less on formal mechanisms
and should include strategies that use informal
coordination more effectively. Tables 2.2 and 2.3
identify the requirements of various organizational
approaches and specify their advantages and
disadvantages. Using these approaches is more
difficult than identifying them because choosing which
set of cues to follow is a political act. It helps
determine who receives which benefits from a project.

The second implication is that to defuse the
explosiveness of any analysis of institutional
problems, the discussion of cues must be conducted
through the use of analytically neutral categories.
Moreover, these categories must be standard enough to
apply to a wide range of situations while not
succumbing to methodological formalism. Two key
categories that provide an appropriate focus are
incentives and resource bases. These categories are
illustrated by the three field experiences at the
beginning of this chapter, with Indonesia representing
incentives and Liberia representing resource bases.

Focusing on these categories is not just a design
activity. Formative evaluations and implementation
workshops should incorporate them into an unfolding
process of organizational learning and capacity
building.[16] The discussions should not assume naive
linear sets of project objectives; instead, they
should highlight the differing agendas of involved
institutions and address the contradictions inherent
in induced rural development.

Confronting Contradictions

The logic of design documents for integrated
rural development projects posits a complex set of
mutually supportive outputs that combine to achieve a
broad, long-range developmental goal. At the same
time, various interacting institutions have different

TABLE 2.2
Formal Mechanisms to Increase Coordination

Formal Mechanisms	Advantages	Disadvantages
Interagency coordination or advisory committees	High-level input for policy support	High opportunity cost, infrequency of meetings
	Potential to enforce (influence) coordinative decisions	Different levels of authority among participants may make it difficult to reach decisions
	Sharing of professional expertise and concurrence in professional norms and standards	
Creation of liaison positions or groups	Can select groups or individuals for specific coordination issues	Often caught without authority to make decisions
	Value in having an independent (nonaligned) perspective	
Interagency task force	Can focus on specific issues or problems	Depends greatly on capability of task force leaders
	Brings relevant disciplines and expertise to bear on problems	May lack authority to affect policy or make binding decisions for agencies involved

TABLE 2.2 (continued)

Formal Mechanisms	Advantages	Disadvantages
	Usually includes operational personnel	
Binding cooperative agreements (fixed reimbursement agreements)	Greater potential for compliance	Enforceability may depend on a power linkage
	Clear specification of resource needs and responsibilities	Inflexible in meeting changing resource needs
Transfer of staff between agencies	Facilitates communication and understanding of different goals and priorities	Transferred personnel adhere to interests of parent agency rather than host or project
	Can generate multidisciplinary focus	Parent agency may fear that personnel will be permanently lost to host institution

TABLE 2.2 (continued)

Formal Mechanisms	Advantages	Disadvantages
Joint training and orientation courses for agency personnel	Facilitates sharing of goals and interagency communication	Minimal resource transfer involved
	Low risk means little resistance to activity	Minimal opportunity for directly influencing decision making
Copies of reports sent to heads of other agencies	Promotes sharing of goals and priorities through feedback	No assurance that reports will be read
	Creates a routine channel of communication	May not deal with critical coordination issues
Single report format used by two or more cooperating agencies	Requires sharing of information and staff interaction	Difficult and time consuming to organize staff and information

TABLE 2.2 (continued)

Formal Mechanisms	Advantages	Disadvantages
	Focuses attention on mutual problems and interdependence	Report format may not serve individual agency requirements or address specific problems
Existence of an independent monitoring and evaluation entity	Value in an independent viewpoint	Can be perceived as a threat to agencies
	Can identify difficult problems and uncover blockages	Costs are associated with setting up a special unit
Merging of agencies	Increases control over resource inputs and alleviates need for coordination	Strong bureaucratic resistance
	May save costs by reducing personnel needs	Inappropriate when the functions of agencies are different

TABLE 2.2 (continued)

Formal Mechanisms	Advantages	Disadvantages
Creation of incentives (financial, promotion-al, professional) to encourage working on joint projects	Motivates individuals to address coordination problems Can lead to creative and flexible approaches to circumvent administrative blockages	May increase implementa-tion costs May build up inequities among staff

TABLE 2.3
Informal Mechanisms to Increase Coordination

Informal Mechanisms	Advantages	Disadvantages
Lending of resources (personnel, transport) by one agency to another on an informal basis	Shows a genuine commitment to cooperate Can provide specific resources	Unreliable over the long term
Use of informal information systems by decision makers	Can build on existing patterns of interaction Nonthreatening to decision makers	Unreliability of information (decision making by anecdote) Timing of information is periodic
Encouragement of informal communication between agency staff (through interagency sports competition, week-end staff retreats, occasional seminars)	Contributes to open management style and sharing of problems Can carry over to work performance through generation of espirit de corps	Difficult to focus communication on coordinative issues Can degenerate into excessive rumors or needless competition

TABLE 2.3 (continued)

Informal Mechanisms	Advantages	Disadvantages
Having participant agency offices in the same location	Better focus on client population Increased communication and sharing of priorities	Difficult to accomplish when separate facilities already exist
Periodic meetings of agency decision makers on an informal basis	Nonthreatening opportunity to share problems Can generate a wide range of solutions in a risk-free environment	Impossible to ensure participation of key decision makers Need to create reasons for meeting an agenda that is unspecified Difficult to link to actual decisions
Staff participation and use of a supportive management style by agency	Encourage commitment by staff to follow through on coordinative decisions	Time consuming for senior management

TABLE 2.3 (continued)

Informal Mechanisms	Advantages	Disadvantages
	Can encourage coordination at lower levels in the organization	Consensus is more difficult to achieve
	Serve as example for coordination with clients	
Use of a bargaining strategy with other actors, rather than reliance on present rules	When power relationships are not equal, gives agency an opportunity to gain needed resources	Cooperation is not voluntary and can be withdrawn
		Bargaining skills may not be evenly distributed among participants

interpretations of their implementation roles and how
the project relates to their own objectives. As a
result, serious contradictions come into play.

Previous discussion emphasized the need to
examine the potential for contradictions to emerge.
Unfortunately, it is even harder to overcome
contradictions than to describe them. Micro-level
approaches such as workshops can be useful, but the
organizational setting itself must be used to overcome
contradictions. The desirability of informal
approaches should not be allowed to obscure the need
to make formal the innovative practices required for
sustainability. Informal communication patterns may
disappear with personnel turnover; institutional
development requires something more. It must begin
with the choice of an appropriate organizational host
for intervention.

Table 2.4 lays out the strengths and weaknesses
of the five types of institutions commonly chosen as
hosts for projects. These choices should not be
viewed as mutually exclusive or permanent. The range
of cues in any specific setting may support the
simultaneous pursuit of multiple placements for
distinct activities within a particular program. In
the Provincial Area Development Program in Indonesia,
for example, the objective was to enhance
institutional capacity in subnational government
bodies. However, this activity could not be conducted
at a single level--the interaction between national
and provincial units greatly influenced project
success. As a result, AID and the technical advisers
devoted resources to adapting national behavior to
support capacity-building initiatives. The
simultaneous use of a nationally based, but temporary,
project management unit and application of assistance
to a permanent, subnational institution were sensible
strategies.

A sequential strategy may also be advisable. For
example, in the North Shaba Rural Development Project
in Zaire, an immediate objective was to build roads
quickly to transport maize. However, a long-term
project objective was to develop local ability to
maintain those roads. To circumvent endemic corruption, an autonomous project management unit was set up
for the first phase.[17] But a project management
unit could not be responsible for long-term maintenance since it had no permanent status. The project's
second phase is addressing this issue by integrating
the road maintenance component into a local
institution, specifically, a cotton-growing company
that is also interested in maintaining a viable
network of roads in the area.

TABLE 2.4
Organizational Placement Alternatives and Tradeoffs

Alternative	Tradeoffs	
Implementer	Major Advantages	Major Disadvantages
National Line Agency (permanent) such as Ministry of Agriculture	Provides a base in a permanent institution	Imposes sectoral focus on project strategy
	Provides for high-level support and direction	Preoccupied with national problems rather than local variations
	Appropriate for sector or infrastructure projects	Reluctance to delegate significant operational authority
	Simplifies initial preparation process and resource flows	Likely to have conflicts with other line agencies

TABLE 2.4 (continued)

Alternative	Tradeoffs	
Implementer	Major Advantages	Major Disadvantages
Subnational Government Entity (permanent) such as a region, province, or district	Provides focus on local issues	Often has low institutional and human resource capability
	Sometimes helps to concentrate authority in project activities	Often has little leverage over line ministries whose activities affect the project
	Can build planning and implementation capability in permanent entity	
Integrated Development Agency (permanent) such as a national authority	Provides comprehensive project overview	Line agency competition can adversely affect performance
	Combines local focus with access to higher level authority	Complex communication needs
	Can avoid overly centralized audit and control procedures	

TABLE 2.4 (continued)

Alternative	Tradeoffs	
Implementer	Major Advantages	Major Disadvantages
Project Management Unit (autonomous and temporary) such as that often created as part of the design of an integrated rural development project	Can be used to concentrate authority in project area	Difficult to institution-alize
	Familiar to engineers who staff infrastructure projects	Temporary nature creates personnel management problems
	Can avoid centralized audit and control procedures	
	Can avoid inappropriate sector boundaries	

TABLE 2.4 (continued)

Alternative	Tradeoffs	
	Major Advantages	Major Disadvantages
Implementer		
Private Voluntary Organization (autonomous and often with permanent status in country)	Authority usually delegated to project site	Frequently not linked to resources from established government agencies
	Tradition of active beneficiary and other local group participation in decision making	Budget sources are often limited and uncertain
	Can avoid centralized audit and control procedures	
	Can work with both private and public sector agencies	

Harnessing Change

It is difficult to change deeply embedded behavior patterns.[18] Although new policies, ideologies, and leaders periodically appear and great successes are proclaimed, the prevailing pattern of organizations is one of persistence rather than change.[19] Nevertheless, experience in rural development suggests that there are some opportunities that, although often missed, still offer hope.

One persistent and universal obstruction to field management is unwillingness to relinquish decision-making authority. At a macro level, the devolution of power is called "decentralization"; at a micro level, it is called "delegation." At both levels, the devolution of power is crucial to harness change and take advantage of emerging situations. However, building capacity may first be necessary, either to ensure that delegation will work or to convince those with power that delegation will work. Providing training and technical assistance to organizations is one way to accomplish this change.

Turnover is usually depicted as a constraint, a disruption of continuity in policy, style, and organizational memory as well as an indicator of low capacity to hold talent.[20] However, it can be useful when it removes incompetents, fosters change, and leads to positive links with other organizations. In fact, long tenure of project staff often produces a rigid approach or over-identification with the need to prove success. For this reason, timing interventions to coincide with turnover is one way to harness change.

One theory of social change locates the motor for development among socially marginal populations, and a corresponding strategy might involve targeting development benefits to these groups.[21] However, the probability of destructive institutional competition is greatly increased when this approach challenges vested political and economic interests. Nonetheless, small-scale efforts using informal beneficiary groups can often avoid the strong resistance that is mounted against large projects, offering attractive targets for predatory organizations.

In other cases, marginal groups may be ethnically distinct entrepreneurs such as the Lebanese in West Africa, the Asians in East Africa, or the Chinese in Southeast Asia. This situation can complicate the issue when they do not have local citizenship and the national government is trying to displace them.

But no choice should be final. Flexible, process-oriented projects, rather than rigid blueprints, are needed. Harnessing change requires

creative responses to new opportunities rather than
lock-step implementation of predetermined designs.
   The nature of implementation has been well
described:

> A development project is not like a train trip to
> a ticketed destination. It is more like sailing
> on a ship, hopefully beyond the point where the
> internal rate of return becomes favorable, in the
> direction of a better and more generously endowed
> climate.[22]

If the ship is not to sink, serious attention must be
given to the role of institutions.

CONCLUSION

   National income, crop harvest tonnage, or road
network mileage are not the sole indicators of development. The essence of development is to increase the
ability of people to determine their own living conditions and achieve their own objectives. This goal, in
turn, requires enhanced institutional and organizational capacity. Unfortunately, present project
approaches often impede institutional development.
   At the same time that project approaches fail to
address the institutional nature of development,
production technicians are frustrated by insufficient
management performance. This situation leads to a
focus on the problem of organization. However, the
emphasis on formal management processes, such as the
preparation of job descriptions and organization
charts, rather than on behind-the-scenes decision-
making patterns and cues, misses the essence of the
performance problem.
   Two levels of action are required to alleviate
this situation and promote effective development
programming and implementation: a reorientation of
donor approaches and a change in field-level
management practices.
   Concerning donors, three changes are required:

- Institutional development must receive high
  priority, and immediate production gains
  should no longer dominate project objectives.
  Indicators of success and evaluation practices
  must be altered. Local organizational
  learning must be emphasized, and the purpose
  of evaluations should be recast to reinforce
  this emphasis.

- Project development processes must be changed. Collaborative, long-term designs that explore the local system of cues should become the norm. Instead of automatically establishing a new organization to implement a project, donor agency staff should be required to obtain a waiver and justify any proposal to bypass existing institutions.

- Flexible, dynamic designs are needed. These designs should recognize contradictions and articulate a plan for organizational evolution. Resources for workshops, studies, and the development of new components should be built in.

At the field level, three practices should be strengthened:

- Staff and beneficiary workshops should be used more extensively to improve collaborative action and identify mixed cues and their effects.

- Attention to job design (and redesign) and to staff behavior must be recast in light of capacity-building objectives. Learning and action must be combined to improve performance.

- Informal work groups, communication channels, and social events should be used by field managers to guide the implementation process.

Adopting these recommendations should help to ease the constraints currently imposed by organizational and institutional factors. This is no panacea, but it is a necessary step in rethinking the development paradigm and improving the implementation record.

NOTES

1. Project Assistance Handbook No. 3 (Washington, D.C.: Agency for International Development).
2. Harry Levinson, Organizational Diagnosis (Boston: Harvard University Press, 1971); Robert Chambers, "Project Selection for Poverty Focused Rural Development: Simple is Optimal," World Development 6:2 (1978):209-219; and David C. Korten and Norman Uphoff, Bureaucratic Reorientation for Rural Development (Washington, D.C.: NASPAA, 1982.)

3. George H. Honadle, "Rapid Reconnaissance for Development Administration: Mapping and Moulding Organizational Landscapes," World Development 10:8: (1982): 633-649.

4. Kenneth Little, Voluntary Organizations in West Africa (Cambridge, England: Cambridge University Press, 1968).

5. This was the case in the Second Integrated Rural Development Project in Jamaica, where the project organizations were by far the weakest of those in the local environment.

6. M. Farber and T. Milton, The Careless Technology (New York: National History Press, 1972).

7. Charles F. Sweet and Peter F. Weisel, "Process vs. Blueprint Approaches to Designing Rural Development Projects," International Development Administration: Implementation Analysis for Development Projects, eds. George H. Honadle and Rudi Klauss (New York: Praeger, 1979) pp. 127-145.

8. George H. Honadle, "Development Administration in the Eighties: New Agendas or Old Perspectives?," Public Admiministration Review 42:2 (1982):174-179.

9. David C. Korten, "Community Organization for Rural Development: A Learning Process Approach," Public Administration Review 40:6 (1980): 480-511.

10. Jon R. Moris, Managing Induced Rural Development (Bloomington, Ind.: Indiana University, International Development Institute, 1981).

11. George H. Honadle, David D. Gow, and Jerry M. Siverman, "Technical Assistance Alternatives for Rural Development: Beyond the Bypass Approach," Canadian Journal of Development Studies 4:2: (1983): 221-240.

12. George H. Honadle and Jerry Van Sant, Implementation and Sustainability: Lessons from Integrated Rural Development, (West Hartford, Conn.: Kumarian Press, forthcoming).

13. Dennis A. Rondinelli, "Designing International Development Projects for Implementation," International Development Administration: Implementation Analysis for Development Projects, eds. George H. Honadle and Rudi Klaus (New York: Praeger, 1979), pp. 21-52.

14. Stanley Heginbotham, Cultures in Conflict: The Four Faces of Indian Bureaucracy (New York: Columbia University Press, 1974).

15. Robert Price, Bureaucracy and Society in Contemporary Ghana (Berkeley: University of California Press, 1975), p. 123.

16. Elliott R. Morss, Paul R. Crawford, and George H. Honadle, Toward Self-Reliant Development: A Guide for Evaluating the Sustainability of Project Benefits (Washington, D.C.: Development Alternatives, Inc., May 1982.)

17. Kenneth Koehn, "Project North Shaba: Practicing What One Preaches," Rural Development Participation Review 3:3 (1982): 10-11.

18. Samuel P. Huntington and Joan M. Nelson, No Easy Choice, Political Participation in Developing Countries (Cambridge, Mass.: Harvard University Press, 1976); Normal Long, An Introduction to the Sociology of Rural Development (Boulder, Colo.: Westview Press, 1977); and Goran Hyden, Efficiency versus Distribution in East African Cooperatives: A Study in Organizational Conflicts (Nairobi, Kenya: East African Literature Bureau, 1973).

19. Herbert Kaufman, Are Organizations Immortal? (Washington, D.C.: The Brookings Institution, 1974); and Marshall Meyer, Change in Public Bureaucracies (Cambridge, Mass.: Cambridge University Press, 1979).

20. Dan R. Dalton and William D. Todor, "Turnover Turned Over: An Expanded and Positive Perspective," Academy of Management Review 4:2 (1979): 225-235.

21. E.E. Hagen, On the Theory of Social Change (Homewood, Il.: Dorsey Press, 1962).

22. W.J. Siffin, Administrative Problems and Integrated Rural Development (Bloomington, Ind.: PASITAM Publications, 1979).

3
Personnel Constraints

Elliott R. Morss, Paul R. Crawford, and Gene M. Owens

INTRODUCTION

Many of the implementation problems that arise in large development projects stem from the performance and utilization of personnel. Among the most serious obstacles are shortages of trained personnel, failure to make effective use of available personnel, and mediocre results from the use of foreign advisers. This chapter examines these problems and discusses how they relate to the role of foreign assistance in the development process and to the personnel policies and practices of developing countries.

PROBLEM DESCRIPTION

The human resource problems of developing countries range across a broad spectrum. At one end is a group of countries that can neither supply nor pay for a large portion of the trained personnel needed for development. These countries have little choice but to place direct responsibility for implementation in the hands of foreigners, or to postpone critical development efforts until their people are adequately trained.

The vast majority of countries, in contrast, have a small cadre of trained and capable people. However, because most of their labor force lacks technical and administrative skills, this cadre is severely overextended. The situation creates its own set of problems, not the least of which is the ineffective use of junior personnel.

In other cases, the shortage of skilled personnel may not be as serious as problems that are familiar in the developed countries: the national interest may be subordinated to bureaucratic imperatives, and incentive systems may not reward individuals for working to their full potential.

At least in theory, foreign assistance has important roles to play in alleviating these problems.

It can finance expatriates with requisite skills, provide for the training of nationals, and introduce ways to make more effective use of indigenous personnel and institutions. Development projects appear to be a suitable vehicle for all three roles. Unfortunately, the results have often not lived up to expectations.

A Crippling Ambivalence

Decision makers in many developing countries suffer from an understandable ambivalence about the purposes of foreign assistance. On the one hand, they would like to eliminate their dependence on outside aid; on the other hand, they are anxious to achieve quick development results. Unfortunately, the two generally cannot be accomplished at the same time. This contradiction becomes obvious during the design and implementation of complex development projects.

Immediate development results are most often achieved by relying heavily on capital-intensive technologies, subsidized imports, and specialized expertise, all of which tend to bypass recipient country institutions and personnel. Although this approach usually brings about rapid and visible change, it is unlikely that the recipient country will be able to sustain the benefits when foreign assistance ends. The risk is particularly high when the project leads to broad changes in the production practices and income status of rural populations, as opposed to an investment in physical infrastructure.

A strategy that gives highest priority to sustainability seeks to make maximum use of local resources. It prepares recipient institutions and their personnel to continue critical project activities after foreign assistance ends. Inevitably, this approach takes longer and carries more uncertainty than efforts to generate quick and visible development activities.

When the supply of skilled people in a country is limited and its institutions are weak, there is a real temptation--one to which many countries succumb--to go for quick results. Frequently, this decision is made easier by the tacit collusion of the donor.

Coping with Donor Requirements

Donors often require developing countries to make a formal commitment of institutional and human resources support as a precondition for development assistance. Ostensibly, this donor requirement reflects a desire to involve host country institutions and personnel in the project. In response, the borrower or grantee government agrees to assign

responsibility to institutions for functions in the
project and to provide specified numbers of personnel.
Frequently, these commitments are unrealistic, given
existing personnel constraints. For different
reasons, however, both recipient and donor choose to
overlook this inconvenient fact.

This oversight is not the result of a lack of
knowledge about real institutional capacity.
Estimating the aggregate commitment of human resources
to donor-funded projects is a simple accounting
exercise; similarly, the performance record of
existing institutions is usually not hard to
determine. Instead, this willingness to look the
other way stems from eagerness to disburse aid monies
and to achieve quick development results, albeit at
the expense of long-term efforts that could become
self-sustaining.

Once the project is under way, the country's
inability to fulfill unrealistic promises exhibits
itself in several ways. In many projects, the
promised personnel never appear. A recent study of
thirty-nine AID-supported agricultural research
projects, for example, found that one-third suffered
from shortages of host country personnel.[1] To one
of those projects, the Tropical and Subtropical Fruit
Improvement Project in Yemen, the host country had
promised to transfer a research staff of five
professionals and five subprofessionals in the first
year. In fact, only one researcher was transferred,
and he served only briefly before leaving for training
abroad. Shortly after he returned, he left the
project to become coordinator of all foreign
agricultural assistance to the country.[2]

Equally serious are the delays that take place in
appointing personnel. In an Egyptian project, for
example, the government chose a manager who had to
complete a two-year contract with another donor before
joining the project.[3] In other cases, personnel who
are identified at the planning stage depart or become
committed to other endeavors as start-up problems
delay implementation.

Host governments may respond to donor requests
for personnel by assigning individuals to projects on
a part-time basis. Yet part-time personnel cannot be
expected to give full attention to the needs of the
project or to fulfill their intended functions.
Sometimes, high-level host country officials are
nominally assigned to projects. However, as a result
of their positions, they have other, more demanding
administrative responsibilities that conflict with
their project roles. In Jamaica, for example, the
original project director for Second Integrated Rural
Development Project was the senior soil conservation
officer of the Ministry of Agriculture. The project

was only one part of his duties, and the ministry would not relieve him of his other tasks or permit him permanent transfer to the project site. Eventually, he had to be replaced by a full-time project director who had management, rather than technical, skills.[4]

Another common host government response is to assign junior personnel who do not have the proper training for the job. In the North Shaba Rural Development Project, for example, the staff provided by the Zairian government was young and far less experienced than called for in the project design. This meant that considerable time in the early phase of the project had to be spent training the new staff and exposing them to rural conditions.[5]

The demands by different donors that recipient countries make good on personnel promises may result in rapid staff turnover. This occurs when the recipient country's strategy is to make occasional gestures of compliance to the various donors. In the Arusha Planning and Village Development Project in Tanzania, for example, almost all of the senior technicians assigned to the project were transferred to other regions within a year. At the end of four years, only one senior Tanzanian official who had been with the project when it started remained. High turnover interferes with the staff continuity required to master the details of project activities.

More is involved here than just technical knowledge. If a project approach is to survive and be replicated in competition with other ministry and donor initiatives, support for that approach must be instilled in the project staff of the recipient country. High turnover rates reduce the chances that an innovative approach will be internalized and implemented by host country staff.

In retrospect, the assumption that donor requirements for host country personnel can and should be met often reflects wishful thinking. Governments have continued to promise personnel to fill positions, but these people have not appeared at the projects. And donors, unwittingly, have further intensified the pressure on host countries to make hollow promises.

Misuse of Available Personnel

The problems caused by personnel shortages are compounded when available people are not used effectively. For example, one study of the utilization of personnel in Tanzania concluded that although only 50 percent of the listed job openings in government service were filled, the productivity of personnel already employed could be increased by at least that much if certain changes were made.[6] The report

identified poor deployment, lack of adequate super
vision, and inadequate incentives as the critical
problems.

Another study, also in Tanzania, highlighted poor
deployment as it related to road construction and
maintenance.[7] The study criticized the practice of
having road crews spend too little time maintaining a
given road (crews would often spend less than a week
in one location before being moved 100 miles or more
to another site). As a result, roads soon fell into
disrepair. The study urged sufficient work time for
each geographic area.

A study of a project in Jamaica pointed out
shortcomings in the project management structure.[8]
The study foresaw problems for a project employing 300
people but having only three people with decision-
making authority.

Other studies comment on the problems of
inadequate personnel supervision in developing
countries. The point is made that qualified
supervisors are needed to make effective use of
abundant semiskilled and untrained workers. Many
self-help or village brigade projects have failed for
lack of effective direction. The problems are
exacerbated when this lack of direction coexists with
shortages of funds and materials, as when, for
example, extension workers have no gas for their
motorcycles. In these cases, even though the workers
cannot perform all the tasks in their job description,
they can be productive if they have a supervisor who
can redefine the tasks.

Incentive structures often work against effective
use of the available staff. Usually, there are no
rewards for personnel who find imaginative solutions
to implementation problems. In the absence of these
rewards, the staff member usually interprets regulations literally, regardless of the implementation
problems that this creates or perpetuates.

Institutions that have been assigned roles in a
large project often have goals of their own that do
not correspond to the formal objectives of the
project. If a regional division of the Ministry of
Works, for example, is committed to maintaining the
primary road network linking major towns and villages,
it will deploy staff and equipment accordingly. These
objectives may conflict with activities in a newly
introduced project emphasizing construction and
rehabilitation of farm-to-market roads. Even if formal
assurances are given at the central government level
that ministry staff in the region will coordinate
their program with the new project, there is no
guarantee that this will happen. Mobilizing the
resources of institutions already in place to fulfill
desired roles in a project requires a subtle and

pragmatic understanding of their agendas; it cannot be assumed that their agendas are perfectly matched with those of the project.[9] A more detailed examination of the conflicting agendas theme appears in Chapter 8 of this volume.

Often, donor-financed development projects are located in isolated rural areas that are unattractive to potential staff. The absence of urban amenities such as housing, schools, and health facilities can be important disincentives. In a project in Egypt, for example, fifteen of the sixty-seven district agronomists trained by AID resigned from a project when they were asked to leave Cairo and go to their respective districts. Most of them cited inadequate housing as the reason.[10] In countries in which public service salaries are inadequate, assignment to a rural area may decrease the opportunities for finding additional work to supplement a staff member's salary or for employment of a spouse. Thus, potential staff face a loss of real income.

Finally, good field performance is often rewarded by a promotion that entails greater responsibility and authority. In almost all cases, this involves a move toward the locus of power within the agency or ministry concerned, and thus a physical move toward a regional or national capital. Ironically, successful performance in rural development can have the effect of drawing talented technicians and managers away from the field and into urban centers. This process persists, even though someone who performs well in a rural setting will not necessarily be equally effective in a more senior bureaucratic position.

OVERCOMING PERSONNEL PROBLEMS

The experience of the 1970s shows that signifi- cant costs are associated with the practice of recipient countries making unrealistic personnel commitments to projects. Donors share the blame because they have accepted these commitments at face value, even when they knew them to be unrealistic. Personnel shortages exist, and projects should be designed accordingly.

Being More Realistic

When there are shortages, at least four alterna- tives for coping with them should be considered:

- Make training a major project component;

- Simplify project activities;

- Do not initiate a new project; or

- Use foreign advisers to perform project
  activities.

When training is emphasized in the design of a
project, the timetable for field activities—such as
delivering extension advice to farmers, rehabilitating
roads, and performing on-farm trials of new crop
varieties—will be more gradual than in the case of
conventional project designs. The same will be true
for disbursement schedules: effective use of project
funding, if large amounts are involved, will depend on
the results of the training; thus, expenditure may be
slow in the early phase of the project and accelerate
in the second or third year.

This approach assumes that the investment in
training commands a high priority at the beginning of
the project and that, even if other components are
delayed, the long-term prospects for sustainability
make it worthwhile. This perspective is a radical
one, in terms of conventional project analysis, which
discounts the value of investments over time and
cannot easily accommodate to a gradualistic model of
development.

A second approach, reflecting the simple-is-
optimal school of thought, would restrict the project
to activities that available personnel can
perform.[11] This approach presumes that no major
investment will be made to upgrade skills. It
concentrates instead on low-maintenance, low-cost
technologies that can be sustained by local organizations and junior government personnel.

Personnel shortages can dictate a temporary
moratorium on new projects. Little is to be gained
from asking an overtaxed group of people to assume yet
another project responsibility. It may be more useful
to determine how foreign aid can assist in implementing the existing project portfolio.

By using foreign advisers as implementers, a
project can sidestep a local shortage of skilled staff
and achieve rapid results. However, foreign advisers
are expensive, and unless they are used properly,
their presence can breed dependence rather than self-
sufficiency.

Training. The immediate purpose of training in a
donor-supported project is to make personnel able to
implement project activities and ensure that those
activities, and the benefits that flow from them, will
continue when foreign aid is withdrawn. From the
perspective of the recipient country, training has
several different purposes. One is to increase to the
maximum degree the number of people who gain access to
overseas education. Donor support for projects is one

of the few sources available to developing countries for foreign travel; therefore, host government officials often attempt to broaden a project's training mandate to include programs that have little relation to project activities.

In addition to sending persons overseas, training goals can be achieved by in-country academic training, short courses, and on-the-job training. Each approach has its advantages and disadvantages, which are spelled out below.

Overseas Training. The needs of developing countries will continue to make degree-level formal education an important part of many donor portfolios. The cost of university training in donor countries is skyrocketing, however. As of 1983, the total cost of providing a single participant with a two-year Master's degree in the United States was over $30,000. Clearly, the cost-effectiveness of out-of-country training must be weighed against that of educational alternatives.

There are reasons to question the utility of donor-country training as a way to meet the needs of project implementation. First, the subject matter and techniques learned in donor countries often are not relevant to the needs of the developing country, much less to those of the project. Second, by being overseas, personnel may miss the opportunity to work with and learn from foreign experts participating in project activities. A solution to this problem is rotation of both junior and senior personnel; each group takes turns at out-of-country training and in-country work with foreign advisers.

Third, the high rates of vertical and lateral mobility in most host country civil services make it improbable that returning trainees will work on projects very long. As a result, degree training in donor countries may not be appropriate to meet narrow project needs. This type of training is more effective when given its proper role: the development of managerial, planning, and analytic skills.[12]

In-Country Training. In-country training can take several forms. There may be courses at formal academic institutions or at research and training centers, or there may be short courses on specific topics, given either within or apart from an institution or a project setting.

In-country academic training may suffer from the same lack of project relevance that afflicts academic programs in donor countries. However, a country's academic institutions usually become the foundation of its human resource development efforts, providing the knowledge base on which more specialized training programs can build.

Formal short courses and workshops can be used effectively to teach specific, project-related skills. The major difficulty with the formal workshop approach is that frequently a standardized package of lectures and exercises is presented, dealing with topics of general interest to a broad range of personnel. Although this keeps the cost per participant low, it decreases the relevance of the training.

Development literature includes a number of recommendations for improving the relevance and effectiveness of short-term, in-country training.[13] The training should be based on the explicitly identified needs of the trainees. The training program should be planned in discussions between those responsible for giving the training and those receiving it. The course materials should address situations faced by the trainees in their jobs. During the training sessions, the instructors should revise the materials in cooperation with the participants, based on participant perceptions of their relevance.

In Jamaica, a workshop was aimed at training project staff to solve problems as they saw them. Rather than relying on hypothetical examples, trainers used staff definitions of issues and attempted to create an environment in which mutual learning could take place. Thus, the exercises were based on real situations, and project staff generated their own plans for action.[14]

Similar workshops have been conducted in Indonesia, Egypt, and Tunisia. In all cases, evaluations by local government participants indicated strong support for this approach. In the Tunisian case, a team of foreign advisers gave a series of management seminars that drew material for practical exercises from the participants' current work. With guidance from the advisers, the participants designed projects, implemented a project monitoring system, and conducted evaluations. A key aspect of this effort was that the seminars were spaced a few months apart. This timing was to give the participants time to apply the skills learned in the previous session and to avoid either the appearance or the reality of their becoming dependent on the foreign advisers.[15]

On-the-Job Training. A third approach is on-the-job training. This includes informal coaching by foreign advisers and host government superiors and more structured exercises, such as temporary assignments to widen employee experience. Often the most

effective on-the-job training takes place when government officials and outside advisers work together
closely, each learning from the other.

The wisdom of assigning personnel who are
less qualified academically than their expatriate
counterparts depends on the nature of the assignment.
Where a high level of visibility, contact with
officials, and specialized skills are required, highly
qualified persons are needed. When the position is
field oriented and requires limited technical
knowledge, however, able candidates with less formal
training can do the job and learn while doing.

For example, the host-country counterpart to
the credit adviser of the Eastern ORD Rural
Development Project in Upper Volta had the equivalent
of an eighth-grade education. However, he performed
well in his post and, since he was proud of his newly
found skills (setting up a computerized credit
system), he was likely to remain content in that
role.[16] Continuous training and improved
supervision can help individuals with limited
backgrounds gain experience and become effective
technicians and managers.

Table 3.1 summarizes the advantages and
disadvantages of the training approaches discussed
above.

Simplifying Project Activities. Another strategy
for dealing with human resource limitations is to
design projects that can function by drawing primarily
on the available personnel pool. In many countries,
there is an abundant supply of junior personnel who
are underemployed because of shortages in supervisory
staff and supporting services. Through training and
supervision, senior project staff can help junior
personnel contribute to the project. A growing body
of literature discusses ways in which useful roles may
be found for inexperienced workers.[17]

Deferring New Projects. A recent study conducted
in Kenya found that six ministries were each implementing 177 donor-financed projects.[18] Managing
such a large number of projects, each with its own
objectives and clients, places tremendous demands on
the limited number of skilled ministry personnel. The
study pointed out that adding more projects would only
contribute to the supervision problem and result in a
breakdown in ministry control of activities and
policies.

Kenya is not an isolated case of project proliferation. Instead of contributing to this problem,
donors should consider ways to consolidate

TABLE 3.1
Advantages and Disadvantages of Various Training Approaches

Type of Approach	Advantages	Disadvantages
Out-of-country degree programs	Political benefits for donor as it strengthens ties and mutual understanding between donor and present and future decision makers in recipient country	Costly in terms of time and money; only a small number of individuals will benefit
		Candidates will be away from their posts for a considerable time and must be replaced or reabsorbed into the organization when they return
		Training is limited to those who speak the language of the donor country
		Training in donor countries is often geared to problems and solutions appropriate to that country, and not to those of importance to the developing countries
		Relevance of the training to the immediate needs of the project may often be low
		Difficult to coordinate the return of long-term trainees with the departure of the expatriate technicians to ensure project continuity

TABLE 3.1 (continued)

Type of Approach	Advantages	Disadvantages
		Potential danger of a brain drain increases with long-term overseas training if individuals become accustomed to standards of living that cannot be supported by public service employment in their own country; persons with advanced overseas degrees are often promoted rapidly into administrative positions and thus no longer use the disciplinary expertise that they have acquired
In-country short courses or work-shops	Can be inexpensive, especially when indigenous instructors are used	Limited to standardized topics and approaches that will be of interest to a relatively wide range of staff; cannot be easily tailored to individual needs
	Certificates of attendance or performance can be given, thus improving the credentials of trainees	Requires the absence of the trainees from their posts at times which, although convenient for the instructor and the class as a whole, may be inconvenient for the individual and the program to which he or she is attached
	Language problem is eased, assuming that the instructors are fluent in the local language	

77

TABLE 3.1 (continued)

Type of Approach	Advantages	Disadvantages
		Difficult to identify individuals who have the technical and training skills, as well as the language ability to conduct the training sessions
On-the-job train-ing	Is very specific to the needs of the project	Requires the development of a sound interpersonal relationship and incentive on the part of both parties to serve as teacher or student; these are difficult to mandate or structure into a project
	There is no interruption of the work schedule; trainee continues performing his routine tasks	No academic credentials are accorded so that the training does not benefit the trainee directly in obtaining promotions or increased responsibility
	Low cost, assuming that an expert available to assist in project implementation in any case	Language may be a problem if expatriate is not fluent

project activities, perhaps by contributing to the implementation of the existing project inventory.

Substituting Foreign Advisers. Foreign advisers can be substituted for host country personnel as implementers of development projects. Often, this will accelerate the pace of development activities. However, this approach also creates problems. In part, these stem from the advisers themselves and the roles donors have asked them to play. But in part they are caused by ambivalence felt in developing countries about the role of the adviser.

National leaders are under pressure to obtain immediate results. If achieving these results is the primary task of advisers, they will have little time to train host-country personnel to do the job themselves. This can lead to resentment and jealousy. In addition, host-country personnel may fear that the performance of foreign advisers will outshine their own. Of course, national leaders want to increase the capabilities of indigenous personnel, but it is sometimes too easy to place a higher priority on the achievement of observable results than on less dramatic capacity-building efforts.

Finally, some developing countries believe, rightly or wrongly, that they do not need foreign advisers. Government officials accept them because donors insist that the advisers be part of the foreign assistance package. This issue may be submerged during negotiations before project implementation begins, but if outside technical assistance is really considered superfluous—part of the price for obtaining material resources and foreign exchange—the advisers assigned to the project face a long, uphill battle. If the donor and the host government disagree on this point, it should be brought out before both sides formally commit themselves to the project. The earlier this is done, the better: donor and host country resources can be conserved by aborting the design process when the two sides have drastically different understandings of the project's personnel requirements. When the design is nearly complete, however, the pressure on both parties to obtain funding approval and proceed with the project may be irresistible.

Making Better Use of Available Personnel

Developing countries frequently do not make effective use of their limited human resources. There are two reasons for this. First, persons skilled in management, including both system designers and those with supervisory qualifications, are often in short supply. This situation could be improved by devoting more attention to management training.

Second, incentive structures in developing countries often work against the purpose they are intended to serve. Incentives need to be reviewed to make them appropriate to the intended task.

CONCLUSION

Personnel shortages are an important constraint to progress in developing countries. These shortages have contributed to the problems of implementing development projects. This chapter has described the nature of the problem and indicated how changes in policies, actions, and attitudes can alleviate it.

In the following chapter, attention is shifted from the role of developing countries to the role of donors and how changes in their policies might enhance the contributions of development assistance.

NOTES

1. Paul R. Crawford, Implementation Issues in Integrated Rural Development: A Review of 21 USAID Projects, IRD Research Note no. 2 (Washington, D.C.: Development Alternatives, Inc., May 1981), pp. 64-65.

2. Jeremy Hodson et al., Evaluation: Tropical and Subtropical Fruit Improvement Project, Yemen (Washington, D.C.: Ronco Consulting Corporation, July 1981), pp. 10-22.

3. Comptroller General of the United States, U.S. Assistance to Egyptian Agriculture: Slow Progress After Five Years (Washington, D.C.: United States General Accounting Office, March 1981), p. 51.

4. Ronald V. Curtis, James B. Lowenthal, and Roberto Castro, "Evaluation of Pindar River and Two Meetings Integrated Rural Development Project" (Washington, D.C.: Agency for International Development, January 10, 1980), p. 11.

5. Internal Evaluation of Project North Shaba (Washington, D.C.: Development Alternatives, Inc., 1980) pp. 31-33.

6. Liz Wiley, A Profile Analysis of Government Manpower in Arusha Region: General Conclusions and Recommendations (Arusha, Tanzania: Arusha Planning and Village Development Project and the Regional Development Directorate, 1980).

7. John Moris, Managing Induced Rural Development (Bloomington, Ind.: Indiana University, International Development Institute, 1981).

8. Jerry Van Sant et al., Management Support to the Jamaica Ministry of Agriculture Second Integrated Rural Development Project, IRD Field Report no. 13 (Washington, D.C.: Development Alternatives, Inc., April 1981).

9. Overseas Development Institute, "Integrated Rural Development," Briefing Paper no. 4 (London, December 1979); Vernon W. Ruttan, "Integrated Rural Development Programs: A Skeptical Perspective," International Development Review 17:4 (1975): 9-16.

10. Comptroller General, U.S. Assistance, pp. 19, 89.

11. Robert Chambers, "Project Selection for Poverty-Focused Rural Development: Simple is Optimal," World Development 6:2 (1978): 209-219.

12. George H. Honadle, "Manpower for Rural Development in Malawi: An Integrated Approach to Capacity-Building" (Washington, D.C.: Development Alternatives, Inc., July 1980), pp. 14-15.

13. John P. Hannah, Gene M. Owens, and Donald R. Mickelwait, Building Institutional Capacity for Project Planning in Central Java, Indonesia (Washington, D.C.: Development Alternatives, Inc., January 1981); George H. Honadle and John P. Hannah, "Management Performance for Rural Development: Packaged Training or Capacity-Building?," Public Administration and Development 2:4 (1982): 14-15.

14. George H. Honadle et al., Implementing Capacity-Building in Jamaica: Field Experience in Human Resource Development, IRD Field Report no. 9 (Washington, D.C.: Development Alternatives, Inc., September 1980).

15. John M. Buck and Claude I. Salem, Central Tunisia Development Authority Project Management Training (Washington, D.C.: Development Alternatives, Inc., November 1982); John M. Buck, William A. Rutherford, and Kenneth E. Koehn, Central Tunisia Development Authority Project Management Training II (Washington, D.C.: Development Alternatives Inc., March 1983); and John M. Buck and Claude I. Salem, Central Tunisia Development Authority Project Management Training IV (Washington, D.C.: Development Alternatives, Inc., November 1983).

16. Crawford, Implementation Issues, pp. 111-112.

17. Milton J. Esman and John D. Montgomery, "The Administration of Human Resource Management," Implementing Programs of Human Development, World Bank Staff Working Paper no. 403, ed. Peter T. Knight (Washington, D.C.: The World Bank, 1980), pp. 183-234; Robert W. Iversen, "Personnel for Implementation: A Contextual Perspective," International Development Administration, eds. George H. Honadle and Rudi Klauss (New York: Praeger, 1979), pp. 87-98.

18. Elliott R. Morss, "Institutional Destruction Resulting from Donor and Project Profileration in Sub-Saharan African Countries," <u>World Development</u> 12:4 (1984): pp. 465-470.

4
Technical Assistance Shortcomings

George H. Honadle, Jerry M. Silverman, and Donald R. Mickelwait

INTRODUCTION

Technical assistance (TA) is the provision, on a temporary basis, of qualified outside personnel to help with tasks for which people with necessary skills are not available in sufficient numbers. A lack of trained personnel is common in the isolated areas in which most development projects take place. Often a significant portion of a project's budget is devoted to TA, and foreign personnel occupy visible positions in the project organization.

The intended functions of TA in the design of most development projects can be divided into two categories:

- <u>Technology transfer</u>: the provision--formally or informally--of technical education that local staff require to perform their functions; and

- <u>Systems and organizational development</u>: the provision of assistance in the design of structures and procedures that integrate the activities and tasks needed to achieve project objectives and sustain results. When successful, most of this design work consists of adjustments in current structures and procedures rather than creation of new systems and organizations.

Most international donors have traditionally viewed TA in terms of technology transfer. Many large-scale development projects, however, are based on the need for significant changes in the context and manner in which tasks are performed and therefore also require an investment in systems and the development of organization.

Criticism of TA--in terms of its philosophical justification and practical application--is currently

widespread within donor agencies and recipient govern
ments. This criticism results from dissatisfaction
with the quality of TA personnel, confusion about the
appropriate functions of TA, and disagreement over the
roles that TA personnel should play.

This chapter addresses these problems and their
impact on project implementation. It identifies them,
examines their roots, and suggests ways they might be
alleviated.

IDENTIFYING THE PROBLEMS

TA is only one of many aspects of development
theory and practice subjected to criticism. Dissatisfaction with TA is symptomatic of a more fundamental
crisis in development: the contradiction between the
perception of development as a bottom-up, outward-
pushing process and the application of TA as though
its goal were merely to transfer technology. One
study suggests that marshaling folk-management skills
could eliminate the need for much TA and enhance local
capacity. Another study has explored the indigenous
technical knowledge, which is often overlooked by
outside experts.[1] Both approaches question the
value and underlying rationale of TA.

Strategy versus Fire Fighting

Although many studies and commentaries stress
that development is a long-term process involving
capacity building rather than just performance, field
activity often focuses on daily operational problems:

> In the midst of a forest fire, there is often
> little opportunity for the fire-fighting team to
> reflect objectively on the future implications of
> present tactics and the most appropriate uses of
> TA. The view from the small end of the telescope
> often magnifies the immediate problem but results
> in a narrow field of view. The team leader may
> accept constraints that should not be allowed to
> stand, or overrun guidelines which are legitimate
> project parameters. Given the hundreds of
> pressing decisions facing the TA manager each
> day, the long view can be very shortsighted.[2]

This sort of observation is understandable: the
conditions that cause TA to be required in the first
place also make it difficult to carry out.

Quality, Cost, and Loyalties

In 1980, the World Hunger Commission wrote that
there has been "a significant decline in the Agency

for International Development's capacity to deliver high-quality TA to help recipient nations sustain self-reliant national agricultural systems."[3] In response, AID's Board for International Food and Agricultural Development (BIFAD) reviewed its experience with TA personnel drawn from land-grant universities in the United States. The BIFAD report identified problems resulting from institutional factors within universities; the relationships among donor organizations, host governments, and universities; and the quality of TA personnel supplied by universities.[4] These observations support the contention that the quality of TA can be a problem and that institutional mechanisms for delivering it often fail to meet expectations. New approaches are needed.

The cost of TA personnel is also controversial. Usually TA funding is included in the grant portion of donor-assisted development programs. As a result, TA funding is often mistakenly viewed as a free good. In many cases, however, TA imposes real costs on the host government. Services and facilities, such as office space, secretarial assistance, housing, vehicle maintenance, and counterpart personnel, are normally provided as the government's in-kind contributions. Sometimes the real costs of TA personnel are apparent only after their arrival in the country.

A broader issue has been raised: "a project cannot be considered well-designed unless it is manageable by indigenous personnel."[5] From this perspective, heavy reliance on expatriate TA is a symptom of poor design. In fact, donor agencies often require recipient governments to accept foreign TA. Although the donor may believe that sophisticated skills provided by foreigners are necessary, recipient country personnel often view the foreigners as project spies, loyal to the donor rather than to local project management.

That perception is compounded when TA personnel are selected in compliance with regulations that require that goods and services be procured from specific geographic sources. In bilateral programs, TA and commodity line items are often linked directly to donor-country products and protected by complex waiver procedures.[6] In multilateral programs, such as those of the regional development banks, portions of specific member contributions are often tied in a similar way. Recognition of this fact, and frustration with its effects, led to the following recommendations:

> There should be no political conditions attached to development assistance and both donor and recipient countries should have full autonomy in this regard. The recipient countries should be

able to decide themselves on the use of development assistance and on where to obtain equipment
and experts.[7]

Many of these problems fall on field staff.
Contract management issues, project regulations such
as tied-aid purchasing requirements, and a host of
administrative details may distract or overwhelm the
TA personnel so that they lose sight of the long-term
rationale for their presence. A study of organization
and management in a large, ten-year project in
Tanzania found many of the symptoms of ineffective
TA:[8]

- Project technicians tended to act as independent individuals rather than as members of an
  integrated team;

- Work programming was often nonexistent, seldom
  realistic, and almost never undertaken jointly
  with either the team or the local personnel;

- Chiefs of party were mainly technicians rather
  than managers or planners;

- Locals and expatriates tended to apply different standards when judging expatriate job
  performance: Tanzanians stressed ability to
  communicate (language facility indicates both
  commitment and effectiveness) and interaction
  with local organizations and individuals,
  whereas Americans stressed technical competence and sophistication;

- Conflict resulted from different views of
  the performance of technicians and the
  desirability of renewing their contracts;

- TA team members did not have career prospects
  with the contracting organizaton;

- Accountability in the TA team was at a
  minimum;

- On-site orientation for TA personnel was not
  provided, although both Tanzanians and
  expatriates considered it to be a fundamental
  requirement;

- There was a noticeable lack of appreciation
  for others' problems and for the give and
  take of the development process; and

- Expatriate personnel turnover was high (see Table 4.1).

TABLE 4.1
Contract Team Tenure in the Masai Range Management Project

Months	Chief of Party	Technicians
0-12	3[a]	7
13-24	--	12
25-36	1[b]	2
37-48	1[c]	--
49-60	--	1
61-72	--	--
Over 72	--	1

Notes:

a One previously spent fourteen months as a technician and another subsequently spent nineteen months as a technician

b Previously served as a technician for nineteen months

c Previously served for seven months as a technician

This project's experience with TA was conflict ridden and poorly managed. These failings are usually measured by short-term, micro-level criteria such as those noted above. Attempts to improve the application of TA will remain superficial, however, unless they address long-term, strategic issues that are the underlying causes of the problem.

THE ROOTS OF THE PROBLEM

Three common failings afflict TA efforts:

- TA personnel adopt inappropriate roles;

- TA teams have inadequate structure and support; and

- Project designs and design processes are inappropriate.

Inappropriate Roles

Although most conventional project designs emphasize the technology transfer role of TA, in practice the advisers often interpret their role narrowly. Rather than transferring skills to local counterparts, TA personnel do the job themselves in the hope that local officials will be able to imitate them later. This approach is commonly used for large infrastructure projects: a person or team is simply hired and told to perform an activity. The focus is on a product that results from the activity, such as a road or a report, and no attempt is made to build local skills.

This is essentially a production model. It encourages technicians to perform rather than instruct, and it reinforces the tendency toward short-term project perspectives. It also implicitly defines development as a process of buying products from outside sources, rather than as one of stimulating the use of internal resources.

This model may achieve the project's immediate objectives; however, it will not contribute in any significant way to long-term, local capacity building. Unless experts are recruited, supported, and evaluated with other roles in mind, technology transfer objectives will not be achieved. Alternatives to this performer model are needed if the practice of TA is to be improved.

Inadequate Structures and Support

Many development projects use the services of foreign experts who have no affiliation with, and receive no support or direction from, an outside institution. Generally hired on personal services contracts, these advisers are directly responsible to a project directorate, such as a project management unit or a government ministry, and work without help or interference from a home office. In projects with limited scope, in which only one or two advisers are needed in specialized fields, this individual strategy can be cost-effective, provided that the project directorate or donor can identify and contract for the needed TA skills. Thus, when activities are well defined and are composed of relatively discrete tasks, the individual strategy has merit.

Most multi-million dollar development projects, however, require large and diversified teams of TA personnel. These teams are difficult to staff, and

project activities are even more difficult to
coordinate, if each specialist must be recruited
individually.

Thus, TA services for large-scale projects are
likely to be furnished by institutions that have large
staff resources of their own, or specialize in
locating and placing temporary staff in project
assignments. These institutions range from
universities to private voluntary organizations to
consulting firms that operate for profit. Each is
generally believed to have comparative advantages in
supplying certain types of TA. Their involvement in
project implementation is intended to relieve both the
donor agency and the host government of administrative
burdens. When as many as ten or twelve advisers and
their families must be recruited, placed, housed, and
supported in a remote rural area, those burdens are
substantial.

The options for acquiring TA through a contracting institution carry different implications for
the management and effectiveness of the TA team. A
university-based strategy calls for a good fit between
the research interests of the academic institution and
the goals and implementation requirements of the
project. This type of fit is not automatic; indeed,
conflicting agendas have plagued several projects in
which the academic strategy was applied. This
occurred because often the TA staff assigned to the
project were junior faculty or graduate students (and
thus failed to meet host country expectations of
expertise), or the research did not deliver results
that could be applied in the lifetime of the project.

A second variant of institutional contracting can
be described as a bodyshop strategy. This model
requires that the institution's home office carry out
a set of basic functions to find TA personnel and
deliver them to the project area. Once this happens,
the institution's role diminishes: it performs
routine administrative functions, it pays team
members' salaries, and it leaves the business of
project implementation entirely in the hands of the TA
team leader in the field. When this model in adopted,
the team leader has considerable latitude in decision
making, and can be confident that his or her judgment
will not be second-guessed by the home office. The
bodyshop strategy thus appears to be an efficient and
relatively cost-effective way of obtaining TA
personnel and letting them do their jobs.

In terms of the requirements of most complex
development projects, however, the bodyshop strategy
has serious drawbacks. Although job descriptions may
seem clear cut in project documents, the field
situation in a typical project contains surprises,
disappointments, conflicting expectations, confusion

over lines of command, and a host of other factors
that complicate the roles of TA personnel. The team
leader is thus challenged by the need to reconcile, or
at least balance, the following interest groups:

- Team members, with their own individual needs,
  strengths, and weaknesses;

- Donor agency representatives who wish to
  influence the project without taking
  responsibility for decision making;

- A constellation of host government agencies,
  each with its own objectives and priorities;

- Senior project personnel of the host country
  who are charged with achieving targets on a
  schedule that is often unrealistic; and

- Project beneficiaries, often not formally
  organized as a group, who nonetheless have
  high expectations for, and make large demands
  on, the project.

The combined effect of these demands generally
prevents the TA team leader from concentrating on the
project's long-term development goals, particularly
the important effort to build local capacity. The
contractor's home office may be preoccupied with other
matters, including billings and cost control, publications, development of new business, and donor-client
relations, many of which are not relevant to the
project. The home office may also lack an overview of
the project's strategy and performance. Certainly the
bodyshop model places no requirement on the home
office to deal with the larger picture; yet team
leaders in large projects usually need precisely this
kind of substantive support and feedback--in fact,
they crave it. When field staff are left to act
autonomously, without a supportive professional
network and home office management that is committed
to the broad mandate of the project, the tendency to
act as performers is strong, because encouragement for
other roles is lacking.

Inappropriate Designs

The design of a project influences the effectiveness of TA in at least three ways. First, TA personnel must be located with easy access to appropriate
organizations within the local system and to appropriate local counterparts responsible for management
decision making and performance of specific tasks.
Second, the scope of work and specification of TA

qualifications must be appropriate to roles that TA personnel are expected to perform. Third, the timing of specific TA contributions must correspond to the proper sequence of project implementation phases.

Often a project is designed to avoid interference from both the established bureaucracy and the private sector. Project designers can achieve this situation by creating an autonomous project management unit outside the ministerial structure and emphasizing the performer model of TA. Local counterparts are then recruited out of a permanent organization, placed in a temporary and vulnerable one, and then expected to ingest knowledge by observing the TA experts at work. But by the time this transfer of knowledge has taken place, the project management unit may be making plans to disband, and the local counterparts are set adrift. In this situation, the project design undercuts the long-term impact of TA, although the design may have been technically effective.

In the case of large-scale development projects that cross sectoral boundaries, the problem of organizational structure is compounded. In the absence of a new project-specific organization, some mechanism is usually established at a higher level to coordinate activities of these agencies. Although a coordinating body may be important in establishing policy and resolving interagency disputes, it seldom has any authority over implementation. TA personnel assigned to this body, therefore, have little impact on implementation, whereas those assigned to sector-specific agencies have little impact on policy.

In many projects, the scope of TA roles is too narrowly specialized. A typical team is composed entirely of specialists such as agronomists, agricultural engineers, and road and bridge engineers. From among these specialists, a chief of party is chosen, usually on the basis of age or extent of previous experience in the country. As a result, the chief of party often has no significant team management skills and, more important, lacks the strategic vision necessary to integrate the various sector-based efforts into a coherent whole.

Other problems result from the dual desire to keep advisers in the field for at least two years and to keep the team small. The scope of work may assign to one individual the responsibility for providing a wide range of expertise within a sector. For example, because an agricultural engineering adviser assigned to a project in Indonesia was the best qualified of the three-person TA team, he was required to advise counterparts in four separate government agencies on all rural public works, animal husbandry, secondary field crops, and horticultural subprojects.

This overuse of TA personnel often results from their long-term status. The normal justification for using TA over an extended period rests on one or more of the following arguments:

- TA personnel must become familiar with the project environment, including local culture, structure, and procedures of project-related organizations and personnel, and this process takes time.

- TA, to be effective, must be consistent in its content and approach over an extended period.

- TA contributions must be integrated, and this integration results only when TA personnel are together over time.

- Effective TA requires trust between expatriate and host country personnel, and the development of this relationship takes time.

- Long-term TA is less expensive per day than short-term TA because fixed costs (such as for transportation and living) are spread over a longer period.

However, when personnel on long-term assignments provide most of the TA, the following negative consequences often result:

- The expertise of one resident specialist is more limited than would be available from a variety of short-term experts;

- As the project moves through implementation, the requirements for specific skills and approaches change, but the expertise provided by TA personnel remains unaltered. Thus, skills appropriate during the first year may be irrelevant during the third year; and

- TA personnel associated with a project over a long period often insist on acting out their performer roles, even in the absence of donor agency pressure to attain production objectives.

Many implementation problems are reflections of design decisions, and many TA failures reflect poor project strategies and organizational arrangements. In evaluations that emphasize production targets, TA tends to be judged by performer standards--which do not support capacity building. Thus, project design often inhibits TA efforts to encourage local initiatives and nurture viable processes.

ALLEVIATING THE PROBLEM

Substantial improvements in TA may be brought about by:

- Adopting alternative, and more appropriate, roles for TA;

- Improving the mechanisms used to supply TA; and

- Adopting new approaches to the donor's process of developing projects.

Adopting New Roles

The performer style of TA and its limitations were noted above. Three other models can be identified: the substitute, the teacher, and the mobilizer.[9]

The substitute model provides people to fill positions until local talent is recruited and trained. For example, OPEX (operational expert) personnel are provided as stand-ins for trainees in AID-assisted projects in Zambia, Botswana, and other southern African countries. This is also a common feature of British aid.

The substitute model resembles the performer approach because it places a person in a ministry, staff unit, or operating agency with responsibility for doing a job. It differs, however, in that the substitute is expected to focus more on caretaker functions than on high quality results. The substitute approach has been applied using colonial service personnel who are long on contacts and experience, but often short on technical skills, in countries in which an indigenous bureaucracy has been slow to develop.

An alternative role for TA is that of adviser, although teacher is a more accurate description. This model, based on the diffusion or transfer of skills and technologies, places the outsider in an advisory rather than a direct decision-making role. The key factor is the interaction between the local counterpart, who receives the advice, and the adviser. Because success is defined as the transfer of skills to the counterpart, the adviser model has a personal focus, rather than a product or job focus.

The use of short-term advisers of this type mixes a person and product emphasis. For example, an outsider may be engaged to conduct a cash-flow analysis of the operations of an irrigators' association. Under the performer model, the report would be the only consideration. Under the teacher model, however, preparing the report would become a device to impart an analytic skill. A teacher would most likely consider a counterpart's ability to replicate the study, perhaps writing the study in a way that would help the reader reproduce the methodology in a new setting. Thus, the teacher approach places a high priority on the writing and teaching capabilities of TA personnel.

Although the teacher model is often espoused by TA staff and their employers, it is not commonly practiced. Long-term advisers slip into performer roles when their counterparts are unassertive or unavailable. Moreover, even when the long-term strategy emphasizes the teacher mode, short-term components of the strategy may be based exclusively on the performer model.

The final TA model is the mobilizer, which has its roots in community development, organizational development, and institution-building traditions. Mobilizers combine advisory and advocacy functions. Their purpose is to help a segment of a community, organization, or government increase its capacity to influence other sectors. Thus, coalition building, motivation, and surrogate leadership are key activities.

Since this model emphasizes the ability of TA personnel to motivate others to act, it focuses on the establishment and institutionalization of processes that enhance existing local skills and develop new ones. Effectiveness in the mobilizer role requires an ability to interact smoothly with multiple organizational levels. Academic credentials and seniority, combined with personal commitment and the ability to relate to and communicate with villagers, are all important. The ability to use informal decision-making networks is paramount.

The mobilizer model shares some but not all of the characteristics of the teacher role. An effective mobilizer, like a teacher, has conflict management skills and the ability to analyze and articulate the process dimension of the assignment. Although a teacher is usually a technician, such as an agronomist, engineer, economist, or geologist, a mobilizer is more likely to be a generalist with expertise in community development, public administration, or management training. Table 4.2 summarizes the advantages and disadvantages of each TA model.

TABLE 4.2
Alternative Technical Assistance Roles

Role	Advantages	Disadvantages
Performer	Allows freedom from kinship ties	Bypasses local organizations and fails to build capacity
	Offers high technical performance standards and quick results	Results in recommendations that are often ignored
	Is a familiar role for most technicians	
	Allows unpopular technical recommendations	
	Is easy to evaluate	
	Serves watchdog function	
Substitute	Allows freedom from kinship ties	Perpetuates local employment of colonial civil servants without needed skill levels
	Allows long-term participant training	Fails to build capacity
	Can utilize volunteers	
Teacher	Allows freedom from kinship ties	Depends on counterpart relationship and availability
	Builds individual capacity	Is sometimes uncomfortable for local government
	Is usually an accepted and common role	May be sensitive to age or sex differentials

96

TABLE 4.2 (continued)

Role	Advantages	Disadvantages
Mobilizer	Allows freedom from kinship ties	Is easily politicized
	Builds organizational capacities	Is difficult to evaluate
	Improves chances that newly emerging project opportunities will not be missed	Is an unfamiliar role for many TA personnel
	Does not require a significant resource base	Requires projects supportive of role

Using New Mechanisms

An emerging and potentially more promising alternative to the traditional TA contracting mechanisms is
the management team strategy.[10] Effective use of
this strategy in a development project depends on four
preconditions:

- The team leader has a stake in the institution
  that is contracted to carry out the TA. A
  "stake" is defined as a staff position with
  employment that continues after the assignment
  ends and allows the team leader to influence
  decision making within the home office. This
  precondition improves the chances that the
  field team will listen and respond to
  substantive direction from the home office.

- The home office has management staff with
  development experience and capability, who can
  review the progress of the project, provide
  short-term assistance on a regular basis,
  conduct evaluations, and contribute to the
  development of strategy. This precondition
  precludes those contracting organizations with
  experience limited to proposal writing and
  resume review. It assumes that home office
  management has something useful to say to the
  field team.

- Both field and home office staff agree on a
  prevailing development approach that provides
  a unifying theme for undertaking a rural
  development project. This precondition lowers
  strategy conflicts between home office and
  field and among the field team members.

- The donor agency, client government, and TA
  organization all recognize that development
  involves changes, some of which are unpredictable and unprogrammable early in the project
  life cycle. This calls for adaptive field
  testing, experimentation, and modification of
  original plans during implementation. If met,
  this criterion reduces the likelihood that any
  party will hold sacred the original project
  blueprint, which was written years earlier.

The purpose of a management team approach is to
ensure that TA has the greatest possible impact on
project success. The approach depends on strong links
between the long-term team, which has been identified,
recruited, oriented, and placed in the field, and a

home office system with the capability to provide administrative, logistical, personnel, and financial support to maintain the field team. Discussions of development strategy can easily be sidetracked if the home office is unable to pay salaries, ship goods, process travel vouchers, or expedite insurance claims. If these activities are under control and if the preconditions discussed above are satisfied, members of the home office staff can turn to managing substantive TA efforts.

The home office portion of the management team must recognize that field teams live and work under more difficult conditions than those at the home office. A variety of factors can divert TA personnel from their tasks. These include host country politics; conflicts with counterparts; commodity shortages; inadequate planning, funding, and staffing; and a harsh physical environment. These factors increase stress and thereby make apparent the team's own human inadequacies.

The task of supporting a long-term field team is not simple. There must be a balance between attention to daily detail and to strategy. Therefore, home office management should set out clear administrative policies and guidelines. With these in place, most daily, weekly, and monthly team management decisions can be vested in the field leader. In the final analysis, the division of responsibility between home office and field teams is usually a negotiated settlement; it always reflects project circumstances and the personal characteristics of managers on each side.

The mechanisms by which the home office can make meaningful contributions to the project are few; all involve face-to-face contact and the investigation of field-level problems. One mechanism is short-term project assignments for senior home office staff. This approach provides the field with informed support from colleagues in the organization, allows personal communication between field and headquarters, and increases home office understanding of the details of critical TA activities. It requires home office staff who can provide TA; provision in the contract for this assistance; and its acceptance by the field team, donor, and host country.

This technique can easily be misused if managers at headquarters attempt to use staff members on these assignments to conduct unofficial (and unrequested) evaluations. They should not unilaterally analyze project direction or suggest improvements in the TA team's performance. The short-term specialist should follow the team leader's rules of territoriality: when in the field, report only to the field team leader.

A second mechanism by which the home office can make meaningful contributions to the project is through home office management visits. Regularly scheduled visits to the project by home office staff can be useful, particularly when the visits are made by staff with different perspectives. One helpful outlook is the team builder, who can help the team coalesce around project objectives and interact in a positive way. The second helpful outlook is the project officer, who oversees all project activities and is responsible for support within the home office. A third role for the home office visitor to play is the decision maker, who can absorb criticism from the host country government or the donor agency for unpopular but necessary project decisions.

Field teams feel ambivalent about these visits. They want recognition for their effort and success, but they do not appreciate judgments. Experience suggests, however, that unless one home office visit takes place every three to four months the field team becomes disconnected from the home office. This increases the possibility that a team member or team leader may diverge substantially from a consensus strategy for the project; if this occurs and persists over time, there may be no choice but to change personnel.

Finally, the management team strategy enables the TA team to make maximum use of the benefits and reduce to a minimum the disadvantages of both long- and short-term TA by creating the most efficient mix of both. If the managing organization maintains a home office staff of development professionals who are available for short-term assignments under the direction of long-term field team managers with whom they share a common development philosophy and methodology, it will be possible to:

- Limit the size of the long-term field team by including generalists whose qualifications correspond to strategic project requirements;

- Rely on a wide variety of recurring short-term assignments by home office specialists who are guided by long-term TA generalists; and

- Adapt to changes in the scope of work of long-term positions as the project evolves by exchanging field personnel and home office personnel, thereby achieving a better fit of expertise for successive project phases.

This last benefit is important because it offers the prospect of continuing employment of field staff

in the home office when the project no longer requires
their contributions. Thus, TA personnel need not be
maintained in the field for an arbitrary contract
period that extends beyond the project's need for
their specific skills.

Of the contracting and management approaches
discussed earlier in this chapter--individual,
academic, bodyshop, and management team--the simple
individual strategy solution has been found to be
insufficient in meeting the demands of large, complex
multimillion-dollar projects. Two of the other
strategies, the academic and the bodyshop, suffer from
conflicting incentives and lack of home office
support. These factors distract team members from
focusing on the primary task of making the project
work through building the capacities of indigenous
leadership. The management team strategy appears to
have the best theoretical prospects because it unites
the responsibilities of field and home office
management.

The strengths and weaknesses of all four
approaches are noted in Table 4.3.

Designing Better Processes

TA is not a panacea for development. When
project strategies are ill conceived or when TA
personnel are pushed into performer roles, TA is often
counterproductive. Moreover, when project designs are
regarded as rigid blueprints, learning and capacity
building are stifled.

Three recommendations will reduce to a minimum
these and other weaknesses:

- Large, long-term TA teams should be replaced
  by small, long-term teams complemented by
  flexible mixes of short-term specialists;

- Projects should be designed to address issues
  of local capacity by adopting mobilizer and
  teacher models of TA; and

- Donor design processes should conform to these
  new approaches.

This last point is important. The design process
should be based on documents that explain that the
project's highest priority is to build capacity, not
to achieve visible, short-term results. Until donors
begin to define capacity building as the project's
primary objective, it is unreasonable to expect TA
personnel to interpret their role as one that extends
beyond the performer model. In addition, evaluations

TABLE 4.3
A Taxonomy of Technical Assistance Strategies

Approach	Strengths	Weaknesses
Personal services contract: "the individual strategy"	Low cost	Limited recruiting pool for individual specialists
	Low profile	Isolation from new approaches to development
	Allows specification of known individuals	Reliance on donor or host governments for procurement
		No mechanism for short-term technical assistance
		Limited support services (insurance, retirement, household storage) for expatriates
		Lack of any tax advantage may affect quality of staff assigned to project

TABLE 4.3 (continued)

Approach	Strengths	Weaknesses
University contract: "the academic strategy"	Link to research networks	Can be opportunity to assign low per-forming faculty
	Can improve quality of development studies program	Reward system may support research but not action
	Field team has permanent base	Usually inexperienced in procurement
		Not easy to deliver short-term technical assistance
Private firm contract with temporary staff: "the bodyshop strategy"	Allows specification of known individuals	Temporary staff limits field management
	Builds talent search capability in domestic organization	Home office aim is to keep costs low; therefore support may be minimal
	Does not require strong capability in home office	

TABLE 4.3 (continued)

Approach	Strengths	Weaknesses
	Can deliver short-term technical assistance	Reliance on donor for procuremnt
		Relatively high cost
Private firm contract with resident team leader permanently employed in home office: "the management team strategy"	Link to project information networks	High cost
	Facilitates field management	Long communication and supply lines
	Facilitates procurement	Requires experienced home office with knowledge and competence in development
	Facilitates short-term technical assistance	Adds another actor into the development assistance project

TABLE 4.3 (continued)

Approach	Strengths	Weaknesses
	Home office account-ability for contract provides strong incentive among field staff for quality work	Extremely difficult to implement, given the demands made on the time of home office management
	Can support capacity-building role models	

Source: Donald R. Mickelwait, George H. Honadle, and A. H. Barclay, Jr., "Rethinking Technical Assistance: The Case for a Management Team Strategy," Agricultural Administration 13:2(1983):16-17.

will continue to reinforce the performer and product approach that predominates design documents.

The following steps will keep development assistance focused on capacity building and sustainability:

- Project designs should avoid bypass mechanisms such as project management units in favor of established government institutions such as provinces, districts, or other permanent bodies;

- Project evaluations should stress the impact on local capacity rather than the achievement of preset production targets; and

- Donor design processes should become capacity-building exercises, extending for up to two years, that mobilize local human resources in the design process. The result should be a flexible document that supports innovative problem solving, creative use of TA, and organizational learning processes.

Without these changes in the TA environment, it is unlikely that new mechanisms or role models will lead to significant changes in performance.

CONCLUSION

This chapter has identified some root causes of problems with the use of TA in large-scale integrated development projects. In addition, the chapter has suggested role models, contracting and management mechanisms, and project design and evaluation approaches to alleviate these problems. The chapter indicates that the problems with TA extend far beyond the TA personnel themselves.

At the same time, personnel are of central importance. Unless committed, skilled, enlightened, and realistic people are encouraged to participate in development, there is little hope for positive outcomes. The task, then, is to create institutional climates that support this participation. This is true for all the sectors--donors, universities, TA teams, developing country governments, and village societies. Only when "development" is redefined as mutual learning, and "TA" is defined as mutual support, will the development process achieve greater success.

106

NOTES

1. Robert W. Iversen, "Personnel for Implementation," International Development Administration: Implementation Analysis for Development Projects, eds. George H. Honadle and Rudi Klauss (New York: Praeger, 1979), pp. 87-98; Robert Chambers and Mick Howes, "Rural Development: Whose Knowledge Counts?," IDS Bulletin 10:2 (1979).

2. Donald R. Mickelwait, Technical Assistance for Integrated Rural Development: A Management Team Approach, IRD Working Paper no. 3 (Washington, D.C.: Development Alternatives, Inc., September 1980), p. 9.

3. Overcoming World Hunger: The Challenge Ahead (Washington, D.C.: Presidential Commission on World Hunger, March 1980), p. 117.

4. Morris D. Whitaker, Toward More Effective Involvement of Title XII Universitites in International Agricultural Development, BIFAD Staff Report no. 1 (Washington, D.C.: Agency for International Development, October 1980).

5. Iverson, "Personnel," p. 88.

6. There is potential for conflict when the capacity to do the job exists locally but procurement regulations require that the donor seek the expertise elsewhere. Theoretically, this approach assumes the lack of local talent or an overriding capability located somewhere else. In practice, it is often used in bilateral programs to generate employment for experts in the donor country. The resulting products also allow the donor agency to demonstrate its performance, responsibility, and good management.

7. Food and Agriculture Organization, Report from World Conference on Agrarian Reform and Rural Development (Rome, 1979), p. 50.

8. George H. Honadle with Richard McGarr, Organizing and Managing Technical Assistance: Lessons From the Maasai Range Management Project, IRD Field Report no. 2 (Washington, D.C.: Development Alternatives, Inc., October 1979).

9. This typology is detailed in George H. Honadle, David D. Gow, and Jerry M. Silverman, "Technical Assistance Alternatives for Rural Development: Beyond the Bypass Model," Canadian Journal of Development Studies 4:2 (1983): (221-240).

10. Donald R. Mickelwait, George H. Honadle, and Albert H. Barclay, Jr., "Rethinking Technical Assistance: The Case for A Management Team Strategy," Agricultural Administration 13: (1983): 11-22.

5
Decentralization and Participation: Concepts in Need of Implementation Strategies

David D. Gow and Jerry Van Sant

INTRODUCTION

The late 1970s and early 1980s have seen a growing interest in decentralization in many developing countries. A significant aspect of this interest is that decentralization is now viewed as a way to:

- Improve the planning and implementation of development; and

- Facilitate effective popular participation in the process of development in a more profound way than envisaged in earlier decentralization efforts.[1]

Decentralization and the participation of beneficiaries are believed to increase the possibility of project success. It is argued that, if the local population--particularly the poor--is to benefit from development and obtain a larger share of government services and resources, the delivery systems for public services must be decentralized and participation in planning and decision making must be elicited from beneficiaries at the local level.[2] Decentralization implies the devolution of decision-making authority and control over the management of development initiatives and resources from the center toward the periphery. Participation implies local autonomy through which potential beneficiaries discover the possibilities of exercising choice and thereby become capable of managing their own future. This type of beneficiary participation, however, is unlikely to take place unless some corresponding participation characterizes the work climate of government staff. This staff participation, in turn, may best be stimulated by decentralization.

Central governments decentralize to attain their political, economic, and social objectives.[3] The same is true for participation, although, as one study has pointed out, having a voice and a role in assessing one's material needs is something to be valued in itself.[4]

Decentralization can contribute to development in the following ways:

- Close contact between potential beneficiaries and government officials allows the officials to respond more effectively to local needs and conditions;

- Local capacity to plan, implement, evaluate, and maintain development activities increases with experience; and

- The balance of political power in a specific locality can be altered by bypassing, strengthening, or compromising with traditional leaders.[5]

Although the potential advantages of decentralization and participation overlap, the same project has only rarely successfully achieved both. Increased participation does not necessarily lead to more decentralization or vice versa, although some form of decentralization seems to be a necessary condition for effective beneficiary participation. Whether pursued together or individually, however, these initiatives have not lived up to expectation, as manifested by the following common project characteristics:

- Unwillingness of central ministries to devolve meaningful authority to project staff;

- Unwillingness of project staff to allow potential beneficiaries to participate in project decision making;

- Reluctance or refusal of potential beneficiaries to participate in project activities;

- Success of local leaders in manipulating project resources and activities for their own ends; and

- Weakening of high-level support for decentralization and participation when local initiative stretches beyond the narrow confines of project decisions.

REASONS FOR THE PROBLEM AND ITS MANIFESTATION

Decentralization and participation initiatives have not met expectations for a several reasons. For example, they have been viewed as a panacea:

> . . . If one surveys any body of relevant litera-ture--theoretical or applied--decentralization is presented as a solution to a rather large number of problems. It promotes geographical equity, increases popular capacity to insure responsi-bility and accountability, enables easier access to decision points, reduces conflict and is more democratic . . . . It improves delivery of service . . . it even eases national planning problems through the provision of a more reliable information base. These are claims: not hard fact.[6]

In addition, decentralization and participation have not been effectively implemented. There are five reasons why this is so: lack of political commitment, bureaucratic resistence, poor project design, inadequate resources, and key constraints in the immediate project environment. Each reason will be discussed below.

Lack of Political Commitment

Unless political will at the national level favors decentralization or participation, there is little chance that either will take place. Political commitment may take several forms, including:

- Articulating participatory development strategies in national policies and legislation;

- Ensuring a high priority for development in routine administrative decisions; and

- Breaking barriers of entrenched interest in the redistribution of resources needed for rural transformation.[7]

Yet even political commitment from the top will not ensure effective decentralization. In countries as different as Tanzania and Panama, for example, decentralization was promulgated by a strong national leader. Nonetheless, in Tanzania it took nearly a decade for President Nyerere's concept of ujaama to be incorporated into national policy and yet another decade for implementation efforts to start.[8]   In

Panama, the concept of _poder_ _popular_, introduced in
the mid-1970s, received a severe setback with the
untimely death of President Torrijos. Decentralization in Panama has taken two forms: geographic
dispersion of line ministries and creation of representative bodies from all levels of society. These
bodies, especially at the local level, have not been
particularly effective, in part as a result of lack of
central support.[9] In Egypt, much of the impetus for
decentralization came from President Sadat. Although
the relevant legislation was introduced in the early
1970s, implementation has been slow and problem-
ridden.[10]

Political commitment from the highest levels can
be two-edged. Although decentralization and participation can translate into widespread rural mobiliza-
tion to support and implement government policy, they
can also serve as effective tools for government
control of the rural population.

In the Philippines, for example, President Marcos
has consistently pushed for limited decentralization.[11] In Indonesia, proposed expansion of the
Provincial Area Development Program to Irian Jaya was
also seen by some in this light. In this tribal
region, non-Irianese civil servants, whose vision of
the process and goals of local development may vary
considerably from that of the ethnically different
indigenous population, would be the likely
beneficiaries.

Bureaucratic Resistance

Even when the political will exists, implementation of decentralization and participation initiatives
may be difficult to effect if the political leadership
has to deal with powerful line ministries that are
unsympathetic, if not openly opposed, to these
initiatives. Opposition may cause a chain reaction:
central government staff are unwilling to delegate
responsibility to field staff, who, in turn, are
unwilling to share their limited authority with
intended beneficiaries.

Since most development agencies existed before
the concepts of decentralization and participation
became part of the development paradigm, many were
designed for the more centralized, control-oriented
needs of colonial powers. As a result, the
structures, systems, and norms of these agencies pose
important barriers to decentralization and
participation.[12] Furthermore, as weak, newly
independent central governments attempted to engage in
nation building, bureaucratic practices become even
more rigid. A study of decentralization in Sudan,
Kenya, and Tanzania reported that the various

bureaucratic tiers through which local plans must pass discourage participation in development planning and reinforce the power of the bureaucracy to veto or modify proposals at each stage.[13]

At the local level, development field staff are said to be poorly trained, poorly motivated, poorly supervised, and poorly served by logistical supply systems.[14] Agricultural extension services are usually run by the government according to a standard set of procedures, rules, and precedents, resulting in inflexibility and slow response to field needs. Prospects and incentives, particularly for those working in the field, are bad. Often pleasing immediate superiors is more important than doing good field work. Field staff, for example, will yield to the bureaucratic emphasis on documenting the completion of facilities, training of farmers, or disbursement of funds rather than concentrate on the impact of these activities.[15] These incentives do little to encourage the civil servant to look beyond procedural compliance. The civil servant, like the small farmer, aims at reducing risk.

Even if central bureaucracies do favor decentralization and participation, lack of trained, experienced personnel may seriously delay, if not impede, effective implementation. The staff problem at the national level is often one of quality rather than quantity: the administrative capacity is weak and technical and managerial skills are scarce. At the project level, the problem is often one of both quality and quantity.

Nor are the international donor bureaucracies blameless in their support of decentralization and participation initiatives. AID personnel, for example, must meet the differing agendas of Congress. This often requires moving money in limited time cycles while paying lip service to the rural poor and participation. Because progress is usually measured in terms of money spent, the emphasis is often on large, complex projects, which tend to be inconsistent with decentralization and participation initiatives.[16] Both take time to implement, and neither is easy to evaluate.

The AID-financed Provincial Area Development Program in Indonesia, for example, has emphasized the implementation of widely scattered subprojects. This emphasis has led to a reluctance to involve low-level officials and organizations, on the grounds that their capabilities are limited.[17] Moreover, the assessment of subprojects has often focused on physical completion and money spent rather than such process issues as participation as bases for AID reimbursements to the government of Indonesia.

The contrasting perspectives of technical project staff and participation-oriented planners are summarized in Table 5.1.[18]

Poor Project Design

Many problems encountered during implementation result from decisions made during design. In fact, so-called management problems are often the results of project organizations that are poorly designed. Problems encountered with decentralization and participation may also have their genesis in the design phase. In some cases, the ambiguity that already surrounds decentralization and participation is left untouched, and no specific guidelines or procedures are provided for achieving these goals.

In the study cited earlier on Sudan, Kenya, and Tanzania, for example, no intensive analysis was done of the types of planning and administrative functions that should be delegated to different levels, or of their capacity to absorb these functions. Furthermore, little allowance was made for changing capabilities over time.[19] One major obstacle to effective decentralization in the Provincial Area Development Program in Indonesia has been the lack of an adequate methodology for including the beneficiaries in the planning process, and consequent uncertainty about how to implement decentralized activities within existing structures.[20] In the design of a large project in Jamaica, the project paper called for local organizations to be linked into the project, but did not specify which organizations.[21]

In the Abyei Development Project in Sudan, efforts to decentralize and enhance local participation were stymied for two basic reasons. First, the proposed Abyei People's Development Organization did not build on any existing pattern of social relationships, local leaders, or institutions. Second, because program outputs were deliberately left undefined and ambiguous, beneficiary participation in selecting goals, establishing priorities, and mobilizing community resources fell below expectations.[22]

Inadequate Resources

The problems encountered in implementing decentralization and participation initiatives are often exacerbated by the central government's reluctance to provide adequate revenue-raising authority to local governments or to share national revenues with them.[23] Without these revenues, it is

TABLE 5.1
Perspectives of Technical Project Staff Compared With
that of Participation-Oriented Planners

Technical Project Staff	Participation-Oriented Planners
Pressure to justify the expenditure of funds through quick and observable projects to ensure continued funding and a favorable work image	Inclination to go slowly to ensure that farmers understand the purpose and goals of the project before it is implemented
Confidence that project goals, techniques, and strategies are based on technologies that have have been empirically verified	Awareness that regardless of how technically correct the project strategy may be, the continued use of the technology over time requires that farmers themselves see its value and utility
The tendency to assume that any rational project will easily be accepted by farmers, once it has been been explained and demonstrated to them	Recognition that the process by which farmers come to accept change is not easy and is based on their observing the project in action and experiencing some success with it
The belief that project innovations will be better for farmers than the old way of doing things	The feeling that the old way is often best because it is consistent with the past experiences of farmers, their values and social norms, and the social realities of their community
The assumption that the suggested innovations hold no risk because of confidence that new technologies will help the farmer	Widespread anxiety that any shift from the tried-and-true way of doing things may be disastrous, especially for the farmer living at subsistence level

unlikely that decentralization and participation
initiatives will ever become self-sustaining.

Although many countries provide a mechanism for
generating taxes at the local level, the amounts
collected are usually small. This is particularly
true if the local population practices a subsistence
economy. In this case, the forms of taxation that can
be imposed are limited and consist primarily of head
taxes and personal property taxes, which are difficult
to assess and collect.[24] Generally, taxes are
channeled to the center, and sometimes a percentage is
returned to the locality.

An exception to this practice occurs in the Yemen
Arab Republic, which has witnessed the proliferation
of local development associations, created in part as
a response to the inability of the central government
to provide better infrastructure and social services.
One major source of funding for public works projects
is the local tax, which is levied on agricultural
production, livestock, and capital assets. The
locality uses the major portion of this tax to finance
public works.[25]

More usual, however, is an administrative
structure in which local authorities depend heavily on
the central government for their financial resources.
For example, in the Philippines:

> . . . Local governments have very limited formal
> authority and financial resources. The doctrine
> of residual powers is not accepted under
> Philippine laws of local government. Therefore,
> authority is limited to only explicit legal
> grants. In addition, local governments rely
> heavily on various forms of national financial
> aid to the extent of 20-80 percent of their
> budgets, depending upon size, wealth, political
> connections, and how 'aid' is defined. Moreover,
> many of the activities normally considered
> 'local' in developed countries are either handled
> by agents of national ministries or by officials
> who have undifferentiated responsibilities to
> both national and local government.[26]

In Jamaica, local governments receive approximately 95 percent of their revenues from central
government grants. Primary responsibility for
agricultural development is centered in the Ministry
of Agriculture, which has established numerous boards,
agencies, and projects--all of which receive their
direction, directives, and financing from the
center.[27] This financial dependency has resulted in
an elaborate system of patronage.

Constraints in the Immediate Project Environment

Factors within the immediate project environment may limit the effectiveness of decentralization and participation initiatives. These include historical factors, the role of local leaders, and the lack of infrastructure.

Historical Factors. Local responses and initiatives, as well as capacities to organize and attempt collective innovation, are all conditioned by the course of history, especially the recent past. In many parts of the developing world, the colonial experience still exerts a strong influence, which may severely constrain development initiatives. The suppression of local leadership, the imposition of forced labor, and the harmful effects of cash cropping on the respective roles of men and women are all part of this unfortunate legacy. As a result, societies with a colonial history are often skeptical about development initiatives introduced by outsiders.

In the North Shaba Rural Development Project in Zaire, the local population was initially suspicious of any increased governmental interest in the area. In the past, this type of initiative had resulted in the abuse of collected data and further efforts to control the population.[28] With the exception of tax collection, outside intervention had been dominated by the one-time supply of health and education services. Government workers would arrive, construct a school, well, or dispensary, and then depart, arguing that the needs of the local population had been served. Thus, from the outset, the North Shaba project was confronted by a passive, somewhat suspicious dependency on the part of the local population.[29]

Previous developmental experience, although negative in the short run, can also have positive long-term implications. A recent study of grassroots development projects in Latin America noted an apparent contradiction: how do you explain collective efforts at grassroots development when there is no evidence of any threat, physical or otherwise, in the immediate project environment? Closer investigation showed that many of the people involved in local organizations had participated in previous forms of collective action. Although these earlier experiences might have aborted or even ended successfully, the desire for social change through collective action had never left them.[30]

Role of Local Leaders. The ability of governments to control social and political relations at the district level and below is frequently negligible, because of powerful local leaders who often use their power for personal gain.[31]   Even if the government did wish to bypass these leaders, it would be virtually impossible.   These elite groups will be overrepresented in any process of decision making on a formal or informal basis.[32]

Elites are made up of various economic, political, religious, and military groups.[33]   Some may make concessions to the poor majority out of enlightened self-interest that will yield them future payoffs.   If there are conflicts among these local leaders, some may seek support from the local population, thus providing participation in decision making.   Some may be in the positions they occupy because of their ability, and these people are crucial for encouraging participation.   In seeking support and legitimacy for their actions, they may spread the benefits of projects to a large number of people.[34] This has been the case in the Yemen Arab Republic, where both sheiks and local leaders have strongly supported the local development associations.   A study of 25 land reform programs in the developing world concluded that decentralization had played an important role in benefit distribution.   The most effective approach was to devolve power to local political leaders.[35]

In essence, a participatory process is actually a system of decentralized decision making by local leaders.   This system is different from genuinely representative decision making and equitable benefit distribution.   Depending on the type of project, these leaders may decide to monopolize the services, goods, and benefits proffered.   For example, in agricultural projects that offer scarce and divisible goods such as credit, production inputs, and machinery services, local leaders are likely to monopolize these goods. In contrast, collaboration between these leaders and other community members is necessary for another group of projects, including those designed to eradicate contagious diseases and those in which the goods are collective, such as churches, soccer fields, footpaths, and feeder roads.   Otherwise, these projects cannot function.

In another group of projects, there is no inherent reason why the interests of the local leaders and those of other community members should conflict if the project is well designed.   This situation may well occur with health and education projects. Nevertheless, control by local leaders of these projects may result in a more restricted distribution of benefits.[36]

Lack of Infrastructure. The poor physical
infrastructure found in many rural areas of the
developing world impedes decentralization and
participation:

> Inadequate . . . transportation facilities, roads
> and communication network . . . make coordination
> among decentralized decision-making units nearly
> impossible and effective interaction between the
> central government and local administrators
> extremely difficult. Moreover, it creates enor-
> mous difficulties for local administrators in
> mobilizing resources, supervising field person-
> nel, distributing services, and disseminating
> information.[37]

In the Yemen Arab Republic, for example, local
government is decentralized and independent, but
receives little assistance from the central
government, partly a result of the country's daunting
physical barriers and widely dispersed settlement
patterns. The ratio of central places to villages is
estimated to be 1:631, compared with 1:307 in Syria,
1:204 in Iraq, and 1:4 in Israel.[38] In a proposed
project area in Panama, one major constraint to
development and decentralization has been lack of
roads. There are 429 settlements in the project area,
77 percent of which contain less than fifty people,
and the majority of which are accessible only by
foot.[39]

In Indonesia, experience with the Provincial Area
Development Program has shown that local participation
is more effectively obtained in Java than in the more
remote outer islands. This difference is largely
attributable to the lack of both physical and
institutional infrastructure in the outer island
provinces. This creates enormous difficulty in
achieving the kind of communication necessary for
decentralized administration and for realizing the
benefits of local participation.

These difficulties occur in many project areas.
As a result, administrators must spend time visiting
and monitoring project activities. Because communication is essential for decentralized administration
and beneficiary participation, transportation problems
represent a major constraint. One way to deal with
this constraint is to begin project activity in
relatively accessible areas and gradually spread to
remote regions as experience, capabilities, and
perhaps infrastructure itself improve. The difficulty
with this approach is the risk that rural areas with
the greatest need will be missed because they are
often the most difficult to reach.

ALLEVIATING THE PROBLEM

The ways in which the problems confronting the implementation of decentralization and participation initiatives can be alleviated may be grouped into five categories:

- National policies;

- The bureacracy;

- Design and organization;

- Generating financial resources; and

- Building capacity in beneficiary organizations.

Each category is discussed below.

National Policies

Neither a donor agency nor its surrogate, a technical assistance team, has the right to force a national government to incorporate a policy of decentralization and participation in its development activities. Foreign specialists can, however, explain the potential advantages of decentralization and participation and ways in which these initiatives can help achieve more equitable development. However, neither initiative should be held out as a panacea for the endemic problems encountered in the process of project implementation. Most authorities on decentralization would agree that:

> . . . The issue of decentralization cannot be put as a simple two-valued choice. It is, rather, how much, where, under what conditions, and toward what purpose. And the answer may vary from situation to situation. Proposals to decentralize are either meaningless or utopian if they are not delimited accordingly--for they include a fundamental restructuring or rearrangement of authority.[40]

Participation initiatives are similarly complex:

> Participation is not something to be provided or planned in the same way that training is provided or expenditure is planned in a project. Because it involves factors beyond the project planner's or manager's control and because it depends on others' perceptions, interests and actions, it can only be provided _for_, or planned _for_. . . .

Participation is a matter of degree, and there
are many different kinds of participation. Not
all are always appropriate or possible.
Providing for participation involves sorting out
what kinds of participation are supportive of
development objectives in specific situations,
for given tasks.[41]

Decentralization and participation initiatives
will have significant political implications. Broader
participation is likely to change the use and
allocation of resources among social groups; indeed,
this is often the reason why participation is
advocated.[42] Decentralization will offset power
relations within government and affect the
distribution of resources among social groups.[43] As
a result, governments are usually reluctant to move
speedily to implement these initiatives. This
reluctance is often based on the assumption that the
periphery's gain will be the center's loss. The real
issue, however, is to negotiate the right mix of
supervision and autonomy.[44]
The ever-present pressure from central line
ministries to promote their own development ideas,
since this is essential for their own power, is not
necessarily inimical to decentralization and
participation.[45] There is a growing consensus that
if decentralization initiatives are to be effective
the center must have firm control.[46] A study of
agricultural administraton in Kenya noted that in a
decentralized administration structure the center
should be as strong as in a centralized one:

The key concept in rural administration is
linkages. The days of autonomous agricultural
development are ended. The development of the
small-farm sector is critically dependent on
government support. The state develops new
agricultural technologies, promotes and finances
their acceptance, and determines the dynamism of
their growth through price and other controls
. . . . Just as the small farmer depends on the
assistance of government, national ministries
need local incentives if rapid development is to
occur.[47]

In the case of the Chilalo Agricultural Unit in
Ethiopia, local elites managed to subvert the project
since the unit had few, if any, linkages with the
national government. In contrast, the Comilla project
in Bangladesh and the Joint Commission on Rural
Reconstruction in Taiwan had these linkages and
therefore could generate the necessary support to
carry out their programs.[48]

What is required, then, is controlled decentralization characterized by strong linkages and a negotiated sharing of responsibility between the center and periphery. This strategy can give project staff the autonomy and resources to demonstrate their capabilities within definite policy guidelines and centrally established standards.[49] A case study from Rajasthan, India, illustrates how this type of controlled decentralization can be successfully implemented.[50] There, the center has a virtual monopoly on funds for rural development projects, while the state has formal constitutional authority. In the case of rural electrification, central power is limited primarily to review of large projects and coordination of those projects involving more than one state. At the state level is a state electricity board, an autonomous technical body within the state government that receives some funds from the state but also raises capital on the open market.

Prior to 1969, the state electricity board in Rajasthan operated under the assumption that rural electrification was a technical problem to be solved by technicians. As a result, it isolated itself from both potential beneficiaries and other state agencies, preferring to use only information provided by its own engineers in selecting villages for electrification. In the late 1960s, pressure to decentralize electrical planning and coordinate it with other rural development efforts increased. Social and political criteria were therefore added to the technical and economic criteria used in the selection process.

In 1969, district agricultural production committees, which included politicians, administrators, and technicians, were given the power to select villages for electrification. This encouraged adherence to political criteria, primarily as a result of the increased accessibility of decision makers. Because more villages qualified under the stated economic criteria than could be electrified in any one year, the district agricultural production committees were able to expand the criteria and include the concerns of local constituents. Although the committees could not countermand the criteria imposed nationally, they were able to choose among priorities that lay within the general guidelines.

Controlled decentralization can strike a viable balance between the center and the periphery, retaining the best features of centralization and decentralization by:

- Combining the long-range perspective of the center, which establishes technical criteria, with the short-range perspective of the local level, which establishes additional sociopolitical criteria;

- Stimulating officials to be more responsive to the local population;

- Increasing efficiency; and

- Achieving economic and political goals.[51]

On this last point, this strategy has been called decentralization within centralization. With this approach, decentralization is regarded, at least in part, as a way to bring into harmony the interests of both national and local development. On the one hand, decentralization can improve the management of rural development, essential for the well-being of the country as a whole and of the beneficiaries of specific projects. On the other hand, it can achieve popular participation as well as national unity.[52]

The Bureaucracy

Even with strong national support for decentralization and participation initiatives, the attitudes and behavior of development field personnel must change for these initiatives to be successful:

> In part, and sometimes in large part, the observed behavior and manifest attitudes grow out of the structural situation in which government staff find themselves--the role expectations communicated in training programs and contacts with their superiors, the reward structures they face, the sanctions threatened, the performance measures against which they are assessed. While BRO [bureaucratic reorientation] will to some extent involve attitude and value changes, the more important element involves changes in job definitions, incentives, procedures, organizational responsibilities and the like. Indeed, it is likely to require that decision making within government become more participatory, as organizations tend to replicate in their external relations those styles of operation prevailing internally.[53]

How is this staff participation to be encouraged? It involves:

- Access to power, specifically the capacity to mobilize resources to accomplish tasks; and

- Opportunity, specifically, changes for advancement, contributions to important decisions, and increases in skills and rewards.[54]

Colombia's integrated rural development program,
which is administered by a special unit located within
the National Planning Department, a powerful and
respected government ministry, provides an example of
this type of staff participation. An outstanding
characteristic of this program has been its ability to
attract and keep well-trained, motivated professionals. This professional behavior appears to result
from the following factors:

- Some financial control over participating
  agencies in the program;

- Security of employment;

- Opportunity to present and implement one's own
  proposals; and

- Opportunity to complain and be heard.

Beneficiaries have played an increasingly
important role in planning activities for integrated
rural development in Colombia. Although they do not
control the budget, they do have some influence in how
it is allocated at the local level.[55] In this case,
staff participation did, in fact, encourage
beneficiary participation.

But this is not always the case. INVIERNO, an
integrated rural development project in Nicaragua
whose main component was supervised, computerized
credit, also managed to attract and keep highly
qualified, motivated personnel. INVIERNO offered its
staff opportunities for self-improvement, including
training, financial renumeration, and promotion.
Although INVIERNO did not necessarily offer them much
power, it did invite some staff participation in
planning and evaluation. Participation by beneficiaries, however, was limited almost exclusively to
using the services offered--in this case, primarily
agricultural credit and technology.[56] Even acceptance of the services was limited, perhaps a
consequence of the project design, which was based on
sophisticated technologies.

This approach has been called a retreat to
technology. In this case, delivering credit to large
numbers of small-scale farmers was seen as a technical
approach amenable to the advanced technologies of
information processing and communication.[57] The
evidence indicates that when a project is highly
complex it is less likely that project staff will
encourage intended beneficiaries to become involved in
project implementation, except as recipients of
proffered services.[58]

In light of the bureaucratic constraints to
beneficiary participation, more attention should be
paid to participation by project staff as one means of
addressing the problem. Key objectives of this
approach would include:

- Enhanced staff commitment to organizational
  goals and operational targets;

- Greater staff support for decisions and
  problem-solving initiatives;

- Increased exchange of information;

- Better use of staff knowledge in planning;

- More appropriate individual job designs; and

- Reduced resistance to change.

Types of management development activities that
support these participatory staff objectives include
team building, intergroup problem solving, joint goal
setting and planning, and training.
    The importance of basing these activities in the
actual context in which staff must perform was
emphasized in an evaluation of the Arusha Planning and
Village Development Project in Tanzania. The
evaluation's recommendations concerning training
activities included the following:

- Training should be based on the trainees' own
  explicitly identified needs;

- Throughout the training sessions, the material
  used should be subject to revision by the
  trainees themselves, based on their perceptions of the relevance of the material to
  their actual job requirements; and

- Materials and exercises should be based almost
  exclusively on the actual materials the
  trainees will use in their work.

Meaningful staff participation of this type, supported
by appropriate incentives and decentralized authority,
is one important way beneficiary participation in
rural development may be enhanced.[59]

Design and Organization

Many problems encountered in the implementation
of decentralization and participation initiatives have
been blamed on poor design and inadequate organiza-

tional arrangements. Some of these problems can be anticipated early, but others cannot, as the process is complex. Some general guidelines, however, can be prescribed.

Following a Process Approach. In the development field, there is growing evidence that creating effective decentralization and participation is a gradual, evolutionary process in which both project staff and potential beneficaries try some alternatives, discard them when they prove unworkable, and try others. This type of approach assumes considerable uncertainty and is characterized by an openness to redesign and adaptation to changing circumstances. The approach relies on a quick study and an interactive style of problem solving, rather than remote expertise. This approach rejects the blueprint concept of project design and implementation.[60]

A process approach has the following strengths and potentials:

- It is rooted in dialogue with the rural population and thus is responsive to local potential and needs;

- It allows variation in bureaucratic structures and thus can be adapted to political, social, economic, and physical changes that take place during implementation;

- It is based on learning and capacity building and thus is well fitted to the promotion of self-sustaining development;

- It transfers ownership of the program to implementers and thus creates an environment that supports innovative problem solving rather than routine application of pre-determined solutions; and

- It avoids negative side effects by eliminating design components that are deemed inappropriate.[61]

This approach, of course, requires designers and implementers to admit that, given the complexity of the problems to be solved, they still have much to learn. The approach implies, however, that both are prepared to try to find solutions by following a "dynamic, living theory of knowledge that requires us to set new facts into the world."[62]

If a process approach is to be effective, an information system that provides relevant, timely, and

succinct information to those with the authority to
use it is essential. Two elements of this system
should be stressed. First, careful planning is
important. A process approach does not mean
de-emphasizing planning. Without clear specification
of the structure and timetable for decision making,
the use and management of information will be
inefficient, crucial decisions will be deferred or
made precipitously, and implementation will drift.[63]
Second, an information system should provide a
two-way information flow between the staff of a
project and its beneficiaries. This interchange
should help temper the arrogance of outside experts,
who often assume that local information and knowledge
are intrinsically inferior and therefore to be
ignored--to the detriment of the development
initiatives.[64] An example of the importance of
these information flows is illustrated in the abortive
Tonosi Integrated Rural Development Project in Panama.
The government was unable to implement this project
effectively because of local opposition. This
opposition eventually erupted in a violent confronta-
tion between project staff and potential beneficiaries
in which a national guardsman was killed. The project
was abruptly terminated. This project had been
designed in a top-down manner, and the local population had not been consulted about the proposed
project components. One component, land distribution,
provided the catalyst that solidified local
opposition.[65]

Simple Is Optimal. If a project is highly
complex, it is less likely that donor agencies or
national governments will encourage decentralization
and participation, principally because complex
projects demand more effort on the part of project
staff and also take longer to demonstrate visible
results.[66] Furthermore, within the international
donor community, the emphasis continues to be on
large, capital-intensive projects that rely heavily on
imported technology.[67]
These projects invariably follow a blueprint
approach and are biased against decentralization and
participation from their outset. In reality, the more
complex a project is the greater the number of unforeseen problems. Thus, flexibility and adaptability are
required. They can best be provided by an approach
that starts with small, relatively simple activities
that respond to local needs and produce results
quickly.
Potential beneficiaries are more likely to
participate in development initiatives if they obtain
tangible, relatively immediate benefits. In this way,
they can gain the confidence and capability to under-

take more complex, long-term activities.[68] Simple
and small, in this context, are not advocated as ends
in themselves. When resources are dispersed to fund
numerous small activities, limited management capacity
may be spread so thinly that it is depleted instead of
enhanced. This situation can lower the chances that
any activity will become self-sustaining because
technologies will be ignored, benefits monopolized,
and lessons lost.

Often, the priorities of project planners differ
markedly from those of potential beneficiaries. The
project goal may be to improve human well-being by
increasing productivity; the beneficiaries' goal may
be to improve quality of life through more amenities.
For example, small-scale farmers are not usually as
concerned about the price or quality of basic staples
as are urban dwellers and the central government:

> They themselves can usually eat, no matter who
> else goes hungry . . . . What rural people see as
> scarce are good roads, good water supplies,
> health and educational facilities, and public
> buildings, the goods which the better-off urban
> dwellers can now take for granted.[69]

Not surprisingly, many rural inhabitants
downgrade farming as a way of life and prefer schools
that teach children skills they can use in town.
Off-farm employment means that children can provide
support for parents and other kin.[70] Clearly, there
is a need to improve conditions in rural areas and to
develop technologies that will ensure a better return
from farming. One way that this may be achieved is by
project staff negotiating with potential beneficiaries
to establish some common priorities.

This process of negotiation will involve tradeoffs. Experience in Tanzania indicates that when
villagers become aware of the tradeoffs that must be
made to achieve project objectives, they may decide
that achieving these objectives is no longer
desirable. This situation sometimes leads to
unexpected failures during implementation.[71] These
failures could be avoided by a process of dialogue and
negotiation between project staff and potential
beneficiaries before the proposed activity receives
final approval and funds are obligated.[72]

Working with Existing Organizations. Local
organizations of farmers are commonly regarded as the
most practical and effective means to achieve participation. These organizations can play positive roles
in the development process by acting as vehicles for:

- Maintaining two-way flows of technical information; this reinforces individuals who try new approaches and breaks down barriers between groups or individuals;

- Reducing risk to a minimum and practicing economies of scale;

- Adapting project activities to local conditions;

- Marshaling local resources;

- Achieving greater political and economic influence for local people by exercising influence over local administrators and asserting claims on governments;

- Sustaining project benefits; and

- Coordinating and spreading the benefits of outside assistance.[73]

Opinions differ on whether participation can be most effectively encouraged by working through existing organizations or by creating new ones.[74] The most important criterion for selection of an existing organization is its amenability to change. The extent to which the organization is willing to reorient its activities toward tasks different from those for which it was formed is difficult to predict. Moreover, few existing organizations are likely to appear fully satisfactory as a result of their domination by elites, uneven participation by their members, or poor performance. However, the introduction of new organizations takes considerable time, and they may well suffer from the same defects as their predecessors.

Three criteria that may help in selecting existing organizations are:

- The purpose for which the organization was formed;

- The organization's resource base; and

- The organization's ability to mobilize the local population.

One study has distinguished between active and defensive organizations: the former exist to advance members' interests and are, therefore, more amenable to change; the latter exist primarily to protect

members' interests.[75] If an organization already
has some productive assets, this indicates the
existence of resources and some managerial capacity to
undertake new or additional activities. Active
organizations include those that generate capital for
lending and savings as well as those that pool
productive assets to use land or water better.
Finally, an organization that has demonstrated its
ability to mobilize the local population to provide
funds, labor, or skills has capacity to undertake
additional activities.[76]

This strategy of working through existing
organizations has been successfully implemented in
Colombia through its integrated rural development
program, which functions in five regions of the
country. At the local level, the most prevalent
organizational form is the community action board,
which is dedicated exclusively to rural works
projects. If a community wishes to participate in the
program, the community action board must agree to
broaden its activities and become more production
oriented. If the board agrees, then the program works
directly through it. If the board does not agree, a
parallel group is set up, often with overlapping
leadership. Success to date appears to have resulted
primarily from two factors: the relatively apolitical
nature of the intervention at the local level and the
caliber of the technicians involved.[77]

In several Latin American countries, communities
form civil improvement associations to plan and
implement specific rural works projects. An
individual community commits some of its own resources
to these projects and petitions the government or
other funding agencies for additional resources. Once
a project is completed, these organizations may lie
dormant until they act on the next felt need.

These groupings can also form the basis for a
more permanent, production-oriented organization.[78]
It has been argued that these temporary organizatons
are successful because the members perceive themselves
to be cooperating to achieve a specific goal rather
than to create an organization.[79] If they succeed
in achieving their initial goal, the potential exists
for expansion into other activities. But this
transition to a broader, more permanent status will
not be automatic; it requires a patient, thorough
organizational effort.

If the decision is made to establish a new
organization, designers and implementers should be
aware of some possible pitfalls. First, a project
should not assume that a new organization will
automatically be understood and supported, unless it
meets some recognized need and the activities
involved are familiar and simple. Second, the use of

external resources should be kept to a minimum to
avoid the creation of a dependency relationship.
Third, when a new organization is introduced from
outside the community, the leadership roles (including
president, chairman, secretary, and treasurer) appear
to members and leaders alike to have outside authority
behind them. As a result, these roles are likely to
be exercised with less restraint and consideration
than if they were created by the members
themselves.[80]

   Dealing with Local Leaders. One common fear of
decentralization is that project staff and local
leaders will receive more than their fair share of
scarce development resources, that is, conditions will
be ripe for corruption. There is no evidence,
however, that decentralized administration and
decision making result in more corruption than do
centralized approaches.[81] Indeed, if decentralization is accompanied by greater openness in local
budgetary and other transactions, opportunities for
corruption may be reduced. In Indonesia, the Save the
Children Federation Community Based Integrated Rural
Development Project used a strategy of combining open
records with rudimentary training in bookkeeping and
management for members of local organizations. The
result was the exposure and removal of a corrupt local
official, triggered by the local participants themselves.[82]
   Nevertheless, decentralization and participation
imply the potential for conflict, particularly if they
are to be implemented through local organizations:

      Organizations are sources of power and a major
      purpose of community organizing is often to build
      the power of the poor to challenge the entrenched
      interests. The potential for conflict is self-
      evident and any community organizing activity
      should be carried out with recognition that if
      the group begins to take on any political char-
      acteristics there is likely to be a backlash
      which may result in withdrawal of official
      recognition, loss of resources, or even physical
      coercion.[83]

   In this situation, the leaders of the most
important factions--elites or otherwise--must be
included. Some of these leaders will have obtained
their positions as a result of their ability.
Consequently, the skills and experience they can bring
to development may be crucial. In addition, they may
often be those best placed to take advantage of
development initiatives. Some may be motivated to
help their fellow villagers because of enlightened

self-interest, others because they need a certain local constituency to support and implement their views. Whatever their motivation, local leaders will be represented--if not overrepresented--in any process of decision making.

One study has proposed a specific process strategy for a project area with little social cohesion, arguing that in this case an intervention should be geared toward an identified social grouping at the outset. This should not be overdone so as to generate irrevocable opposition from other groups; it should, however, represent a temporary concession to social realities. In time, the intervention strategy can become less exclusive, particularly by including activities that are important to more than one group but cannot be completed by any one group alone.[84]

The project may offer distinct social groups different types of technical assistance. In the Provincial Area Development Program in Indonesia, for example, one approach entails offering forms of assistance that would be of interest only to the rural poor, for example, technical assistance to those with no irrigation and the provision of low-value animals, such as ducks and goats, to those with no cows.[85] A similar strategy to reach the rural rich was designed into a proposed integrated rural development project in Panama. Directed toward helping small-scale farmers, the preliminary project design was strongly criticized by the large landowners in the area, who threatened to scuttle the project if they were not allowed to participate. As a result, an agribusiness component was designed into the project, primarily to satisfy their demands.[86]

Another possibility is to play one organization off against another. This approach requires consid-erable political sophistication.[87] In the Philippines, one municipality contained three active community organizations: the first was agressively anti-mayor, the second vigorously pro-mayor, and the third supportive of a young, activist priest. By working through this last group, which served as a balance for the other two, the mayor was able to obtain widespread community support for his projects.[88]

Even where local leaders dominate local organizations, they will not necessarily obtain a monopoly on the benefits. A case in point is the local development associations (LDAs) of the Yemen Arab Republic. These associations are responsible for designing and implementing public works projects. The LDAs are usually led by the local sheik, a hereditary position that, although similar to that of a feudal lord in medieval Europe, entails a considerable degree of reciprocity and moral responsibility for his

followers. It appears that these sheiks and the local
elites who support them usually act in the public
interest: most LDA decisions reflect the public will,
factionalism and corruption are surprisingly low, and
development projects generally benefit most of the
local population. Part of the explanation may lie in
the fact that the local population has channels
through which to obtain redress of grievances and
influence decisions.[89]

In most cases, even when groups are formed
specifically to serve the interests or defend the
rights of the disadvantaged, effective leadership is
most likely to emerge from those individuals who are
relatively more advantaged and closely allied with the
local power structure. However popular in theory,
programs that attempt to simply undercut or bypass
traditional leadership are not feasible. Either they
fail or outside authority in the form of project
agents takes the place of the traditional local
leaders. The key is to make leaders accountable to a
broad constituency, regardless of their group of
origin. This accountability may be defined by both
local and more centrally determined norms and
standards. It will be more effectively enforced if
incentives and sanctions are determined and applied
from below as well as from above. For sanctions to be
enforced by constituencies of rural poor, there must
be an open mangement style in which all members have
access to community activities and records. Training
may also be required to equip persons to review and
understand information newly made available to
them.[90]

Generating Financial Resources

Financial resources can be made available in
several ways, such as revenue sharing or block
grants.[91] In the former, a percentage of the local
taxes is returned to the locality to be used for
development activities, as is done in the Yemen Arab
Republic. In the latter, the central government makes
a grant directly to the local authorities to finance
these activities. The only way to help project
staff--and beneficiaries--realize their potential is
to give them adequate autonomy and resources. These
resources can be made available in the form of a
block grant for them to use at their discretion on
projects that fall within jointly negotiated
boundaries.[92] Where this has been done for small
rural works projects in Egypt, Nepal, and Indonesia,
for example, the reported misuse of funds had remained
within tolerable limits and the benefits have been
significant.

Experience with poverty programs in the United States provides some interesting insights into the options open to the central government. There are three distinct types of grants: categoric, block, and revenue sharing. Categoric grants, tightly controlled by the center, have been most effective at stimulating local activity to meet national priorities:

> Block grants and general revenue sharing with less federal control have enabled local governments to design programs which meet their own priorities. These grants increase local governmental power and discretion and enhance local capacity but have been less effective at targeting programs to the needy and promoting innovations . . . categoric grants have been found to be more stimulative then the other two types. [93]

Strong support from the center is thus important. In fact, many U.S. observers recommend not using block grants when the center cannot trust the localities to have the same priorities. [94]

Another way to generate financial resources is to have potential beneficiaries commit resources of their own. This is desirable for a number of reasons. First, governments do not have the resources to support all worthwhile development activities. Requiring an initial resource commitment indicates that this is not going to be another government giveaway program. Many activities would probably function better without any government involvement. Second, committing resources will make the contributors more concerned for the success of the development initiative than they otherwise might be. Finally, this commitment will indicate how interested the community members are in a new initiative. [95] Findings from an earlier study demonstrated the positive correlation between this type of resource commitment and overall project success. [96]

These commitments can be either in cash or in kind and can be generated in a variety of ways: from membership fees, quotas determined by family size, or some form of recycling of project benefits. It has been recommended that contributions be related to economic status and be limited to those who are expected to benefit. Often, in fact, it may be appropriate to link local farmer investment in projects to income gains derived from project benefits. [97]

In some countries, these resource commitments may be made formal by a contract between the beneficiaries and the outside funding agency. In Nepal, for example, participation in rural public works was generated in this manner. The contract laid out the costs, inputs, timing, and resource commitments from both the local population and the funding authority, in this case the district government. The funds were disbursed in installments, and progress reports, prepared by the district engineer, were submitted before further disbursements were made. Although not infallible, this type of contractual arrangement provides both parties with leverage.[98] Whatever the specific mechanics of this type of resource commitment, a commitment of some kind should be made to prevent the accentuation of paternalism and dependency.

In the area of resources, it is important to distinguish between resource commitment and income-generating activities. Resource commitment is usually some sort of contribution--either in cash or in kind--made at the time of project start-up. Income-generating activities produce income on a regular basis to cover operating costs of ongoing activities and to finance new ones.

These income-generating activities can cover a wide spectrum, from charging a user's fee for services provided (as happens in many indigenous water-users' associations and cooperatives) to establishing an enterprise specifically devoted to raising funds for the local organization and its activities (such as a store, a communal plot, lending money, or hiring out labor). These activities should evolve alongside the building of organizational capacity. What is important is that participants control how these locally generated resources are allocated and used. These resources can play a crucial role in achieving organizational sustainability.

The provision of external resources should be kept to a minimum to encourage self-reliance. In an irrigated rice project in Haiti, the opposite strategy was followed, with disastrous results. Small farmers were given food in payment for their participation in this project. Once the food stopped, so did their work and the rice was left unharvested: the participants did not view the project as their own, but as that of the implementing agency.[99]

A similar problem affected a major rural development project in Jamaica. The participation of farmers was essentially purchased through payments to them for terracing their land. Later, in the absence of these financial incentives, the farmers neglected to maintain their terraces. In this case, the terracing idea came from foreign specialists on a design team sent by an international donor agency. No real local participation in either project design or resource commitment was called for. Thus, the roots of farmer involvement in the scheme quickly withered when the incentive payments stopped.[100]

This project in Jamaica also illustrates that if the issue of sustainability is ignored--as it often is--some benefits can be provided without local resource commitment. In this case, external resources flowed to local organizations, benefits reached the small farmer, participation was low, and resource commitment was virtually nonexistent. The principal reasons for this lack of participation were the high degree of centralization, dependence on the government for the provision of goods and services, and the importance of patronage as a means of securing benefits. All of these patterns were already established through the experience of small-scale farmers with earlier organizations. Although the project could have worked to overcome this dependence syndrome, this would have called for the modification of many traditionally held understandings about the political system, involving costs to the project, the leaders, and the farmers.[101]

There is little evidence that the project's designers ever fully considered the long-run implications of their strategy. Typical of many large, donor-assisted projects, this project emphasized large up-front resource transfers that relied heavily on imported technology and technical assistance. Not surprisingly, the project was locked into a set of quantitative component targets. This type of project is intrinsically anti-participatory, since its focus is on short-term measurable targets. Attention to these targets precludes strategies aimed at involving farmers in a meaningful, long-term way.

Although those involved in development generally agree on the importance of a local resource commitment, they differ on the amount of assistance that should be provided to local organizations:

> It is not a question of substituting government for local patrons, especially in the frankly exploitative role which many local patrons adopt. It is a question of non-directive support and the gradual growth in confidence. It would be absurd to believe that the weak, in their weakness, can march ahead without such support.[102]

The indications are that this support can be effective in the form of project funds to be used for improving organizational capacity and stimulating income-generating activities, two conditions necessary to achieve sustainability.

Building Capacity in Beneficiary Organizations

Much of the emphasis on capacity building is directed toward project staff rather than

beneficiaries. Yet the need at the beneficiary level
may be just as great, if not greater.

In many project areas, there may be a lack of
organizational skills--particularly those required for
organizing meetings, reaching consensus, choosing
capable leaders, keeping records, or handling organizational funds.[103] One response to this problem is
to emphasize capacity building to improve the ability
of local people to deal with their own problems. In
general terms, capacity is the ability to:

- Anticipate and influence change;

- Make informed decisions;

- Attract and absorb resources; and

- Manage resources to achieve objectives.[104]

To utilize these capabilities, people often form
organizations. These groups allow capabilities to
continue independently of the individuals who are
members at any one time. Requirements for a capable
organization include, but are not limited to:

- Organizational skills, such as the ability to
  forge effective links with other organizations
  and to make it possible for local residents to
  participate in decision making;

- Information for decision making and the
  ability to use this information;

- Staff or a stable membership; and

- Processes for solving problems and
  implementing decisions.[105]

When the capacity of an organization to undertake
particular tasks is assessed, two dimensions should be
examined. The first dimension is organizational
stock, that is, what resources the organization
controls. An organization with adequate assets is
more likely to perform well then one without them.
The second dimension is organizational behavior, that
is, what people actually do. This is important
because high levels of stock do not automatically lead
to high levels of performance. Many factors may deter
capable people with superior facilities from acting in
ways that support a particular project. Thus,
effective capacity-building efforts must look beyond
inventories of organizational stock to actual human
behavior.[106]

The link between stock and behavior is represented by organizational incentives: what incentives are there for people to participate in the organization? In the project in Jamaica, the incentives were few, since resources and benefits were allocated on an individual rather than a group basis. In the Yemen Arab Republic, the reverse was true. Incentives to join an LDA were strong, since this is the only way to obtain vital services for the locality.

The concern for capacity building largely parallels the move toward greater participation. This is not surprising since decentralized administrative arrangements may overwhelm existing organizational capabilities in two ways. First, requirements for coordination are greatly increased. Local self-help groups may find themselves competing with one another for scarce resources. Communication demands are multiplied to serve joint planning needs of local residents, project staff, and government personnel.

Second, a broader role in decision making draws persons into the process who possess limited formal managerial skills. In addition to all the normal management demands of development projects, participatory arrangements add such elements as ambiguity about the respective roles of staff and local leaders, lack of clarity about specific responsibilities, and the tendency of local elites to obtain a monopoly on project benefits.[107] Addressing these and other problems in a project setting calls for dynamic, flexible approaches to the process of building capacity throughout the project system.

The requirements for capacity building and stimulating quick-impact, production-oriented project activities are not always complementary, although the two objectives are frequently linked. This is the case in the Provincial Area Development Program in Indonesia. The result is often a certain inconsistency between targeted organizational behavior and the incentives to support that behavior. Although considerable commitment to capacity building may be evident in the rhetoric of high-level project leaders, staff in the field may respond to project success criteria of a more traditional nature. A key task is therefore to establish a consistent set of incentives to support targeted behavior at all levels of the project management structure. Compensation and promotion systems for local project staff that reward efforts to work with local organizations and strengthen their capacity to address community needs will help generate this kind of behavior.

A case in point is the Small Agricultural
Projects Program in Botswana. Essentially, the
program provides small grants to groups of farmers to
purchase inputs for projects that will benefit the
whole group. Enterprising agricultural staff in one
district, aware of the concern of local farmers about
cattle damage to crops and the farmers' concomitant
interest in fencing, began to encourage the formation
of local farmers' committees. These committees, in
turn, raised local funds and provided labor to build
fences. From the outset, a 50 percent local
contribution in cash or in kind, in addition to labor
requirements, was the norm. The project provided the
balance of cash required. Farmers' committees
generally worked together to set quotas for each
participating group and requested project funds for
the balance. Over time, similar projects developed in
over 100 communities in the area, with the result that
extensive areas of arable land are now protected
against animals.

But this process of capacity building, for both
extension agents and local committees, took time:

> Tremendous investments of manpower, planning,
> training, retraining, and follow-up, and support
> activities from agricultural and local government
> personnel and resources were required. The
> groundwork that led to projects . . . came from a
> long-term effort . . . to re-orient extension
> staff away from their traditional one-to-one
> advisory approach based on exhortation, demon-
> stration, and persuasion, to one focusing on
> groups and their careful organization into
> functioning management units.[108]

This process took about five years, and
government and donors were concerned that not enough
money had been spent. Their response was predictable.
The criteria for grant approval were relaxed,
guidelines on how to obtain funds were published, and
workshops on funding procedures were organized:
spending money had become more important than building
capacity.

CONCLUSION

The experience of development initiatives
throughout the developing world underscores the
importance of decentralization and participation for
project success, reveals several major constraints to
achieving them, and points to some strategies for
alleviating the problem.

Several factors represent deterrents to both
decentralization and participation in rural devel-

opment. These include a lack of visible political
commitment to development, bureaucratic resistance,
inappropriate project designs, inadequate resources,
emphasis on quantitative targets, and a variety of
constraints in the immediate project environment that
are outside the direct control of rural development
managers. These constraints include historical
factors such as recent historical heritage and
unfavorable experiences of earlier development
efforts, sociological factors such as domination by
local elites, and physical factors such as a poor
communications network.

Several factors can facilitate participation and
decentralization, including supportive national
policies and a bureaucratic culture that promotes
negotiation between the center and local
jurisdictions. Project designs that are flexible and
relatively simple and use existing institutional
resources also facilitate effective decentralization
and participation. Local authority to generate
resources, combined with resource commitments by
beneficiaries, is important, especially if augmented
by efforts to build local capacities to manage these
resources.

NOTES

1. D. Conyers, "Decentralization: The latest
fashion in development administration?," Public
Administration and Development 3:3 (1983): 97-109.

2. D.A. Rondinelli, Administrative Decentrali-
zation and Area Development Planning in East Africa:
Implication for United States AID Policy, Regional
Planning and Area Development Project Occasional Paper
no. 1 (Madison: University of Wisconsin, Regional
Planning and Area Development Project, 1980), p. ii.

3. S.S. Cohen et al., Decentralization: A
Framework for Policy Analysis (Berkeley: University
of California, Project on Managing Decentralization,
1981), p. 84.

4. N.T. Uphoff, Providing for More Participation
in Project Planning and Implementation (Ithaca, N.Y.:
Cornell University, Rural Development Committee,
1981), p. 9.

5. These justifications are discussed in more
detail by the following: C. Bryant and L.G. White,
Managing Development in the Third World (Boulder,
Colo.: Westview Press, 1982), pp. 160-163; Cohen et
al., Decentralization, pp. 36-92; D. Conyers,
"Decentralization for Regional Development: A
Comparative Study of Tanzania, Zambia, and Papua New
Guinea, Public Administration and Development 1:1
(1981): 107-120; and Rondinelli, Administrative
Decentralization, pp. 7-10. His ideas are summarized

in D.A. Rondinelli and G.S. Cheema, "Implementing
Decentralization Policies: An Introduction,"
Decentralization and Development: Policy
Implementation in Developing Countries, eds. G.S.
Cheema and D.A. Rondinelli (Beverly Hills: Sage
Publications, 1983). pp. 9-34.
    6. M. Landau and E. Eagle, On the Concept of
Decentralization (Berkeley: University of
California, Project on Managing Decentralization,
1981), p.10. It is also important to remember that
the concepts of decentralization and participation may
also have their basis in romantic illusions about the
nature of society and human potential:

    Underlying the decentralized model is usually a
    romantic concept of society focused on the
    locality - the village, the town, the regional
    urban center - as the embodiment of a national
    culture that has taken form across successive
    generations. Coupled with this view is an image
    of the State which frequently identified its
    existing administrative apparatus with bureau-
    cratic rigidities, procedural delays, excessive
    paper work divided responsibilities, and self-
    serving officials . . . . At the local level it
    is not uncommon to find this idealized view of
    autonomy linked to the image of a more virtuous
    rural, small town society and to a concept of man
    as a dynamic resource for development whose
    potential for work and participation needs to be
    realized in a more productive fashion. (L.S.
    Graham, "Centralization versus Decentralization
    Dilemmas in the Administration of Public
    Service," International Review of Administrative
    Sciences 47:2 [1981]: p. 220.)

    7. D.A. Rondinelli and K. Ruddle, "Political
Commitment and Administrative Support: Preconditions
for Growth with Equity Policy, Journal of
Administration Overseas 17: 1 (1978): 43-60.
    8. Rondinelli, Administrative Decentralization, p.
61.
    9. David D. Gow et al., Differing Agendas: The
Politics of IRD Project Design in Panama, IRD Field
Report no. 17 (Washington, D.C.: Development
Alternatives, Inc., 1981).
    10. Donald R. Mickelwait et al., Monitoring and
Evaluating Decentralization: The Basic Village
Services Program in Egypt (Washington, D.C.:
Development Alternatives, Inc., 1980), pp. 19-20.
    11. A.R. Williams, Measuring Local Government
Performance: Assessing Management, Decentralization,
and Participation (Ithaca, N.Y.: Cornell University,
Rural Development Committee, 1981), pp. 92-96.

12. F.J. Korten, "Community Participation: A Management Perspective on Obstacles and Options," Bureaucracy and the Poor: Closing the Gap, eds. D.C. Korten and F.B. Alfonso (Singapore: McGraw-Hill, 1981), pp. 181-200.

13. Rondinelli, Administrative Decentralization, p. 71.

14. M. Esman and J.D. Montgomery, "The Administration of Human Development," Staff Worrking Paper no. 403, Implementing Programs of Human Development, ed. P.T. Knight, (Washington, D.C.: World Bank, 1980), pp. 185-234.

15. J. Jiggins, "Motivation and Performance of Extension Field Staff," Extension, Planning, and the Poor, eds. J. Jiggins, P. Develt, and G. Hunter (London: Overseas Development Institute, 1977), pp. 1-20.

16. C. Bryant, "Organizational Impediments to Making Participation a Reality: Swimming Upstream in AID," Rural Development Participation Review 1: 3 (1980): 8-10.

17. Jerry Van Sant et al. Supporting Capacity-Building in the Indonesia Provincial Development Program, IRD Field Report no. 12 (Washington, D.C.: Development Alternatives, Inc., 1981), p. 15.

18. D. Hopkins, "People's Participation in PDP" (Jakarta, Indonesia: Report to Provincial Development Program Workshop, May 18-20, 1981).

19. Rondinelli, Administrative Decentralization, p. 98.

20. Van Sant et al., Supporting Capacity-Building, p. 15.

21. A. R. Goldsmith and H.S. Blustain, Local Organization and Participation in Integrated Rural Development in Jamaica (Ithaca, N.Y.: Cornell University, Rural Development Committee, 1980), pp. 2-11.

22. Gene M. Owens et al., The Abyei Rural Development Project: An Assessment of Action Research in Practice, IRD Field Report no. 14 (Washington, D.C.: Development Alternatives, Inc., 1981), p. 26.

23. Rondinelli, Administrative Decentralization, pp. 68-69.

24. Ibid. p. 82.

25. J.M. Cohen et al., Traditional Organizations and Development: Yemen's Local Development Associations (Ithaca, N.Y.: Cornell University, Rural Development Committee, 1981), pp. 14-17, 86.

26. Williams, Measuring Local Government Performance, p. 21.

27. H.S. Blustain, "Participation and Political Culture in Rural Jamaica" (Ithaca, N.Y.: Cornell University, Rural Development Committee, 1981) pp. 10-11.

141

28. Kenneth Koehn, "Project North Shaba;
Practicing What One Preaches," Rural Development
Participation Review 3:3 (1982): 10-11.
29. Five Years Later: Progress and Sustainability
in Project North Shaba (Washington, D.C.: Development
Alternatives, Inc., 1982), pp. 66-67. See also G.
Gran, Development By People: Citizen Construction of
a Just World (New York: Praeger, 1983), chapter 4.
30. A.O. Hirschman, "The Principle of Conservation
and Mutation of Social Energy," Grassroots Development
7:2 (1983): 3-9. Hyden has offered something similar
when he suggests that a viable strategy may be to
create limited local organizations that can be
abandoned in favor of another similar structure in a
"wash-and-wear" fashion. See G. Hyden, No Shortcuts
to Progress: African Development Management in
Perspective (Berkeley: University of California
Press, 1983), p. 125.
31. Bryant and White, Managing Development, p.
102.
32. N.T. Uphoff, J. M. Cohen, and A.A. Goldsmith.
Feasibility and Application of Rural Development
Participation: A State-of-the-Art Paper (Ithaca,
N.Y.: Cornell University, Rural Development
Committtee, 1979), p. 77.
33. C.L.G. Bell, "The Political Framework,"
Redistribution with Growth, eds. H. Chenery et al.,
(New York: Oxford University Press, 1974), pp. 52-72.
34. Robert K. Chambers, Managing Rural
Development: Ideas and Experience from East Africa
(Uppsala: The Scandinavian Institute of African
Studies, 1974), pp. 109-110.
35. J. Montgomery, "Allocation of Authority in
Land Reform Programs," Administrative Science
Quarterly 17 (1972): 62-75.
36. Judith Tendler, Turning Private Voluntary
Organizations Into Development Agencies: Questions
for Evaluation (Washington, D.C.: Agency for
International Development, 1982). pp. iv-v.
37. Rondinelli, Administrative Decentralization,
p. 83.
38. Cohen et al., Traditional Organizations and
Development, p. 30.
39. Gow et al., Hidden Agendas, p. 18.
40. Landau and Eagle, On the Concept of
Decentralization, p. 13. See also Graham,
"Centralization versus Decentralization," pp. 222-223;
Rondinelli, Administrative Decentralization, p. 95;
and Uphoff and Esman, Local Organization for Rural
Development, p. 76.
41. Uphoff, Providing for More Participation, p.1.
42. Uphoff et al., Feasibility and Application, p.
284.
43. Chambers, Managing Rural Development, p.113.

44. H.W. Blair, "Rural Development, Class Structure and Bureaucracy in Bangladesh," World Development 6:1 (1978): 65-82.

45. Elliott R. Morss and R.F. Rich, Government Information Management: A Counter-Report to the Commission on Federal Paperwork (Boulder, Colo.: Westview Press, 1980), chapter 2. There is, of course, a considerable body of literature indicating that bureaucracies are interested primarily in their own survival. In a review of a book by Joseph Califano, President Carter's Secretary of Health, Education, and Welfare and author of much of the Great Society's legislation under President Johnson, the writer had this to say;

> One question left by that tale is whether any
> bureacracy, no matter how benignly conceived,
> does not soon take on a self-interest and life of
> its own wholly isolated from those it was meant
> to serve. At the least, Califano shows us that
> bureaucracies are a kind of organic form that one
> suspects could have outlasted the dinosaurs--they
> acquire a thick, stubborn survivability that
> could endure a glacial age intact. (M. Frady,
> "The Buck Stops Here," The New York Review of
> Books 28:15 [1981]: 15.)

46. N.T. Uphoff and M.J. Esman, Local Organization for Rural Development: Analysis of Asian Experience (Ithaca, N.Y.: Cornell University, Rural Development Committee, 1974), p. 76.

47. D.K. Leonard, Reaching the Peasant Farmer: Organization Theory and Practice in Kenya (Chicago: University of Chicago Press, 1977), pp. 209-210. This point is developed more fully in his later work. See D.K. Leonard, "Interorganizational Linkages for Decentralized Rural Development: Overcoming Administrative Weaknesses," Decentralization and Development: Policy Implementation in Developing Countries, eds. G.S. Cheema and D.A. Rondinelli (Beverly Hills: Sage Publications, 1983), pp. 271-293.

48. D. Brinkerhoff, "Participation and Rural Development Project Effectiveness: An Organizational Analysis of Four Cases" (Ph.D. dissertation, Harvard University, 1980), pp. 166-215.

49. Robert K. Chambers, "Project Selection for Poverty-Focused Rural Development: Simple is Optimal," World Development 6:2 (1978): 209-219.

50. S.G. Hadden, "Controlled Decentralization and Policy Implementation: The Case of Rural Electrification in Rajasthan," Politics and Policy Implementation in the Third World, ed. M.S. Grindle

(Princeton: Princeton University Press, 1980), pp. 170-191.

51. Ibid., pp. 188-189.

52. Conyers, "Decentralization: The latest fashion," p. 101.

53. David C. Korten and N.T. Uphoff, Bureaucratic Reorientation for Participatory Development (Washington, D.C.: National Association of Schools of Public Affairs and Administration, 1981), pp. 6-7.

54. D. Brinkerhoff, "Inside Public Bureaucracy: Empowering Managers to Empower Clients," Rural Development Participation Review 1:1 (1979): 7-9.

55. Donald R. Jackson et al., IRD in Colombia: Making It Work, IRD Working Paper no. 7 (Washington, D.C.: Development Alternatives, Inc., 1981).

56. D.D. Bathrick. Agricultural Credit for Small Farmer Development: Policies and Practices (Boulder, Colo.: Westview Press, 1981), pp. 65-83.

57. J.C. Ickis, "Structural Responses to New Rural Development Strategies," Bureaucracy and the Poor, eds. D.C. Korten and F.B. Alfonso (Singapore: McGraw-Hill, 1981), pp. 4-32.

58. J.M. Cohen, The Administration of Economic Development Programs: Baselines for Discussion (Cambridge, Mass.: Harvard Institute for International Development, 1979), p. 66.

59. Jerry Van Sant, David D. Gow, and Thomas Armor, "Managing Staff to Promote Participation," Rural Development Participation Review 3:3 (1982): 4-6.

60. For example, see Bryant and White, Managing Development, pp. 107-134; D.C. Korten, "Community Organization and Rural Development: A Learning Process Approach," Public Administration Review 40:6 (1980): 480-511; M.J. Esman and N.T. Uphoff, Local Organization and Rural Development: The State of the Art (Ithaca, N.Y.: Cornell University, Rural Development Committee, 1982), pp. 96-97; and C.F. Sweet and P.F. Weisel, "Process Versus Blueprint Models for Designing Rural Development Projects," International Development Administration: Implementation Analysis for Development Projects, eds. G. Honadle and R. Klauss (New York: Praeger, 1979), pp. 127-145.

61. George H. Honadle et al., Integrated Rural Development: Making It Work? (Washington, D.C.: Development Alternatives, Inc., 1980), p. 95.

62. J. Friedman, "The Epistemology of Social Practice: A Critique of Objective Knowledge," Theory and Society 6:1 (1978): 75-92.

63. Owens et al., The Abyei Rural Development Project, p. 20.

64. A classic example of this is provided by S. Conlin, "Peasant Participation in Agricultural in Peru: The Impediment of 'Expertise'," _Rural Development Participation Review_ 2:3 (1981): 10-12. For a discussion of the importance of local information for development planning, see Jerry Van Sant, "Local Needs and the Planning Process for Rural Service Delivery" (Research Triangle Park, N.C.: Research Triangle Institute, 1981).

65. Gow et al., _Hidden Agendas_, pp. 1-3. These painful lessons were not lost on the government. A new project area was selected, and during the redesign, the design team spent a considerable amount of time talking with the various groups who would be included in the project: the landless, small farmers, medium farmers, large farmers, local businessmen and politicians, the national guard, the governor, and government agencies responsible for implementing specific components of the project.

66. Uphoff and Esman, _Local Organization for Rural Development_, p. 25.

67. Chambers, "Project Selection," p. 211.

68. This is well documented in the literature. See Bryant and White, _Managing Development_, p. 218 and Judith Tendler, _Inter-Country Evaluation of Small Farmer Organizations: Ecuador Honduras_ (Washington, D.C.: Agency for International Development, 1976), pp. 7-12.

69. L. Ralston, J. Anderson, and E. Colson, _Voluntary Efforts in Decentralized Management_ (Berkeley: University of California, Project on Managing Decentralizaton, 1981), p. 42.

70. David D. Gow, _The Rural Poor in Haiti: A Social Analysis_ (Port-au-Prince, Haiti: Agency for International Development, 1977).

71. Donald R. Mickelwait, Elliott R. Morss, and Jerry M. Silverman, _A Formative Evaluation of the Arusha Planning and Village Development Project_ (Washington, D.C.: Development Alternatives, Inc., 1980), pp. B-11-12.

72. The importance of negotiation is discussed in more detail in Landau and Eagle, _On the Concept of Decentralization_, pp. 45-50; in E.J. Miller, "A Negotiating Model in Integrated Rural Development Projects," _Exploring Individual and Organizational Boundaries_, ed. W.G. Lawrence (Chichester, England: John Wiley and Sons, 1979); and in J.D. Montgomery, "Decentralizing Integrated Rural Development Activities, _Decentralization and Development: Policy Implementation in Developing Countries_, eds. G.S. Cheema and D.A. Rondinelli (Beverly Hills: Sage Publications, 1983), pp. 231-269.

73. Honadle et al., _Integrated Rural Development_, pp. 129-139.

74. Table 2.1 lists the advantages and disadvantages of working with existing organizations.

75. K. March and R. Taqqu, Women's Informal Associations and Their Potential Role in Rural Development (Ithaca, N.Y.: Cornell University, Rural Development Committee, 1981).

76. Cohen et al., Traditional Organizations p. 24.

77. Jackson et al., IRD in Colombia.

78. David D. Gow, Elliott R. Morss, and Donald R. Jackson, Local Organizations and Rural Development: A Comparative Reappraisal, 2 vols. (Washington, D.C.: Development Alternatives, Inc., 1979), 1:127-152.

79. Tendler, Inter-Country Evaluation, p. 9.

80. Esman and Uphoff, Local Organization and Rural Development, pp. 78-79.

81. Uphoff et al., Feasibility and Application, pp. 73-74.

82. Jerry Van Sant and P.F. Weisel, Community Based Integrated Rural Development (CBIRD) in the Special Territory of Aceh, Indonesia, IRD Field Report no. 4 (Washington, D.C.: Development Alternatives, Inc., 1979), pp. 18-19.

83. F.J. Korten, "Community Participation," p. 196.

84. J.D. Stanfield, "Notes on a Base Organization Strategy," mimeographed (Madison: University of Wisconsin, Land Tenure Center, n.d.).

85. Elliott R. Morss, New Directions and Beyond: A Review of Accomplishments and an Agenda for the Future (Washington, D.C.: Development Alternatives, Inc., 1980), pp. 13-14.

86. This was no idle threat, given the previous IRD experience in Panama. In addition, however, AID wanted to include the private sector, narrowly defined. As the design team pointed out, all the farmers in the project area, whether they had one-half a hectare or one thousand, belonged to the private sector. See Gow et. al., Hidden Agendas, pp. 29-30.

87. Some might criticize this approach as political meddling. But, in reality, decentralization and participation are inescapably political since they deal with the reallocation of resources within society. Furthermore, to a much greater extent than in the United States, project implementation in the developing world is often a focus of political participation and competition:

> This is true because of characteristics of the political systems themselves, such as the remoteness and inaccessibility of the policymaking process to most individuals and the extensive competition engendered by widespread need and very scarce resources. Thus, while in the United States and Western Europe much

146

political activity is focused on the input stage
of the policy process, in the Third World a large
portion of individual and collective demand
making, the representation of interests, and the
emergence and resolution of conflict occurs at
the output stage. (M.S. Grindle, "Policy Content
and Context in Implementation," Politics and
Policy Implementation in the Third World, ed.
M.S. Grindle (Princeton, N.J.: Princeton
University Press, 1980), p. 15.)

88. Williams, Measuring Local Government
Performance, pp. 44-45.
89. Cohen et al., Traditional Organizations, p.
26.
90. Honadle et. al., Integrated Rural Development,
pp. 142-143.
91. David D. Gow and Jerry Van Sant, "Beyond the
Rhetoric of Rural Development Participation: How Can
It Be Done?," World Development II:5 (1983): 439.
92. Chambers, "Project Selection," p. 215.
93. D.R. Marshall, "Linkage Lessons from U.S.
Poverty Programs," Linkages to Decentralized Units,
eds., D. Leonard and et al. (Berkeley: University of
California, Project on Managing Decentralization,
1981), p. 5.
94. Jennifer Bremer, "Evaluation and Monitoring
for BVS," internal memorandum (Development
Alternatives, Inc.: Washington, D.C. July 29, 1981).
95. Gow et al., Local Organizations, vol. 1, p.
149.
96. Elliott R. Morss et al., Strategies for Small
Farmer Development, 2 vols. (Boulder, Colo.:
Westview Press, 1976) 1: chapter 3.
97. Chambers, Managing Rural Development, p. 110.
98. David D. Gow, An Information System for the
Rural Area Development - Rapti Zone Project, IRD Field
Report no. 8 (Washington, D.C.: Development
Alternatives, Inc., 1980), p. 11.
99. Gow, The Rural Poor in Haiti, p. 22.
100. Jerry Van Sant et al., Management Support to
the Jamaica Ministry of Agriculture Second Integrated
Rural Development Project, IRD Field Report no. 13
(Washington, D.C.: Development Alternatives, Inc.,
1981), pp. 15-18.
101. Blustain, "Participation and Political
Culture."
102. G. Hunter, ed., Agricultural Development and
the Rural Poor (London: Overseas Development
Instiute, 1978), p. 43.
103. Korten, "Community Participation," p. 191.
104. Beth W. Honadle, "A Capacity-Building
Framework" (Paper prepared for the White House Task
Force on Capacity-Building, Washington, D.C.:

USDA/ESCS/EDD State and Local Government Program Area, U.S. Department of Agriculture, 1980).

105. Honadle et al., Integrated Rural Development, p. 189.

106. George H. Honadle, Fishing for Sustainability: The Role of Capacity Building in Development Administration (Washington, D.C.: Development Alternatives, Inc., 1981), p. 22.

107. C. Bryant and L.A. White, Managing Rural Development: Peasant Participation in Rural Development (West Hartford, Conn.: Kumarian Press, 1980) pp. 34-39.

108. M. Odell, "How to Kill Local Investment: A Case Study of Local Action in Botswana," mimeographed (Washington, D.C.: Development Alternatives, Inc., 1981), p. 2.

6
Timing

Elliott R. Morss and Jerry Van Sant

PROBLEM DEFINITION

Three types of timing problems interfere with effective implementation of development projects:

- Delays between project identification and start-up;

- Delays during project implementation; and

- Inappropriate time phasing of project activities.

Project managers can address some of these problems more readily than others. Better project planning, for example, can improve the time phasing of project inputs and activities. In contrast, the political and administrative realities of the project approval process are less amenable to influence by project planners and implementers. Nonetheless, better estimates of the time required for project approval can forestall some of the problems associated with delays. In all cases, greater understanding of the magnitude and pervasiveness of timing problems in development projects is needed.

Delays between Project Identification and Start-Up

Two studies conducted for AID have highlighted the importance of delays between project identification and start-up.[1] The first examined the review and approval process for development projects initiated in 1974-1976. The study found that the average time lapse between completion of the project identification document and the project agreement for nine projects was just over two years. The second study was based on a representative sample of AID projects and concluded that the average time from project identification to the obligation of funds was twenty months.

A protracted approval process can create serious implementation problems for the following reasons:

- Enthusiasm for the project diminishes;

- Host-country officials at both the national and the local level involved in project preparation become involved in other activities;

- Interested donor officials are replaced;

- Political, economic, and other conditions change in ways that should generate a change in project design;

- Potential project beneficiaries become impatient and skeptical; and

- Politicians demanding quick results force unrealistic implementation scheduling.

Some causes of delays are beyond donor control, such as recipient country approval and contracting mechanisms. However, the first study discussed above pointed out that far more project documentation is assembled than is ever used and that arguments between donors and their own field missions over specifics of project design often continue for long periods with no apparent mechanisms for resolution.

This criticism, coupled with recommendations made in the second study, led to the following procedural reforms in AID:

- Delegating authorization authority to field missions;

- Improving funding procedures;

- Revising project design requirements;

- Making standard all project agreements;

- Moving toward incrementally funded activities to reduce design work loads;

- Reducing the number of projects in each country; and

●   Developing incentives for project paper
    reviews and response times.

For several years, AID has attempted to apply
recommendations that include further decentralization
of authority to approve projects. However, three
obstacles to this decentralization have remained:

●   Little has been done to reduce the paper work
    for project proposals;

●   Little has been done to increase the account-
    ability of mission directors for the projects
    they approve;[2] and

●   AID staff need additional training to under-
    stand the regulations under which they
    operate, particularly as these are modified
    and streamlined.[3]

Table 6.1 documents the limited degree of
decentralized project approval during fiscal years
1980 and 1981.

TABLE 6.1
AID Projects Reviewed and Mission Authorizations,
1980-1981

Bureau	Project Identification Documents Received in Washington	Projects Authorized by Mission
Africa	89	5[a]
Asia	46	1
Latin America	31	1
Near East	16	3
Total	182	10

Source: AID internal documents.

Note:

a   Mission requested authority to authorize; three
    projects authorized by mission were later
    canceled.

An additional consequence of delay is the effect on project planning. Planners increasingly prefer to submit project plans in phases to allow design flexibility. But they also fear that lengthy approval delays, aggravated by changes in the political climate, will disrupt future implementation. As a result, they submit complex blueprints in an attempt to secure one-time, long-term approval. This increases the risk of locking project implementers into inappropriate designs and host country counterparts into unrealistic expectations.

Project Implementation Delays

The development of realistic project implementation schedules has received limited attention. One manifestation of this is the absence of a timetable of critical activities in many project design papers. The timing estimates that exist have been extremely optimistic when compared with actual rates of project accomplishment, for example:

- A review of nine AID-supported projects found that for seven of them actual expenditures in the first year averaged only 20 percent of estimates made in the project design papers;[4]

- The average time to complete 250 World Bank projects audited between 1975 and 1979 exceeded estimated time by more than 40 percent, despite a reduction in the scope of some of these projects;[5] and

- The World Bank estimated that, for a sample of 120 projects in its 1980 portfolio, 78 would require 50 percent more than had been estimated for completion.[6]

AID mission staffs make annual project expenditure estimates, which presumably should be more accurate than those made in project design papers. Table 6.2 compares planned and actual expenditures in 1980, based on this annual planning exercise. Although there are wide discrepancies among AID's regional bureaus, planned expenditures exceeded actual expenditures in all cases. The results for the Near East Bureau are largely attributable to the Egypt program, which experienced a dramatic expansion of AID commitment in the late 1970s.

TABLE 6.2
Planned and Actual AID Project Expenditures by
Regional Bureau, 1980

Regional Bureau	Amounts ($000) Planned	Actual	Actual as a Percent of Planned
Africa	278,278	232,104	83.4
Asia	430,000	285,937	66.4
Latin America	219,303	208,850	95.2
Near East	527,301	304,124	57.6

Source: AID computer data.

Table 6.3 shows cumulative AID project disbursements as a percentage of cumulative obligations for projects beginning in fiscal year 1977 through fiscal year 1980. These data show an expenditure profile far slower than expected. For the regional bureaus combined, only 2.1 percent of obligated project monies were spent in the first year of fiscal year 1980 projects. The World Bank analysis concluded that an average of two to four years was needed to utilize the first quarter of project monies, even for projects planned for completion in five to six years.[7]

Admittedly, comparisons of commitments and expenditures provide imperfect indicators of the adequacy of project planning. For political, administrative, or budgetary reasons, project funds are often committed well in advance of expected disbursements. Table 6.4 shows expenditures and undisbursed aid commitments for AID, the World Bank, and the International Development Association (IDA). The table shows a significant increase in undisbursed commitments relative to expenditures. This finding suggests that time delays have increased, and planning-budgetary procedures have deteriorated. Another possibility for delays in disbursement is that, with a change in the composition of recipient countries, the overall absorptive capacity has fallen.

It does not make sense to earmark funds for particular projects if they are not to be used until years later, unless the agencies employ four- to five-year planning cycles. But none of these agencies does this systematic planning, and all are concerned with these delays.

Given tendencies for annual donor obligations to exceed expenditures, pipelines are likely to become

TABLE 6.3
AID Project Expenditure Ratio, by Region and Year of Project Start-Up,
1977-1980

(1)	(2)	(3)	(4)	(5)
Year of Project Start-up	Regional Bureau	Cumulative Obligation ($000)	Cumulative Expenditure ($000)	Disbursement as a Percent of Obligation, (4) ÷ (3) x 100
1980	Africa	797,741	24,050	3.0
	Asia	1,259,059	17,290	1.4
	Latin America and Caribbean	765,403	51,958	6.8
	Near East	2,257,968	11,424	0.5
	Total	5,080,171	104,722	2.1
1979	Africa	660,660	110,561	16.7
	Asia	1,083,201	150,835	13.9
	Latin America and Caribbean	571,793	57,902	10.1
	Near East	1,279,436	169,152	13.2
	Total	4,231,131	411,138	9.7

TABLE 6.3 (continued)

(1) Year of Project Start-up	(2) Regional Bureau	(3) Cumulative Obligation ($000)	(4) Cumulative Expenditure ($000)	(5) Disbursement as a Percent of Obligation, (4) ÷ (3) x 100
1978	Africa	513,749	193,156	37.6
	Asia	808,076	304,038	37.6
	Latin America and Caribbean	341,445	89,670	26.3
	Near East	1,279,436	169,152	13.2
	Total	2,942,706	756,016	25.7
1977	Africa	219,881	143,849	65.4
	Asia	188,964	104,368	55.2
	Latin America and Caribbean	105,569	42,066	39.9
	Near East	507,390	143,442	28.3
	Total	1,021,804	433,725	42.4

Source: AID computer records; data as of June 1981.

TABLE 6.4
Comparative Data on Pipeline Problems from AID, the World
Bank, and the International Development Association,
1975-1980

Expenditures (000)	1975	1980
AID	$ 947	$ 1,320
World Bank	1,995	4,363
IDA	1,026	1,411
Undisbursed Commitments, End of Fiscal Year (000)		
AID	$1,551	$ 5,118
World Bank	6,617	22,280
IDA	2,886	8,777
Pipeline as Percentage of Expenditures		
AID	164%	388%
World Bank	332	511
IDA	281	622

Source: Data from AID computer; World Bank and IDA data
           from World Bank Annual Reports.

further clogged. A reduced flow in the pipeline,
however, is not necessarily a goal in itself. In the
absence of better planning, increases in the flow of
money will frequently increase implementation
difficulties and resource waste. Pipeline delays are
best understood as symptoms of unrealistic planning
and cumbersome procedures.

Time-Phasing Problems

The importance of carefully sequencing inputs and
activities in complex, multisectoral development
projects is often overlooked. Even relatively small
and unsophisticated projects can run afoul of time-
phasing problems.

There are many examples of the failure to use a
sound, time-sequenced plan. In the North Shaba Rural
Development Project in Zaire, for example, farmer
groups were organized to increase maize production
before research had been carried out to determine the
technological packages to raise yields. Once formed,
the organizations started to lobby for social services
that, if provided, would have consumed a large portion
of the project budget. The same project received an
expatriate technical assistance team almost a full
year before housing and other essential supporting
services were available in the project area.

Many projects require local labor for activities
such as road construction and rehabilitation.
However, when these requirements are not phased to
coincide with periods of slack agricultural activity,
few laborers are available and the work cannot be
completed.[8]

Another example of the time-phasing problem is
found in an AID-sponsored project to help develop an
appropriate long-term agricultural mechanization
policy for Egypt. The project had a media component to
communicate its findings to farmers. Unfortunately,
this component was managed by an expatriate whose
contract expired before any policy conclusions had
been reached.

Similarly, government authorities in Upper Volta,
impatient over the delayed arrival of the credit
adviser who ultimately arrived eighteen months late,
issued loans in the Eastern ORD Integrated Rural
Development Project with insufficient procedural
safeguards.[9]

These examples of time-phasing problems are not
unusual. Poor sequencing of activities often results
when planners and implementers fail to understand the
interaction of the following elements in a complex
project:

- The institutional base (administrative capability);

- The resource base;

- The research (technology) base;

- Technical assistance; and

- Seasonal factors.

REASONS FOR THE PROBLEM

Thus, planners have seriously underestimated the time required to implement development projects. One reason is that inadequate research has been conducted on timing issues, but the persistence of the tendency toward underestimation indicates that other forces are at work.

The most obvious source of this bias is the political environment in which AID, the World Bank, and other foreign donors operate.[10] Design teams feel pressure to fit projects into the traditional time frame of the bureaucracies that approve project funding. The legislative sponsors of foreign assistance exhibit a strong preference for programs that show quick impact. Pressure for quick results is just as great in recipient countries, and this pressure also contributes to overly optimistic time estimates.

Part of the problem also stems from the characteristics of typical multisectoral projects: complex procurement requirements; emphasis on individual and institutional capacity building; and focus on the poorer, weakly organized elements of rural society. These characteristics affect timing estimates, particularly in the later stages of project implementation.

Recently, a number of studies have attempted to pinpoint specific reasons for project delays.[11] The reasons identified include:

- Institutional squabbles;

- Political and economic policy decisions;

- Organizational and administrative problems;

- Deficiencies in project preparation and design;

- Procurement delays (often as a result of complex procedural and contracting requirements); and

• Recruitment delays.

A review of major World Bank and AID rural development projects implemented during 1981 identified 66 projects with reported timing problems. The reasons for these problems, summarized in Table 6.5, reflect the factors listed above. Although they are at times difficult to overcome, most of these problems can be dealt with through better advance planning and improved management. This section addresses the planning issue, with particular attention to design flaws, donor procedures, multiple project objectives, and institutional development needs.

TABLE 6.5
Primary Reasons for Delay in World Bank and AID
Projects during 1981

Reasons	Number of Projects	
	World Bank	AID
Institutional squabbles	1	8
Policy decisions	3	4
Administrative problems	2	12
Design deficiencies	9	9
Procurement delays	4	9
Recruitment delays	0	5
Number of Projects	19	47

Source: Compiled by the authors from World Bank and AID project documents.

Design Flaws

Several broad conclusions can be drawn concerning the accuracy of time estimates made in project design documents:

• More time than anticipated is necessary to place outside personnel and host country personnel and to develop good working relationships;

- Delays in the delivery of supplies from the outside are not anticipated;

- As a result, the delivery of goods and services proceeds in a haphazard fashion that at times violates the underlying project rationale (for example, the provision of expatriate technicians prior to the commitment of local resources);

- The local initiatives anticipated do not take place as scheduled; and

- The project team is rarely in the field long enough to work toward the sustainability of project benefits.

Thus, for example, a four-year agricultural research project was designed to test and evaluate citrus, coffee, and cocoa as possible crops for small-scale farmers. However, these crops require from four to six years just to come into production, and another two or three years to assess their profitability. Consequently, the time allowed for the project did not even permit completion of the research, much less ensure that any findings would be used.[12]

Clearly, there is a need for more attention to time phasing in project design. There is also need for greater management flexibility to adapt to progress, or lack of it, during implementation.

In the Second Integrated Rural Development Project in Jamaica, vehicles did not arrive until eighteen months after project approval and six months after the arrival of the expatriate advisory team. This delay seriously limited the team's effectiveness, since team members could not visit farms to establish farm plans based on terracing and extension activities. As a result, most other activities had to be rescheduled. One reason for the delay in the delivery of the vehicles was the turnover of personnel within the AID mission responsible for the project. However, since this type of discontinuity is common, project designs should allow for it.[13]

Technical assistance strategies also reflect rigidity in design. If a project has four primary components, for example, the project paper will typically call for four long-term technicians to arrive in the project area simultaneously, instead of describing their jobs to fit appropriate time phasing of their responsibilities. During implementation, management often fails to see the need for staffing changes, or resists them because the design does not permit these changes without time-consuming adjustments in procedure.

A project in Bolivia illustrates the types of design-related problems that often plague development efforts.[14]   The loan agreement between AID and the Bolivian government for the Subtropical Lands Development Project was signed in September 1974, but the project team was not in place until 1977.   The project suffered from most of the major causes of implementation delays.   The principal impediments were:

- Lack of adequate pre-project communication between the donors and the main implementing agency, and within the implementing agency itself;

- Inadequately planned procurement procedures and late arrival of equipment;

- Excessive centralization of decision making by high-level personnel of the implementing agency;

- Lack of adequate technical staff within the implementing agency, especially in aspects related to engineering and the management of machinery; and

- Lack of aerial photography to deal with the property claims of people who had settled in the area before the project began.

As a result of these delays, the road construction started over two years later than planned and cost $2.9 million more than originally estimated.

It would be unrealistic to expect designers to anticipate all of these problems, but the tendency to budget excessive funds to be spent almost immediately, compounded by the rigidity of most project plans and budgets, aggravates the problems caused by these unanticipated delays.

The failure to foresee delays has been attributed to cultural differences.[15]   In contemporary Western management, time is treated as a resource.   It is segmented, linear, and accounted for.[16] Several studies include methods for planning the work of extension agents based on a reallocation of discretionary time.   However,

Local field staff have almost no control over the timing of their duties due to the almost continual interruptions of vehicle breakdowns, natural calamities, schedules imposed by higher authorities, and visitors.   Key activities can be identified but many depend for beginning and completion on external events when timing is itself unpredictable.[17]

Among the causes of this unpredictability are failure to adhere to schedules, the underlying irregularity of support services, fluctuating seasonal factors, and the incongruity of donor and host government bureaucratic calendars.

Nonetheless, the Western mind, whether of a designer or an auditor, tends to assume a delivery system in which everything arrives on time. When everything does not, the implementer has few tools with which to cope with the problem and little leeway for variation from design expectations.

Multiple Objectives

The concern for design flexibility to help cope with delays does not preclude a design framework. The absence of any structure or priorities may dissipate resources with little effect. In the Abyei Development Project in Sudan, for example, an action-research framework used by the project deliberately offered little structure or phasing of activities. Priorities were to be established after the identification of critical areas (based on needs, potentials, and external constraints). However, no hard choices were made, and the project attempted to carry out a diversified set of activities instead of concentrating its limited resources on a distinct set of priorities.[18]

For political reasons, projects with multiple objectives often encounter timing problems:

A first characteristic of ideological programs is that they are expected to realize a multitude of goals at the same time. They represent the first working models of the new society, and are therefore expected to introduce changes in many aspects of existing social relationships. In addition to being numerous, the goals set for ideological programs are also ambiguous in that national elites rarely have a clearly worked out view of what is required to move from the existing state of affairs to the new one. There is no hierarchy of goals, no clear statement that goal A is more important than goal B, or at least that goal A should be achieved before embarking on goal B. The ambiguity of goals presents the implementing organization with the clear message that everything must be done at once and that there are no priorities that can be used to orient implementation.[19]

Institutional Development

It takes time to create a viable beneficiary
organization or rural health clinic, train host staff,
develop a new seed variety, or construct a small-scale
irrigation system. Some activities take longer to
complete than others, and thus certain types of
projects require a longer commitment than others.[20]
Time estimates can be made through discussions with
experts or a review of project literature.

Many current development projects focus on decentralization or institutional development. The best
institutional development efforts seem to be those
that provide for incremental changes through trial and
adoption; yet few projects allow time for this process
to take place. Ten years is probably a minimum time
span for a project with a significant institutional
development component. Traditional four- to five-year
project cycles are simply inadequate.

As the donor supporting the Indonesia Provincial
Area Development Program (PDP), AID recognized this at
the end of the originally planned four-year project
life:

> We now realize that a four-to-five-year life-of-
> project time frame is unrealistic with respect to
> establishing strong local government planning and
> management capability and for achieving sustained
> rural development objectives of the magnitude
> required by the PDP. PDP will therefore follow a
> 'building-block' approach for upgrading local
> government based on the recognition that each
> province requires assistance for approximately
> ten years to (1) design, test, refine, and expand
> concrete mechanisms for assisting rural poor
> groups to increase their productive capabilities
> and incomes; and (2) train personnel and upgrade
> institutions, and perfect and master necessary
> administrative procedures.[21]

Donor Procedures

Project time lapses often result from documentation, review, and approval procedures. Procedures
that delay project implementation include:

- Far more project documentation is assembled
  than is ever used;

- Arguments between AID/Washington and missions
  over the project design often continue for
  long periods with no apparent mechanism for
  resolution; and

- Full and complete project plans are generally
  required prior to the disbursement of any
  project funds (for example, Section 611[a] of
  the Foreign Assistance Act).

These procedures are manifestations of behavior
characteristic of large bureaucracies. Excessive
documentation reflects a belief that large amounts of
paperwork will legitimate any project and protect its
sponsors from outside criticism. Seemingly unending
arguments reflect the lack of a well-defined decision
process. Elaborating on these patterns, a recent
study examined implementation problems of 702 projects
initiated between 1970 and 1974.[22] Reasons for
project delays included the following:

- Some projects had not reached a sufficiently
  advanced state of preparation at the time of
  loan presentation. A majority of delays were
  related to procurement procedures, specifically the issuance and evaluation of bid
  documents. The World Bank and recipient
  countries also had disagreements over the
  selection of contractors and suppliers.

- Complex contracting procedures of the borrower
  contributed to delays: cumbersome prequalifi-
  cation methods, bidding systems, and clearance
  processes emerged as main factors. Financial
  problems, resulting from underestimation of
  costs or price increases, contributed to
  delays in letting contracts and, in some
  cases, to retendering. The situation was
  aggravated by sharp and unforeseen price
  increases in the early 1970s. Because of the
  stringent financial limitations of many
  borrowers, an interacting spiral of time and
  cost overruns had serious implications for
  project implementation.

- Institutional problems were second and
  affected 55 percent of the sample during
  start-up. Major institutional problems
  included those related to the organizational
  structure of the project unit and its fit
  within the borrower's bureaucratic structure.
  Project units were sometimes incorrectly
  located and often did not posses sufficient
  automony to be effective. New units created
  specifically for the implementation of World
  Bank-supported projects were especially prone
  to these problems, compared with organizations
  and project units already in existence.

- A shortage of qualified local staff was a
  major problem, exacerbated by noncompetitive
  salary structures in the public-sector
  organization. Not only was it hard to recruit
  local staff, but it was also difficult to keep
  them for any length of time.

These problems derive in large part from procedures that emphasize programming money rather than
implementing projects. Project design papers are
written to get approval; as a result, they are often
excessively optimistic about how quickly project
activities can be implemented. Moreover, donors seem
to lack monitoring mechanisms to identify these
specific problems at an early stage. Although
decentralization measures have been introduced in AID
to place decision-making authority for projects closer
to the field, the potential for greater realism and
more sophisticated time phasing of project activities
has not yet been realized.

ALLEVIATING THE PROBLEM

The best way to reduce excessive time delays is
for donors to upgrade project planning and management.
This means:

- Developing reasonable implementation plans;

- Monitoring project activities against these
  plans; and

- Rewarding staff for overcoming procedural and
  other barriers that would delay implementation
  activities.

Bureaucratic delays result largely from incentives that encourage programming new money and
adhering to administrative regulations. In addition
to improving management and planning practices, donors
should recognize that development is a sequential
process that includes planning and evaluation as
continuing functions, rather than events occurring at
selected times in the life of a project.

Development as a Sequential Process

Project activities should follow a sequential
pattern for many reasons. For example, personnel
should arrive in the field only when living quarters
are available; establishing the capacity to market
additional produce should precede increasing agricultural production. If one accepts the premise that

farmers should learn to help themselves and that the purpose of outside assistance is to facilitate this process, then the delivery of goods and services through a project should follow, not precede, the organization of small-scale farmers and resource commitments by them.

At a strategy level, other sequencing issues merit consideration. Evidence suggests that the impact of increased health, education, and nutrition is to increase the population growth rate signifi- cantly in the short term [23] and reduce it in the long term.[24] The provision of social services is expensive. Therefore, from a policy viewpoint, it is critical to know how long it will take to move past short-term population increases and achieve long-term growth reduction. Unfortunately, no longitudinal studies have been carried out that would help make this determination. Ideally, this information would be available for consideration in the planning of project timing. The key question is whether a project can afford to initiate the delivery of social services prior to the introduction of income-generating activities.

A sequential approach to development is desirable because it helps to:

- Focus attention on the frequent need for broad-based development of the subsistence sector;

- Highlight the crucial role of indigenous human resources and institutional capability for effective use of outside interventions; and

- Increase understanding that an increase in productivity of the subsistence sector frequently constitutes a major, but only the first, step toward improvement for subsistence-level rural populations.[25]

A better understanding of gestation periods also helps phase the withdrawal of external resources from projects. Although much foreign assistance is considered beneficial strictly because of resource transfer effects, what happens when the funding period ends? The probable timing of withdrawal should be made clear as early as possible in the project planning. Lack of sustainability may be the major failing of development activities initiated in the last thirty years; in large part, it is caused by unrealistic timing.

In an attempt to deal with the issue of development as a sequential process, one study outlines a learning process approach to community

organization and rural development.[26] Organizations
must learn to be effective, then learn to be
efficient, and finally learn to expand as they mature.
These learning cycles overlap, but progress toward
high performance should follow this sequence. Some
effectiveness will be sacrificed in the interest of
efficiency and expansion. In this third phase,
efficiency will likely suffer as a result of tradeoffs
with the requirements of expansion. But attempts to
reorder the process--that is, expand an organizational
base before it achieves improved levels of
effectiveness and efficiency--are likely to meet with
failure.

It is common to see fledgling administrative
structures overwhelmed by an excessive infusion of
resources and multiplication of tasks. In PDP in
Indonesia, sizable credit programs were introduced in
several participating provinces. In some cases,
particularly in Java, these programs have been
successful. In some outer island provinces, however,
the attempt to expand credit programs prior to
developing a more effective or efficient
administrative base failed. For example, a report on
PDP in the Province of Bengkulu notes that:

> Credit difficulties have had a serious impact on
> the plans of the sectoral services responsible
> for related subprojects. This is particularly
> true for certain agricultural initiatives where
> seasonal factors are of great importance . . . .
> The problem lies in the attempt to institute a
> program that requires a relatively sophisticated
> and mature organizational base before that base
> exists. Credit programs should be a long-term
> product of successful PDP institution building,
> not a mechanism for it. The risk of front-ending
> widescale credits is too high and the cost too
> great.[27]

Finally, a sequential approach to development
requires new approaches to project design. Short-term
design teams can do little more than identify an
appropriate project area, assess the general feasibility of a project concept, and identify possible
counterpart organizations. Adding the substance of
the design should be the first phase of project
implementation--a task that should be performed by the
people who have a stake in the success of the overall
project.

Scheduling

Closely related to the strategic considerations
discussed above are the tactics of appropriate

sequencing and scheduling. Realities of the developing world preclude tight linear scheduling of project activities. Nevertheless, several lessons can be drawn:

- Foreign technicians should not be brought in before counterparts, housing, and supporting services are available;

- The development of sound technological packages must precede effective extension work;

- Efforts to build or repair roads should avoid the rainy season, and plans that require a local labor commitment should not be scheduled at harvest time;

- Efforts to promote the growing of certain crops should not be undertaken prior to the elimination of government pricing policies that make it financially unrewarding to produce these crops; and

- Impact evaluations should not be scheduled before some manifestations of impact can be measured.

In the case of an irrigation project managed by a farmer group, an identifiable transition occurs when infrastructure is completed and work shifts from construction to operation; another identifiable shift takes place when the basis for the water fee goes from public sector stewardship to an independent system. The fee basis is a dimension that can be used for marking transitions: stage 1 is no fee; stage 2 is legal fee; stage 3 is economic fee. Two other useful dimensions that may change over time are "functions performed" and "who has primary responsibility for each function."[28]

This case shows the sorts of techniques that may be used to conceptualize and monitor time-phased activities. Also, standard management techniques such as PERT and critical path analysis may be employed to deal with time delays and phasing problems. Because scheduling techniques may be used in widely varied ways, project managers should understand the purpose of the techniques, the potential benefits of their use, and the costs associated with their implementation. Management must participate in the following functions:

- Selection of appropriate scheduling techniques;

- Education of project personnel in uniform use
  of the techniques;

- Development of a coordinated plan to identify
  potential technical difficulties in the use of
  techniques; and

- Establishment of progress monitoring and
  reporting procedures using the techniques to
  facilitate replanning as technical and
  administrative problems emerge.[29]

Scheduling techniques should also be used with an
awareness of their limitations. Such techniques as
PERT, critical path analysis, and Gantt charts are
largely prospective, that is, they do not require data
other than estimates of the typical duration of
various events.[30] These methods force managers to
identify components clearly and show sequential
linkages, but the time estimates often become
irrelevant in the face of donor and host government
priorities or other unexpected complications. In
fact, the decision paths of a project can rarely be
predicted at the outset. Even if project designers
have an idea of what early decisions will be necessary
and who must make them, their outcome is hard to
predict.[31] In many cases, it is therefore useful to
draw up a range of timing options to be used when key
project stages fall behind schedule.

Dealing effectively with contingencies requires
"compensatory management techniques."[32] These
techniques suggest that the ability to improvise and
anticipate budding crises are key attributes of a
successful project manager:

- Pay attention to detail since almost
  everything can go wrong;

- Follow up all important matters personally;

- Build a large redundancy factor into all
  aspects of the operation;

- Adjust daily activities to fit immediate
  opportunities instead of arranging schedules
  far in advance; and

- Use simple but effective control devices to
  ensure that organizational resources do not
  melt away.

Evaluation

Evaluations are usually scheduled at intervals in the lifetime of a project and, in some instances, after the completion date. Formative evaluations determine whether projects are proceeding on a path that is likely to bring success. Because of the numerous delays that occur in project start-up, an early formative evaluation--within a year of start-up --is desirable.

Impact evaluations determine whether the project is having the desired results. To determine when these evaluations should be scheduled requires further consideration of project gestation periods.

In Figure 6.1, project benefits are portrayed vertically, whereas time is measured horizontally. For most projects, there are two benefit impacts. The first, measured in Figure 6.1 by OC, results directly from foreign assistance (money, personnel, or equipment) provided to the project area. This impact can be called the resource transfer effect. It fades rapidly when foreign assistance comes to an end (at time C in the figure).

FIGURE 6.1
Two Benefit Profiles: Resource Transfer Effects versus Sustainable Benefits

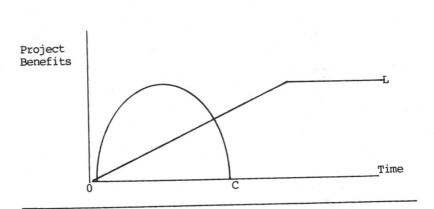

Sustainable benefits are likely to follow a different time profile. As line OL in Figure 6.1 suggests, they do not appear until a considerable time after foreign assistance has begun, if they appear at all, and they usually peak several years after foreign assistance has ended.

Clearly, there are different benefit profiles or gestation periods. In all cases, however, the point at which a project is evaluated makes an important difference in how it appears to be progressing. An impact evaluation should not be scheduled until sustainable impact can be measured or accurately predicted. As a general rule, impact evaluations should not take place until eighteen to twenty-two months after project outputs have been attained.[33]

This argument is particularly applicable to institution-building projects. In the absence of clear criteria for measuring institutional capacity, the tendency is to apply traditional criteria such as budget compliance or physical project completion as measures of success. In the short run, however, such measures may be inappropriate, for managers may have chosen to defer outputs while pursuing good process.

CONCLUSION

Project designers routinely underestimate the time required to initiate sustainable development processes, even when procedural delays do not occur. It takes time for expatriate technicians to develop good working relationships with counterparts; it takes time to transfer problem-solving capabilities to others. Generating and introducing ideas to increase income and productivity are not easy, and it frequently takes decades to create the sorts of local institutions capable of sustaining development initiatives.

Recognition of timing problems and their effect on project performance and impact has begun to filter back from the project level to the institutions and actors responsible for planning, design, and program management. Within the implementation phase itself, some remedies are at the disposal of project managers, although these are mostly tactical in nature. At a strategic level, the most critical need is for donors and host government agencies to create and utilize incentives that support sound implementation practices with a long-term orientation. These incentives must outweigh the shorter-term considerations--loan approval and disbursement targets, for example--that currently govern the process of project design and lead to unrealistic, inflexible project implementation plans that are poorly sequenced.

172

NOTES

1. Donald R. Mickelwait, Charles F. Sweet, and Elliott R. Morss, New Directions in Development: A Study of U.S. AID (Boulder, Colo.: Westview Press, 1979); "Study of Selected Aspects of the Project Assistance Cycle" (Washington, D.C.: Booz, Allen, and Hamilton, 1978).

2. Mickelwait, Sweet, and Morss, Ibid., pp. 209-218.

3. Victoria A. Morss, "The Special Problems of Projects With Significant Implementation Problems: An Examination of Evaluation Findings and Lessons" (Washington, D.C.: Agency for International Development, Office of Evaluation, April 1982).

4. Paul R. Crawford, AID Experience in Agricultural Research: A Review of Project Evaluations (Washington, D.C.: Development Alternatives, Inc., May 1981).

5. Operational Policy Review: Delays in Project Implementation, Operations Evaluation Department Report no. 2946 (Washington, D.C.: The World Bank, 1980).

6. Sixth Annual Review of Project Performance Audit Results, Operations Evaluation Department Report no. 3117 (Washington, D.C.: The World Bank, 1980).

7. World Bank, Operational Policy Review.

8. Robert Chambers, Longhurst, and Pacey, eds., Seasonal Dimensions to Rural Poverty (Towata, N.J.: Alanheld, Osmun, and Co., 1981).

9. Paul R. Crawford, Implementation Problems in Integrated Rural Development: A Review of 21 USAID Projects, IRD Research Note no. 2 (Washington, D.C.: Development Alternatives, Inc., May 1981), p. 84.

10. Aaron Wildavsky, The Politics of the Budgetary Process (New York: Little, Brown, and Co., 1979).

11. World Bank, Operational Policy Review; World Bank, Sixth Annual Review; Booz, Allen, and Hamilton, "Study of Selected Aspects."

12. Crawford, AID Experience, p. 56.

13. Ronald V. Curtis, James B. Lowenthal, and Roberto Castro, Evaluation of Pindar River and Two Meetings Integrated Rural Development Project (Washington, D.C.: Agency for International Development, January 10, 1980), pp. 10, 26.

14. "Project Evaluation Summary - Subtropical Lands Development (77-9)" (Washington, D.C.: Agency for International Development, April 15, 1978), pp. 8-9.

15. Jon R. Moris, Managing Induced Rural Development (Bloomington, Ind.: Indiana University, International Development Institute, 1981).

16. Robert Chambers, Derek Belshaw, and Earl M. Kulp, Designing and Managing Basic Agricultural Programs (Bloomington, Ind.: Indiana University, International Development Institute, 1977).

17. Moris, Managing Induced Rural Development, p. 116.

18. Gene M. Owens et al., The Abyei Rural Development Project: An Assessment of Action Research in Practice, IRD Field Report no. 14 (Washington, D.C.: Development Alternatives, Inc., May 1981), pp. 33, 41-42.

19. Stephen A. Quick, "The Paradox of Popularity: 'Ideological' Program Implementation in Zambia," Politics and Policy Implementation in the Third World, ed. Merilee S. Grindle (Princeton, N.J.: Princeton University Press, 1981), p. 42.

20. Elliott R. Morss, Paul R. Crawford, and George H. Honadle, Toward Self-Reliant Development: A Guide for Evaluating the Sustainability of Project Benefits (Washington, D.C.: Development Alternatives, Inc., May 1982), p. 43.

21. "Draft PID for PDP III" (Jakarta: Agency for International Development, March 24, 1981), p. 73.

22. World Bank, Operational Policy Review, pp. vi-vii.

23. F.L. Mott and S.H. Mott, "Kenya's Record Population Growth: A Dilemma of Development," Population Bulletin 55: 5 (1980).

24. Paul Isenman, "Basic Needs: The Case of Sri Lanka," World Development 8:2 (1981): pp. 237-258.

25. Uma Lele, The Design of Rural Development: Lessons From Africa (Baltimore, Md.: The Johns Hopkins University Press, 1975), p. 192.

26. David C. Korten, "Community Organization and Rural Development: A Learning Process Approach," Public Administration Review 40:6 (1980): 480-511.

27. Jerry Van Sant et al., Supporting Capacity-Building in the Indonesia Provincial Development Program, IRD Field Report no. 12 (Washington, D.C.: Development Alternatives, Inc., February 1981), pp. C16-17.

28. George H. Honadle, Farmer Organization for Irrigation Water Management, Organization, Design and Implementation in Bula and Libmanan (Washington, D.C.: Development Alternatives, Inc., 1978), pp. 21-25.

29. Development Projects Management Center, "Planning Processes for Project Management," Development Project Management: An Integrated Approach to Project Planning and Management (Washington, D.C.: U.S. Department of Agriculture, n.d.), pp. 36-37.

30. Moris, Managing Induced Rural Development, pp. 41-42.

174

31. William J. Siffin, <u>Administrative Problems and Integrated Rural Development</u> (Bloomington, Ind.: Indiana University, Program of Advanced Studies in Institution Building and Technical Assistance Methodology, 1976), pp. 10-13.

32. Moris, <u>Managing Induced Rural Development</u>, p. 118.

33. "The Feasibility and Desireability for Ex-Post Evaluation in the Agency for International Development," draft report (Washington, D.C.: Practical Concepts, Inc., 1979).

7
Ineffective
Information Systems

David D. Gow and Elliott R. Morss

INTRODUCTION

As development projects have grown more complex
and ambitious, the demand for information and
expectations about its utility for project decision
making have risen accordingly. Yet there is ample
cause for skepticism, because quantity is frequently
confused with quality and methodology tends to
overshadow the end uses of information:

> When I look at the future, I flinch. Many people
> do of course, for a variety of reasons. My
> reason is the expectation, more and more confi-
> dently expressed, that the future will be the age
> of information. Already, we are told, an impres-
> sive percentage (estimates vary) of those who
> work no longer grow things or make things or sell
> things. They engage, instead, in 'information
> transfer.' And this we are assured is a mere
> beginning which is why I flinch. Much of the
> information transferred to us now on paper is not
> worth having.[1]

DEFINING THE PROBLEM

The inclusion of a formal information system in a
development project is based on the assumption that
the system will assist project performance, particularly the planning process and the implementation of
development activities. Despite considerable time,
money, and other resources expended on these information activities, however, the returns to date have
been meager. Projects continue to be managed poorly,
which is in part attributable to inadequate information.

Donors are hesitant to act on project information, particularly if it calls for midterm corrections
in project activities or for their termination. To

some extent, this is because information systems are compartmentalized inappropriately. For example, an artificial separation is often assumed to exist between planning, on the one hand, and monitoring and evaluation, on the other. If the planning process is considered to have ended at the time the project was approved, monitoring and evaluation activities will be used to measure compliance with, or deviation from, the plan laid out by the project sponsors. In addition, these activities will not contribute to periodic replanning. Yet most large development projects involve a process of learning and adjustment that calls for modifications (replanning, for example) as implementation proceeds. This cannot be done effectively without information that is geared to the decision-making structure and procedures of project managers and sponsors.

Reasons for the Problem

The basic cause of the problem is that information generated by development projects is often used ineffectively or not used at all: information systems are designed but never implemented; data are collected but never processed; or the results are used only by researchers.[2] The reasons for this situation are both technical and managerial. The technical reasons are two-fold:

- More information-is-good syndrome: more information is a proxy for knowledge, or it is seen as good for its own sake; and

- The excessive cost and complexity of an information system, resulting in methodologies that are inappropriate and impractical.

The managerial reasons for generating useless information are four-fold:

- Project management sees a formal information system as a threat;

- Project management is unable to anticipate its information needs;

- Project staff become intoxicated by crisis management; and

- Project staff are critical of information activities.

The technical and management reasons are discussed below.

More Information is Good. Information has become confused with knowledge: more information is assumed to yield more knowledge. In practice, this has led to an increasing dependence on technology, that is, the more processed information is, the better it is assumed to be. But is it? And, if so, for what purpose can it be used? More information in itself is worthless unless the capacity exists to analyze, criticize, and reflect on it:

> Applied to the planning and management of rural development this easily promotes and justifies unthinking demands for information--demands which misuse executive capacity and culminate in mounds of unused data.[3]

The major culprit has been base-line surveys, usually justified on the grounds that project management needs the data the surveys produce for planning and evaluation. This justification has been roundly criticized

> . . . because the baseline survey is usually so general that the situation portrayed might be more decisively affected by something other than the project itself. Much better would it be to define closely what is to be evaluated (e.g., crop yields after irrigation has been introduced) and then to provide a pre-use baseline for later evaluation.[4]

A further justification for base-line surveys is that the information generated may provide new ways of tackling implementation problems. This rarely happens since surveys do not produce new ideas; ideas do not derive from a mass of facts but come from different perceptions of those facts.[5] In any case, survey results are invariably difficult to interpret-- particularly with regard to the causes of social and economic change.[6]

Moreover, the reliability of data generated by base-line surveys is questionable. In Nepal, researchers, convinced by their experience that survey research data were inaccurate, decided to cross-check survey responses.[7] They compiled a questionnaire drawn from four previously conducted surveys. The questionnaires were administered by experienced interviewers in three communities known to the researchers. Respondents were selected because they were known either to the researchers or to their associates.

In presenting their findings, the researchers noted the survey questionnaire categories in which they found the greatest amount of error as measured against their cross-checked data (See Table 7.1). Beside each category is a "minimum level of error" (MLE)--the lowest level error considered significant for each category. The final column shows the average degree of error for those households in which the errors exceeded the MLE.

Not only did data for over 10 percent of the households contain errors above the level considered significant, but the average magnitude of reporting error was also well over 100 percent for the important categories of land ownership, yields, grain sold, grain exchanged, and annual income.

Excessive Cost and Complexity. A consultant who designs a project's information system typically is not involved in, or responsible for, its implementation. In addition, his contract generally requires him to produce a lengthy document describing an elaborate system. The result is often a design that emphasizes quantity, complexity, and therefore cost, over quality and simplicity.

The integrated rural development program in Colombia provides a good example of this problem. Within the program management unit at the national level is an evaluation group responsible for measuring the impact of integrated rural development activities in five areas of the country. Unfortunately, the methodology selected--the sample survey--proved far too complex for the task at hand. A consulting firm spent a year designing this methodology and an additional five months testing the proposed questionnaire. But both methodology and questionnaire had to be modified during the data collection effort, and processing the data from each area required from six months to a year.[8]

The costs involved in implementing a complex information system are rarely calculated prior to project start-up:

> In East Africa we found that the typical multi-subject baseline survey with a stratified sampling plan and adequate preliminary analysis represents roughly fourteen to eighteen months of work by a team of from two to four senior researchers supported by vehicles and lower level enumerators--i.e., about half the input required for a modest field program.[9]

In the case of the Eastern ORD Integrated Rural Development Project in Upper Volta, the implementing university designed and undertook a large farm survey. The designers tried to provide all things to all

TABLE 7.1
The Reliability of Survey Data in Nepal

Questionnaire Category	MLE	% Households above MLE (N=26)	Average Degree of Error in Household above MLE
Total land owned	10%	54%	240%
Approximate crop yield	40%	22%	184%
Value of grain sold	100%	18%	814%
Grain exchanged	70%	11%	658%
Previous year's income	10%	38%	233%

Source: J. G. Campbell et al., The Use and Misuse of Social
Science Research in Nepal (Kathmandu: Tribhuvan
University, Research Center for Nepal and Asian Studies,
1979), p. 4.

people. The questionnaire had many sections,
including a credit file, a crop production file, an
animal traction file, and a small industries survey,
and the sections were filled out at different times.
The data analysis proved to be unmanageable.
Information was eventually pulled off in little
pieces, but the bulk of it will probably never be
used. The survey was sold in the name of all the
latest innovations in survey design and computer
processing, but it did not satisfy the policy-making
needs of project management. The problem was
exacerbated because few of the results were translated
into French.[10]

   Threat to Management. It would be naive to
ignore that an effective information system--
particularly its monitoring and evaluation functions--
can be seen as a threat by project management. Information is power, and it can be used for good or ill.
Especially threatening is an evaluation system that
grades the overall success of a project or provides
outsiders with evidence to second-guess the decisions
of project managers. Thus, a crucial element in
effective use of an information system is the
willingness of project management to learn from its
mistakes. An information system should show not only
what is going right, but also what is going wrong.
   In Latin America, for example, ORDEZA was a
well-staffed regional organization established to
assist in the rehabilitation of the earthquake zone in
the Huaraz area of Peru. ORDEZA helped communities to
form cooperatives, identify income-generating activities, borrow funds, and implement these activities.
The organization had operated for several years and
had received an AID loan when a consulting firm was
asked to design a comprehensive monitoring and
evaluation system for use primarily by project
management and secondarily by the AID mission in Peru.
   During 1973-1974, the consulting firm's staff
made six trips into the project area to work with
ORDEZA staff. This work consisted of determining
information requirements, designing and testing data
collection instruments, and proposing revisions. The
basic objective was to generate an internal information system, created by ORDEZA staff, for project
management to use.
   The information system was tested and received
enthusiastic responses from the ORDEZA team in the
field; it was then modified to meet the decision-
making needs of the project director. The system was
never completed and never implemented, however. In
part, this was due to a change of directors and other
top officials in ORDEZA and an internal shift of

authority and responsibility. However, there were
other possible reasons:

- The proposed information system reported on
  the activities of field staff without helping
  them to do their job better, that is, the
  control function took precedence over the
  learning function; and

- The system was funded by AID, feeding
  suspicion that the information generated might
  be used to impose external controls on the
  flow of AID funds.[11]

Management Inability to Anticipate Information
Needs. Key project personnel often find it difficult
to specify in advance what information they need for
planning, monitoring, and evaluating project activities. Instead, they may prefer to rely on information
passed through informal channels--a practical alternative in small, straightforward projects, but hardly
reliable in large, complex projects.

The Second Integrated Rural Development Project
in Jamaica, for example, relied too heavily on
informal information systems for daily management.
This informality often had expensive consequences.
Without reliable notification about the time and place
of meetings, people arrived too soon, or not at all,
and meetings had to be postponed. Similarly, a lack
of coordination of transportation left project staff
looking for rides, or several people going to the same
place in separate cars. Extension agents often missed
meetings with farmer groups. In general, staff time
was not effectively used.[12]

Project managers who cannot articulate their
information needs should not necessarily lock to so-
called information experts to assume that responsibility. These experts often do not consider the
different information needs of the various groups
involved in the project. As a result, the systems
they design are likely to the generate information
that is either irrelevant or useless for decision
making.

Project managers have difficulty specifying their
information needs for three basic reasons:

- They are rarely, if ever, involved in the
  design of either the project or the
  information system;

- They may be unaware of the management power of
  an effective information system; and

- They cannot easily decide what data should be collected if the project design does not state explicitly what the project is expected to accomplish.[13]

This last point deserves elaboration, since project goals are often stated in unrealistic terms-- self-sustaining development, increased institutional capacity, and improved human well-being--and usually simultaneously:

Such panaceas can be found all too often in the opening paragraphs of agricultural development proposals. However, translating these goals into specific objectives requires a great deal of skill and knowledge.[14]

The Intoxication of Crisis Management. Some project managers spend much of their time on crisis management--and derive great enjoyment from it. To the extent that they are stimulated by crises, any attempt to reduce the occurrence of crises--for example, by providing relevant information on a timely basis--may be greeted with disdain. Crisis management is a behavioral characteristic, perhaps endemic to project management, that can peacefully coexist with an effective information system, yet be entirely independent of it.

In its purest form, crisis management is charac- terized by a reluctance to undertake planning and the concomitant postponement of decision making until the last minute. Crisis management does not necessarily reflect the quality of project leadership, since it can take place under strong or weak project managers. An external evaluation of the North Shaba Rural Development Project in Zaire characterized the operating style as crisis management and identified the most serious problems as:

- Lack of management planning, resulting in poor decision making;

- An ineffectual accounting system that could not provide accurate data on past expendi- tures;

- Lack of an effective budgeting system, including cash flow management; and

- Lack of documentation for decisions.[15]

Although some of these criticisms deal with information or the lack of it, they do not fully reflect the context of development in a country such as Zaire. Even a simple, timely, effective information system would not have ended the need for the crisis management approach. Other factors simply overruled.

In June 1981, for example, the project submitted to the government of Zaire its budget request, nearly $3.5 million, for the coming calendar year. Six months later the project was granted just over $162,000, which came nowhere near meeting the budget needs of a project with 800 people on its payroll. To avoid temporarily closing down some activities, project management had to spend time and energy securing temporary funding from other sources. In these circumstances, crisis management was a necessity, not an option or a habit.

Internal Criticism by Project Staff. When those responsible for producing information belong to an independent unit that is not an integral part of the ongoing project, chances are that their findings will not be taken seriously. In addition, project staff are likely to criticize both their activities and their findings.

For example, in the Rasuwa/Nuwakot Integrated Rural Development Project in Nepal, a socio-economic unit attached to the project coordinator's office was responsible for collecting information for planning, implementation, and evaluation. As of 1980, this unit was responsible solely to the expatriate adviser attached to the project coordinator's office. This adviser dictated the type of information that the socio-economic unit was to gather. Although most project staff had seen some of the unit's reports, there was no indication they had used the studies for any purpose at the project level. Furthermore, district officers, the highest-level government representatives in the area, criticized the reports on three grounds: inaccurate information, young and inexperienced enumerators, and little supervision of the enumerators while they were gathering data in the field.[16]

ALLEVIATING THE PROBLEM: TECHNICAL ASPECTS

The bottom line for a positive assessment of information activities in development projects should be improved project performance. One condition necessary to achieve improved performance is improved planning capability. Much of the information generated by monitoring and evaluation activities should provide the basis for ongoing planning, including the replanning of those activities that require it.

To achieve better planning, the project's basic
objectives must be stated in terms that can be made
operational. Otherwise, there is little justification
for an information system in the first place. For
example, in the Arusha Planning and Village
Development Project in Tanzania, the goals were
clearly specified:

● To increase village self-reliance, as measured
  by an expansion of village capabilities to
  solve their own problems;

● To improve equity, as measured by poorer areas
  obtaining development benefits in a manner
  that is self-sustaining;

● To promote economic growth, as measured by
  increases in the gross regional product and in
  the generation of foreign exchange earnings;

● To improve regional integration, as measured
  by stronger commercial, institutional, and
  cultural linkages within the region; and

● To protect natural resources, as measured by
  the development of sustainable production
  systems.[17]

Clear project objectives provide management with
a tangible basis for planning and a means by which to
measure progress. However, it is equally important to
allow for unanticipated project effects. Rarely, if
ever, does a project evolve in a linear fashion.
Despite careful planning and expert management, large-
scale development projects may produce unanticipated
effects.

The Caqueza Rural Development Project in
Colombia, for example, collected data on the risks to
small-scale farmers of paying cash for recommended
inputs such as fertilizer, improved seed, and
pesticide. The analysis revealed that, because the
risks increased so dramatically, farmers resisted
applying the new production inputs to their crops.
Instead, they chose to sell the inputs for cash or to
use some of them on crops for which they were not
originally intended. As a result of these findings,
project staff designed and introduced a crop insurance
program, which helped increase the adoption rates for
inputs from 50 percent to 98 percent in the next
season.[18]

This example illustrates the role of an effective
information system in detecting the unanticipated. If
an information system provides timely management and
impact data to project staff and policy makers,

detrimental side effects may be identified early
enough for management to adjust the project strategy
to counteract them.[19] But without a flexible
project design that allows changes in direction, an
effective early warning system is worthless.

Identifying Information Requirements

To develop an effective information system,
project designers should identify the information
requirements of each group of decision makers involved
in the project. These needs differ significantly. For
example, in an agricultural production project,
individual households want some basis for evaluating
the new technologies recommended so they can decide
for themselves if the technologies are worth the risk
involved. This information might include data on
potential advantages and disadvantages, yields, labor
requirements, pricing, marketing, and availability and
cost of inputs. Although project managers realize the
importance of this information to potential
beneficiaries, they often make only cursory attempts
to provide it.

At the other end of the spectrum, decision makers
in the capital (ministries, planning commissions, and
donors) require information on overall progress and
project impact to change or modify their policies.
Because these central actors have the leverage to
demand this information, their needs are the ones most
often met by the information system.

A formative evaluation of the information system
used by the Provincial Area Develoment Program in
Indonesia focused on another barrier to fulfilling
different information needs at various project levels.
At the lowest level, implementing agencies required
specific technical information. At the national
level, although this information was too detailed to
be of much use, it was still routinely provided.

To alleviate this failure to distinguish between
the different information needs of various levels, the
evaluation invoked the principle of "optimal
ignorance."[20] Simply put, this principle states
that the flow of information to any level should be
restricted to what is necessary for informed and
rational decision making at that level. This does not
mean that information most relevant to one level
should never be accessible to other levels, but rather
that it should not routinely be fed into the flow of
reports to all levels. In this way, decision makers
will not be overwhelmed or distracted by irrelevant or
inappropriate information. Although they may be
ignorant of some facets of the project, this is an
asset if they are able to concentrate on addressing
and resolving critical issues.[21]

Relevance and Simplicity

It is easy for project management and other interested parties to become quickly--and perhaps irretrievably--inundated by a flood of data passed off as information. Similarly, experience indicates that project staff quickly become immersed in the daily problems of implementation at the expense of taking time to think through the results and recommendations produced by an information system, regardless of their quality, relevance, or timeliness.[22] The answer is to seek relevance and simplicity.

In the early years of a project, it is vitally important to distinguish between information that is relevant and that which is related. The failure to make this distinction has resulted in the generation of large quantities of related information that have proved useless for decision making. To decide what sort of information is relevant, one analyst has suggested the following:

> It is far easier and more natural to ask for, to gather and to accumulate data, than it is to abstain from asking, to reduce communication, and to limit the information acquired. The challenge here is formidable: it is to reorient thinking radically, to ask . . . . How much does the information cost? Who is going to process and use it? What benefits will accrue? Will the results be available in time? What can be left out? What simplifications can be introduced? What do we not need to know?[23]

Answering these questions is an excellent way to develop a realistic implementation plan for information activities.

Linked to relevance is the issue of simplicity. Those in the simple-is-optimal school argue that current donor practices for project preparation and implementation respond more to technocratic needs for high-cost, sophisticated, and faddish information than to the needs of either project staff or beneficiaries. In other words, complex designs provide more employment for donor-agency staff and Western technicians than for potential beneficiaries.

The advantages of a simple information system can be summarized as follows:

- A greater probability that local management will be capable of implementing it;

- A greater probability of replication since it will not overtax scarce resources;

- A greater chance for beneficiary participation since the information system will be more understandable to the rural population; and

- A higher degree of local control and independence from external experts and powers.[24]

These prescriptions appear eminently logical, and yet there are powerful incentives in the information system business to seek higher degrees of sophistication, quantification, and analytical elegance. As long as project managers and sponsoring agencies remain passive consumers of information services--rather than actively intervening in the design and insisting on timeliness, relevance, and careful adaptation to the real human and financial resources of the project--they are likely to get state-of-the-art services, which are ill-suited to their needs.

Determine the Existing Information Base

Designers and implementers of development projects may choose to ignore the existing information base, particularly as it relates to previous development efforts. In Jamaica, for example, the basic objective of one project was to encourage self-reliance by stimulating self-help farming on church-owned lands. In one rural community in which the project was active, the principal economic activity was truck farming. Although profitable, it was a high-risk, high-gain enterprise. Its success was determined largely by the amount of rainfall, which was highly variable by year. A similar project in the same area had failed a decade earlier precisely because of insufficient rainfall; yet there was no evidence that this information had been considered when the project's sponsors selected the community.[25]

Existing information can be found in various forms: written and oral, formal and informal, qualitative and quantitative. Whatever its form and source, it should be treated with circumspection. Some existing information is worthless--although demonstrating this can be worthwhile. In many of the isolated areas of the world in which projects are implemented, bad information is often all that is available for planning purposes. In the far west of Nepal, for example, the principal data available are the acreage and production statistics published annually by the Agricultural Statistics Division of the Department of Food and Agricultural Marketing

Services. These data are often gathered through a subjective approach by which an individual extension agent may have to guess the acreage and yields for 1,000 farmers.[26]

Existing information systems usually consist of pro forma reports. These "often pay little attention to project implementation and negligible attention to evaluation of impact, tending ritually to record statistics of trivial planning value."[27] Usually these reports provide data to fulfill primary functions such as auditing, controlling finances, and assessing progress toward the attainment of physical targets.[28]

Should these systems be scrapped? It has been argued persuasively that they should not:

> The frontier for planners . . . is in examining the reporting and evaluation systems which already operate within governments and trying to improve them and link them up functionally with remedial action and with future resource allocations.[29]

Finally, information should be sought on similar, ongoing projects within the country as well as on future projects. Information on the activities of research stations, both local and national, should also be gathered. Ideally, all this information--as well as that generated by the information system-- should be carefully guarded in some form of documentation center, thereby creating an institutional memory.

Information Strategies

There is increasing evidence that project managers do not necessarily want data that are 100 percent accurate. A study of East Asian projects reported:

> Project managers at the workshop feel that data on the progress and achievements of rural development projects did not need to be highly accurate. Some felt that an 80 percent and higher accuracy level was acceptable and useful for decision making.[30]

One information strategy gaining increasing acceptance is rapid reconnaissance. The methods utilized include the following:

- Key indicators;

- Indigenous technical knowledge;

- Direct observation;

- Key informants;

- Group interviews; and

- Aerial surveys.[31]

In a recent critique of rapid reconnaissance, two generic problems were pointed out.[32] First, the approach is characterized by an apparent search for universal indicators as a way to promote quick and clean appraisal. In the process, the search loses sight of the contextual nature of indicators. Second, the focus is on cost-effective tools for external actions rather than on the generation and use of data by local institutions to improve their own performance and capacity. These problems can be alleviated:

> First, when using reconnaissance methods, practitioners should pretest the situation by examining the problem context and stating the assumptions linking proxies to phenomena. This requires a high degree of <u>participation</u> by local people and it strengthens the ability to judge the quality of an investigation. Moreover, the participatory and collaborative nature of the exercise can be used to focus knowledge, define problems, and build local organizational capacity. Second, academics should study the contingencies that tend to invalidate different types of indicators. Such studies might improve data collection methods and management systems by identifying warning signals or producing guidelines for indicator selection.[33]

ALLEVIATING THE PROBLEM: MANAGERIAL ASPECTS

To alleviate the managerial aspects of ineffective information systems, three tactics are recommended:

- Overcoming managerial apprehension;

- Overcomming staff apprehension; and

- Participation by beneficiaries.

Each tactic is discussed below.

Overcoming Managerial Apprehensions

Managerial apprehensions can be overcome only if the project manager is actively involved in the design of the information system. Although a project design can sketch the broad outlines of an information system, the manager should develop the plan for implementing it. To do this, management must first clarify project objectives and determine how they are to be made operational. Otherwise, management may find, imposed from on high, a blueprint information system that it can accept or ignore.

In the early stages of a project, it is especially useful to concentrate on gathering information on what has worked and what has not in the project area. Comparative data are needed when a project is quasi-experimental and deliberately tests alternative models simultaneously. For example, a project may try several different extension techniques: including one-to-one, model farmers, and farmer groups. Managers need information on which approach is most effective, as well as the authority to act on the results. This requires enough decentralization for the managers to adapt quickly to changing circumstances and new information without having to seek prior approval from their superiors.

Concerning planning, this approach requires regular updating of the annual implementation plan, perhaps on a quarterly basis. Annual plans should serve as guidelines rather than as prescriptions with fixed objectives to be either slavishly pursued or studiously ignored.

Although these steps should help decrease the level of crisis management often found in development projects, they will not eliminate it--nor should they. An element of crisis management can be stimulating to and demanding of project management and staff. One could argue that some crisis, like some conflict, is necessary to development.

Overcoming Staff Apprehensions

When the unit gathering information is an integral part of the project, and has some responsibility for translating its findings into policy, project staff are more likely to take its findings and recommendations seriously. For example, the information unit in the North Shaba project in Zaire, Systeme d'Analyse et Collecte de Donnees (SCAD), was fully acknowledged by the other project subsystems only after five years. In the early years, other project staff regarded SCAD with considerable skepticism, if not outright suspicion. This was so for two reasons: first, they did not fully understand the extent to which an effective information system could improve project performance; second, since SCAD was organizationally parallel to the other subsystems of the project, staff resented what they interpreted as its snooping, controlling responsibilities.

This situation improved when SCAD was made part of the project management unit, and individual subsystems were allowed some say in the type of information activities it undertook. More important, however, SCAD eventually began to produce information that staff could take seriously. For the 1981 maize harvest, for example, SCAD predicted that aggregate maize production in the project area would be approximately 69,000 metric tons. This estimate was based on data collected from farm journals kept for a sample of project farmers as well as yield tests conducted in farmers' fields.

Project management refused to accept this estimate, arguing that it exceeded by 40 percent the end-of-project (1983) objective of 49,000 metric tons. SCAD was instructed to lower its estimates to conform with the conventional wisdom concerning North Shaba's potential for maize production. SCAD then reanalyzed and revised its data and still came up with the same estimates, much to management's annoyance. However, once the harvest was complete, the data on yields and surplus exported closely matched the original SCAD estimates. From that time on, SCAD's activities have been taken seriously.[34]

Like project management, project staff will take an information system seriously if they are actively involved in it. Although it may take a variety of forms, staff participation in information activities usually has one or more of the following characteristics:

- Shared decision making and problem solving;

- Use of teams to set targets and monitor task performance; and

- Job-related information sharing.

One effective way to increase staff involvement in information activities is to use joint goal setting and planning by project management and staff. This can include systematic performance improvement and target setting as a regular, continuing process. In Indonesia, for example, this method has been used to improve coordination between planning boards and technical ministry personnel at provincial and district levels. The result has been joint development of interim goals and indicators for measuring goal achievement. Although many of these goals have related to enhanced beneficiary participation, the targets and strategies to accomplish this participation are set by project staff rather than project management.[35]

Evaluation is another crucial area in which staff involvement can be improved, not just in the act of evaluating, but also in the process of discussing, accepting, and acting on evaluation results. One comprehensive method to deal with the issue of sustainability is the use of joint programming workshops. These workshops may involve project staff, local community leaders, or government officials, and may last from a few hours to several days. They can have the following uses:

- Presenting results of the evaluation and clarifying the issues;

- Building a consensus among those who will have to carry out the recommendations;

- Planning solutions for problems of sustainability that were identified in the evaluation; and

- Increasing the capacity of those who must carry out the solutions, specifically their ability to respond to future constraints to benefit sustainability.[36]

Participation by Beneficiaries

Much has been written about the importance of establishing the information needs of project beneficiaries and involving them in the planning, monitoring, and evaluation of development activities. In most cases, these ideas have remained in project documents, and beneficiaries have become passive recipients of information passed on by project staff. But what information is likely to interest farmers? In an agricultural production project, for example, it is reasonable to assume that farmers are most likely to be interested in technology transfer.

Until relatively recently, agricultural projects were generally designed to introduce technologies from industrialized countries, or to develop technology within developing countries by drawing on elements of technological packages developed elsewhere. However, these strategies to improve the livelihood of small-scale farmers have repeatedly failed. Furthermore, many agricultural programs have led to an unequal distribution of benefits. Finally, the rising cost of fossil-based fuel has made the use of much Green

Revolution technology prohibitively expensive. In
response to these problems, growing awareness and
interest has developed in what has come to be known as
farming systems approaches.[37]

The primary aim of farming systems research is to
increase the productivity of the farming system by
acknowledging its constraints and potentials. A
systems approach provides a link between the farmer,
the research institution, and the funding agency, thus
counterbalancing the more conventional top-down,
research-station approach. In this way, productivity
can be improved through the development of relevant
technology and complementary policies that increase
the welfare of farm families in ways that are useful
and acceptable to them and society as a whole.[38]

Present farming systems research is characterized
as either upstream or downstream. Upstream research
seeks to generate prototype solutions to facilitate
major shifts in the potential productivity of farming
systems. It often involves several years of research,
both on and off the research station. In contrast,
downstream research is designed to identify rapidly
and to test possible innovations that can be easily
integrated into existing farming systems.[39] Thus
farming systems research offers excellent potential,
providing that farmers are involved in the information
activities:

> Small farmers must actively participate in the
> research and extension activities carried out in
> their area, helping to identify problems and set
> criteria as well as judge results. They can no
> longer be considered the passive recipients of
> material and information handed down to them by
> the professionals.[40]

Nonetheless, a recent commentator has pointed out
that the farming systems research approach has not
proved immune to some pitfalls of information
gathering. Although in principle more participatory
and farmer oriented, some farming systems research
projects are still top-down efforts, with the
researchers defining research priorities and possible
solutions without the participation of farmers. In
these cases, farmers are relegated to the position of
laborers on their own farms and their opinions of
possible solutions rarely elicited. Furthermore, one
common distortion of the farming systems research
methodology is an overriding emphasis on the
collection of data to the virtual exclusion of efforts
to develop appropriate farm-level technologies.[41]

CONCLUSION

This chapter has examined the reasons why formal information systems in large-scale development projects have not lived up to expectations. More specifically, it has uncovered the fallacies associated with the idea that thorough monitoring and evaluation would lead to improved project performance. It appears that information, if collected, has not been used for the intended purposes.

Several factors have contributed to these shortcomings. First, large amounts of information have been collected but not used. Second, information system designs have been excessively costly and complex. Third, managers have not been able to anticipate their information needs, and, more important, they have seen these information system designs more as a threat to their work than as a source of assistance.

Steps can be taken to break out of this pattern of failure. First, a careful study should be made of what information is really needed. With this in hand, a review of existing information should be made. Only when this review is completed should consideration be given to the techniques of collecting needed information that is not already available. Second, managers, staff, and project beneficiaries should be involved to a greater extent than in the past in whatever information activities the project chooses to pursue.

The sponsors of large development projects, that is, donor agencies and host governments, also should modify their expectations and better define their information needs. A mass of detail about project activities tends to obscure the critical issues that the sponsors care most about. This often leads them to intervene in matters in which authority and discretion should be left to project management, or to stress disproportionately reporting against output targets that were written into the design document, but have little relevance thereafter. A realistic information strategy should be based on the prompt delivery of minimum, not maximum, amounts of data analyzed in a form that relates directly to the basic concept, assumptions, and development approach of the project. The other side of the same coin is a willingness by project sponsors to acknowledge uncertainty and flexibility as parameters of development projects.

NOTES

1. Edwin Newman, "O Facilitative New World!,"
Newsweek, Oct. 5, 1981. p. 18.
2. A study of information activities in World
Bank-financed projects in East Asia and the Pacific
reported that only seventeen out of forty-five
projects had specific resource provisions for such
activities. See G. Deboeck and R. Ng, Monitoring
Rural Development in East Asia, World Bank Staff
Working Paper no. 439, (Washington, D.C.: World Bank,
1980), p. 23.
3. Robert K. Chambers, Managing Rural Development:
Ideas and Experiences from East Africa, (Uppsala:
Scandinavian Institute of African Studies, 1974), p.
153. See also, G. Deboeck and R. Ng, Monitoring Rural
Development, p. 10.
4. S. Conlin, "Baseline Surveys: An Escape From
Thinking About Research Problems, And Even More A
Refuge From Actually Doing Anything" (Paper presented
at the Conference on Rapid Rural Appraisal, Institute
of Development Studies, Brighton, 1979), p. 4.
5. Ibid., p. 5.
6. Donald R. Mickelwait, "Information Strategies
for Implementing Rural Development," International
Development Administration: Implementation Analysis
for Development Projects, eds. G. Honadle and R.
Klauss, (New York: Praeger, 1979), p. 199.
7. J. Gabriel Campbell et al., The Use and Misuse
of Social Science Research in Nepal (Kathmandu:
Tribhuvan University, Research Center for Nepal and
Asian Studies, 1979).
8. Donald R. Jackson et al., IRD in Colombia:
Making it Work, IRD Working Paper no. 7 (Washington,
D.C.: Development Alternatives, Inc., June 1981), pp.
20-21.
9. Jon R. Moris, Managing Induced Rural Development (Bloomington, Ind.: Indiana University,
International Development Institute, 1981), p. 43.
10. Paul R. Crawford, Implementation Issues in
Integrated Rural Development: A Review of 21 USAID
Projects, IRD Research Note no. 2 (Washington, D.C.:
Development Alternatives, Inc., May 1981), p. 74.
11. Donald R. Mickelwait et. al., Information for
Decisionmaking in Rural Development, 2 vols.
(Washington, D.C.: Development Alternatives, Inc.,
1978), 1:281-284.
12. Crawford, Implementation Issues, p. 69.
13. G. Deboeck and W. Kinsey, Managing Information
for Rural Development: Lessons from Eastern Africa,
World Bank Staff Working Paper no. 379 (Washington,
D.C.: World Bank, 1980), pp. 16, 23.

14. Kenneth G. Swanberg, _Evaluation Research for Agricultural Development Projects_, Development Discussion Paper no. 127 (Cambridge, Mass.: Harvard Institute for International Development, December 1981), p. 7.

15. Everett Headrick, "Evaluation of the Project North Shaba Project Management" (Kinshasa, Zaire: U.S. Agency for International Development, May 1982). For a somewhat different perspective, see _Five Years Later: Progress and Sustainability in Project North Shaba_ (Washington, D.C., Development Alternatives, Inc, March 1982), chapters 1 and 7.

16. David D. Gow, _An Information System for the Rural Area Development -- Rapti Zone Project,_ IRD Field Report no. 8 (Washington, D.C.: Development Alternatives, Inc., May 1980), pp. 20-25.

17. Charles F. Sweet, _Arusha Planning and Village Development Project, Information Strategy: Past and Future_ (Washington, D.C.: Development Alternatives, Inc., May 1981), p. 4.

18. Swanberg, _Evaluation Research_, pp. 4-5.

19. George H. Honadle et. al., _Integrated Rural Development Making it Work?_ (Washington, D.C.: Development Alternatives, Inc., 1980), pp. 173-180.

20. This principle was first invoked by Warren Ilchman when he wrote about the importance of establishing the "optimum level of ignorance" for making reasonable decisions. See "Decision Rules and Decision Roles," _The African Review_, 2: (1972): 219-246.

21. Michael Morfit et. al., "Toward An Improved PDP Information System," (Report submitted to USAID/Indonesia, April 1982), pp. 7-9.

22. Deboeck and Kinsey, _Managing Information_, p. 48; and Development Alternatives, _Five Years Later_, pp. 53-54.

23. Chambers, _Managing Rural Development_, p. 153.

24. Honadle et. al., _Integrated Rural Development_, p. 39. See also Robert Chambers, "Project Selection for Poverty Focused Rural Development: Simple is Optimal," _World Development_ 6:2 (1978): 209-219.

25. David D. Gow, Elliott R. Morss, and Donald R. Jackson, _Local Organizations and Rural Development: A Comparative Reappraisal,_ 2 vols. (Washington, D.C.: Development Alternatives, Inc., Washington, D.C., 1979), 2:341-350.

26. Gow, _An Information System_, p. 14.

27. Chambers, _Managing Rural Development_, p. 128.

28. For Indonesia, see Morfit et. al., _Improved Information System_, pp. 4-5; for Kenya, see Kenneth Swanberg, _The Kenyan Ministry of Agriculture Monitoring and Evaluation Unit 1976-1980: Objectives, Results, and Lessons Learned_, Development Discussion Paper no. 118, (Cambridge, Mass.: Harvard Institute

for International Development, July 1981), pp. 1,
28-291; and for Nepal, see Gow, An Information System,
p. 12.

29. Chambers, Managing Rural Development, p. 129.

30. Deboeck and Kinsey, Managing Information p.
27.

31. Robert Chambers, "Rapid Rural Appraisal:
Rationale and Repetoire" Public Administration and
Development, 1:1 (1981):95-106.

32. George H. Honadle, "Rapid Reconnaissance for
Development Administration: Mapping and Moulding
Organizational Landscapes," World Development 11:8
(1982): 633-649.

33. Ibid, pp. 644-645.

34. Development Alternatives, Five Years Later,
pp. 53-55.

35. Jerry Van Sant, David Gow, and Thomas Armor,
"Managing Staff to Promote Participation " Rural
Development Participation Review 3:3 (1982): 4-6.

36. Elliott R. Morss, Paul R. Crawford, and George
H. Honadle, Toward Self-Reliant Development: A Guide
for Evaluating the Sustainability of Project Benefits
(Washington, D.C.: Development Alternatives, Inc.,
May 1982), pp. 56-57.

37. David W. Norman, The Farming Systems Approach:
Relevancy for the Small Farmer, MSU Rural Development
Paper no. 5 (East Lansing, Mich.: Michigan State
University, Department of Agricultural Economics,
1980), pp. 1-2.

38. E.H. Gilbert, D.W. Norman, and F.E. Winch,
Farming Systems Research: Critical Appraisal, MSU
Rural Development Paper no. 6 (East Lansing, Mich.:
Michigan State University, Department of Agricultural
Economics, 1980), p. 2.

39. Ibid., p. 10.

40. William F. Whyte, Participatory Approaches to
Agricultural Research and Development (Ithaca, N.Y.:
Cornell University, Rural Development Commmittee,
1981) p. 98.

41. Jennifer Bremer, "But Is It FSR? Potholes on
the Road from Fad to Legitimacy," draft (Washington,
D.C.: Development Alternatives, Inc., 1983).

8
Differing Agendas

Elliott R. Morss and George H. Honadle

PROBLEM DEFINITION

Key players in the development game, both institutional and individual, try to achieve different and sometimes contradictory ends. When agendas differ, project success will rarely receive priority attention. As a result, differing agendas have been a recurring source of problems in project implementation.

This assertion is neither novel nor controversial today. The literature contains numerous theoretical arguments and much empirical documentation to support this point.[1] Management scientists have taken major steps to design and implement strategies that neutralize the negative effects of differing agendas. Consequently, the purpose of this essay is not to assert the seriousness or even the nature of the problem. Instead, it is to:

- Describe the differing agendas that are likely to exist in the context of a large-scale development project; and

- Suggest what can be done to eliminate or neutralize the problems they cause.

Reasons For The Problem And Its Manifestations

To a large extent, differing agendas are the result of the incentive structures in effect. One experienced observer of the development process has made the following assertion:

> The greatest strategic problem of any integrated rural development scheme is not to determine the best collection of component activities. Nor is it to coordinate various specialized agencies and jurisdictions. It is the problem of <u>incentives</u>,

of devising and applying an incentive strategy
for those who must shape and conduct the
activities that will, if successful, produce
desired kinds of results.[2]

Institutional Agendas. The problem of differing
agendas has manifested itself at all levels and in all
phases of the project cycle. The agendas of senior
donor agency executives are a primary example. These
officials tend to be concerned about achieving overall
disbursement targets for their country program; such
technical questions as how the monies are used receive
much less of their attention. This is seen in, for
example, the U.S. bilateral assistance program in
Egypt, with a pledge to transfer annually a specified
amount of money. Another example took place in 1981,
when the World Bank threatened to charge Kenya
interest on the undisbursed portion of committed
monies.

In recipient countries, the central bank and,
frequently, the ministry of finance are similarly
concerned about total aggregate flows. To these
institutions, the most critical question may be the
extent to which foreign aid covers projected balance
of payments and budget deficits.

In these circumstances, when the senior
executives of donor and recipient countries alike
focus on the overall magnitude of aid flows, the
question of how to utilize these monies most
effectively does not receive the attention project
implementers think it deserves. The project matters
that most concern senior executives are issues such as
low disbursement rates and possible project agreement
violations. Unfortunately, pressure to increase
disbursement rates often damages projects, whereas
agreement violations frequently result from honest
efforts to expedite project activities.

Project Design Pressures. The agendas of those
involved in the project design process also present
problems. Projects are usually identified and
designed by donor technicians and their counterparts
in national-level agencies of developing countries.
Both share the common objective of designing projects
that will be approved. In this regard, projects,
unlike programs,

. . . connote purposefulness, some minimum size,
a specific location, the introduction of
something qualitatively new, and the expectation
that a sequence of further development moves will
result.[3]

One analyst further laments the pressure for assertiveness in project design:

> The design processes of technical assistance involve a subtle and complex mixture of analysis and advocacy. The person who defines a problem, shapes a strategy, or creates a project must adopt a strong assertive stance: these are the goals; these are the proper purposes; they will be served by these outputs; and the outputs will be produced by these inputs within the time-frame and this particular setting.[4]

The need to express certainty, largely dictated by the common goal of designing projects that will be approved, mocks the reality of conditions in developing countries. In these circumstances, it is not surprising that project design papers rarely offer useful directions for implementers.

Although foreign technicians and their host country counterparts want to get projects approved, they have to comply with agendas of their parent organizations. Donors, for example, are more likely to approve projects that correspond to their prevailing development strategies. Currently, members of the donor community focus on ways to increase the role of the private sector, to train managers, and to apply new microcomputer technologies. But the development approaches favored and promoted by the counterpart's ministry may not correspond at all to this emphasis. These differences are most frequently resolved through an all-inclusive project design paper. This type of compromise frequently detracts from the soundness of the project concept, thereby creating the potential for implementation problems.

An example of these sorts of problems is the Abyei Development Project in Sudan.[5] The project design called for both experimentation and development results. The contractor, an American university, emphasized experimentation, and incurred criticism from both the donor (Agency for International Development) and the Sudanese government, because anticipated results did not materialize.

The people designing projects are rarely involved to a significant extent in their implementation. Donors usually contract out the technical assistance component of projects, and although they appoint an officer to supervise project implementation, the officer has seldom been much involved in the design. The same situation is true of recipient country personnel: those involved in implementation usually differ from those in design. In Indonesia, for example, a project designed by a national ministry is

often handed over to a lower-level government
institution to implement.[6]

This project design process is a recipe for
disaster. Instead of giving careful attention to
potential implementation problems, the process glosses
over and, at times, suppresses them. The problems, of
course, do not go away, but the size of the project
design document gives the superficial impression that
they have been dealt with. In short, the requirements
of the review and approval process discourage any
attempt to develop a realistic implementation
strategy.[7]

Project Implementation. Once the project is
approved, a new set of actors with different agendas
assumes responsibility for project implementation.
Usually, projects are implemented through a government
entity with the support of a foreign technical
assistance team. Both the donor and the recipient
country appoint people to supervise project
activities. Naturally, the government entity
sponsoring the project wants to control activities.
But because of fiscal constraints, it may be unable to
meet its resource contribution to the project. The
two objectives are incompatible, and compromises must
be made.

Agendas of National Ministries. Frequently,
a number of national-level ministries agree during the
design phase to make significant contributions to
project implementation. Each ministry is interested
in expanding its own power and authority.
Consequently, when asked to play a secondary,
supporting role to some other agency's project, a
ministry may greatly alter or reduce its promised
support. (There is a certain quid pro quo among
agencies--they promise support to others to get their
own projects approved.) In Panama, for example,
serious friction developed between the Ministry of
Planning and Political Economy and the Ministry of
Agricultural Development over their respective roles
in implementing the Tonosi Integrated Rural
Development Project. This friction was largely
responsible for the project's failure.[8]

Regional and local governments also want to
choose project roles that expand their spheres of
influence. The resulting competition among government
entities does not create conditions conducive to
information sharing and collaboration.[9]

Agendas of Foreign Technicians. Project
implementation usually involves assistance from long-
and short-term foreign technicians. The foreigners
are supposed to work with host-country counterparts,

either selected from a central line ministry or hired directly by the project. Chapter 4 addressed the problems of making effective use of foreign technicians, who frequently derive great satisfaction from doing what they are trained to do, such as build roads or conduct agricultural research. Those who are best at getting things done rarely enjoy training others. This problem is compounded when short-term technicians are rewarded for generating paper rather than transferring knowledge. In part, these limitations are the result of personal styles; but they are also the result of incentive structures that guide the technicians' work.

Moreover, the agendas of foreign technicians frequently blind them to the need to ensure that project benefits will be sustained after they depart. The long-term technician who works at his trade until he leaves is rarely motivated to prepare counterparts to take over. By the same token, a short-term technician who spends the last days of his assignment typing a report rather than discussing his work with his counterparts may limit his contribution.

Pressures for quick results often come from the agendas of local political leaders.[10] These pressures only reinforce the foreigners' tendencies to achieve immediate results. Existing incentive structures also motivate foreign technicians to worry more about being criticized for slow results than about their potential failure to build capacity.

Agendas of Host Country Personnel. Problems with recipient-country personnel were addressed in Chapter 3. Briefly, career success often requires organizational allegiance that is inconsistent with the integrated needs of the project. Proximity to the capital city and education in a foreign country pull potential staff away from the project area and can be detrimental to project success.

A number of technical incentives also cause local staff to operate in ways that are not compatible with project objectives. In Indonesia, for example, government workers are given a fixed monthly allotment to maintain and provide fuel for their vehicles. This allotment serves as a disincentive to spend much time in rural areas, where travel is hard on vehicles and requires much fuel. This disincentive--and the resulting lack of rural travel--have impeded the Provincial Area Development Program.[11]

A counterpart hired on a project contract, rather than seconded by a government agency, probably will concentrate on finding another job toward the end of the project. As a result, the counterpart may spend little time seeking ways for project benefits to be sustained when foreign funding is phased out.

Agendas of Donors. Donors frequently insist
on distancing themselves during project implementation, leaving that responsibility to the recipient
country as stipulated by the project agreement.
Frequently, the project coordinator appointed by the
recipient country has neither the information nor the
authority to play an effective trouble-shooting role.
Often, both the donor and the senior officials in the
recipient country know this and tolerate it.

There are few, if any, incentives by which
donor staff are rewarded for finding ways to shorten
or eliminate red tape. As a result, the supervisor of
a donor project can be expected to insist upon literal
compliance with regulations, whatever the costs may be
in project delays and the use of inappropriate
equipment.

Agendas of Beneficiaries. The one group of
people who should have the strongest interest in
project success are the intended beneficiaries.
Unfortunately, there are several reasons why
beneficiaries have not served as effective project
advocates.

First, they usually have not been involved
in the project enough to understand fully what is at
stake and how they might benefit. Instead, they are
often given fragmentary information that comes in the
form of commands. For example, potential beneficiaries might be told that if they change their farming
practices they will qualify for agricultural credit.
Often what they are asked to do does not make sense
economically, however, or they are not adequately
assured that the changes are in their best interest.

Second, intended beneficiaries rarely have
the power to affect the project significantly. Third,
positive effects for some will negatively affect
others. For example, providing any sort of service to
farmers is likely to reduce their dependence on
others. As a result, these other groups may work to
undermine the project.

Thus, many actors with differing agendas are
at work during project implementation. The
unacceptably long delays and egregious mistakes that
occur hardly seem surprising: nobody is in a position
of authority who has, as the chief agenda item, simply
to make the project work. The most important agendas
of key project actors and their likely influence on
the project are highlighted in Table 8.1.

The involvement of numerous actors in
project decision making reduces the chances of getting
anything approved. Even when there is general
agreement that something should happen, the chance

TABLE 8.1
Major Players in the Project Development Game, Their Agendas,
How These Contribute to Implementation Problems

Planner	Agenda	Influence on Project
Donor Agency	Program monies for development activities that comply with substantive directives and procedural regulations	Project design blueprints will be written to obtain approval; as a result, possible implementation problems will will be suppressed
Central Bank/Treasury of Recipient Country	Maximize immediate hard currency inflows, minimize short-run government budget and personnel commitments	High level of project outlays in early years; little concern for project substance or long-term input
National Functional Ministries Lower-Level Government Entities	Each wants to maximize control over resources and how they are used	Little local involvement in project decision making; little cooperation or support for project by government agencies that are not primarily responsible for its implementation
Lower-Level Politicians	Want to take credit for project and ensure that existing power structure remains in place	Distribution of project benefits will reflect desires of existing power structure
Foreign Technicians	Want to perform in their technical area of expertise	Little attention given to capacity building and technology transfer, thereby reducing chances that project benefits will be sustained

TABLE 8.1 (continued)

Planner	Agenda	Influence on Project
Local Project Staff	Want career advancement and quality of life not offered by rural areas	Rapid turnover and absence, which reduces effectiveness of capacity-building efforts and threatens sustainability of project benefits
Intended Project Beneficiaries	Are hesitant to risk existing standard of living for new approaches advocated by project; are concerned about their relationships with other members of local power structure	Resistance to changes advocated by project; project takes longer to achieve sustainable benefits than anticipated
Other Members of Local Population	Threatened by or envious of project activities and benefits	Further delays in getting project to achieve objectives

that it will fail increases dramatically as the number of clearance points increases. Table 8.2 shows different combinations of clearance points and probability of agreement that would cause clearance chances to be less than 50 percent. The table indicates that if the probability of clearance at every point is as high as 80 percent, four clearances reduce the changes for agreement to less than 50 percent. Moreover, in attempts to get approval, requests are frequently changed from their original form or goal.

TABLE 8.2
Clearance Probabilities for Differing Numbers of Clearance Points

Probability of Agreement on Each Individual Clearance Point	Number of Agreements that Reduce Probability below 50 Percent
80	4
90	7
95	14
99	68

Source: J. L. Pressman and A.B. Wildavsky, Implementation: How Great Expectations in Washington are Dashed in Oakland (Berkeley: University of California Press, 1973).

An example of how a large number of clearance points can interfere with effective decision making is offered by the AID-sponsored Arusha Planning and Village Development Project in Tanzania. Although the main AID country office was in Dar es Salaam, direct project supervision rested with a small office in Arusha. Frequently, requests originating in Arusha and relayed to Dar es Salaam were sent to Washington for approval. On the Tanzanian side, the project was working with the regional government, but frequently relatively routine decisions required central government approval. Both sides encountered numerous delays. There were instances in which the request that ultimately reached Washington was significantly different from that made by the project. The forces identified above were very much in evidence.

It is tempting to prescribe "simplicity in project design" as the answer to this problem.[12] Unfortunately, this is not a satisfying solution. Development initiatives, if they are to be sustained, are likely to be complicated and dependent on numerous, different activities that must be orchestrated. Although some techniques permit simplification through partitioning and scheduling discrete activities, the strengths and weaknesses of these techniques must be understood before they can be effectively utilized.

The Role of the Project Manager. Overseeing all of the actors during implementation is the project manager. The toughness of this assignment is intensified because those appointed as managers rarely have received the proper training. Often, project managers come out of one of two molds.

First, there is the colonial manager. This person tends to maintain order, hierarchy, and seniority to the detriment of the project[13]. Second, there is the type of manager who has been characterized as pursuing the Lawrence of Arabia syndrome.[14] This person tends to be autocratic, charismatic, and unable to delegate authority, with the result that when he leaves everything falls apart.

Commonly, project managers emerge as a result of promotion: they are selected because they have distinguished themselves in some technical field of development. They might be road builders, anthropologists, economists, livestock experts, or academics. Unfortunately, training for these fields does not provide the skills to manage large development projects. As a result, project managers rarely have a background that allows them either to anticipate in the most common management problems or to know what to do about them when they arise.

ALLEVIATING THE PROBLEM

It is easy, and perhaps prudent, to be pessimistic about finding ways to alleviate these fundamental problems. The pessimists argue as follows: individuals and institutions understandably have agendas of their own; the only way they will make project success a high priority is to be accountable for it; holding people and institutions accountable for project success requires an acceptable method by which to measure project performance; this measurement technique does not exist, nor is it likely to be developed soon; without such a technique, accountability cannot be ensured, and differing agendas will continue to cause serious implementation problems.

There is much to be said for this line of
reasoning. Anything short of creating accountability
incentives cannot be guaranteed to work. Nevertheless,
several intermediate measures, if taken, could
dramatically improve the existing state of affairs.
Individuals and institutions with differing agendas
will be brought together to design and implement
large-scale development projects. The question, and
challenge, then becomes to find ways to change the
beliefs, attitudes, and behavior of these individuals
and institutions to motivate them to work together
toward achieving project objectives. It is important
to get people to recognize clearly that differing
agendas produce serious problems that can divert the
project from its goals. This initial appreciation of
the potential problems can be followed by explicit
discussions of how to alleviate them.

Changing Donor Incentives

The pressure on donor agency staff to get
projects through the review and approval process
results in inadequate attention to implementation
problems during project design.   The senior executives
of donor agencies and developing countries will
undoubtedly continue to be concerned about the
programming and disbursement of assistance funds.
However, there is a growing recognition that
implementation problems are weakening the effect of
these funds. Even in the absence of sound project
performance measures, the senior executives of these
institutions can give their staffs incentives to focus
more on the implementation aspects of project design
process.
For example, an implementation strategy could be
a required part of the project design paper. At
present, project design papers rarely include more
than an estimate of annual project expenditures, and
many lack even this estimate. Another way to ensure
that implementation plans are included in the project
review and approval process is to establish a separate
committee to review these plans. These reviews might
consider the implementation plans for every project
activity and the methods proposed to carry out the
plans.
An alternative strategy could also be tried.
Instead of sending out large and expensive teams to
design projects, donors and recipients could simply
identify a location for a project. Then a small
project implementation team could be sent out for one
or two years. This team would have limited resources
to engage in local development activities; its main
task would be to work with counterparts to develop an
implementation plan for a far more ambitious project.

This approach could avoid most of the problems associated with designing a project in six weeks or less.

Because of the growing concern with implementation problems, staff should be reallocated to spend more time on these problems. The establishment of an ombudsman office within donor agencies would also help overcome red tape and procedural blockages that now seriously impede implementation efforts.

Actions such as these can have a powerful impact that goes far beyond their direct intent: they can signal to lower-level staff that top management has a new concern for project implementation and that efforts to alleviate implementation problems will be rewarded.

Upgrading Project Management

Below the senior management level, much can also be done at the project site. Again, a good starting point is the project manager.

Development professionals with little or no management experience or training are often chosen to manage projects. In addition to having management skills, a good project manager must know how to deal with people from different cultures, often under conditions of hardship. He or she must make decisions in uncertain conditions. A project manager must deal with bureaucracies. In addition, it would help if he or she were a development expert. Not many persons have all these prerequisites. This means that managerial candidates should be screened for both their strengths and weaknesses and ways should be found to support them in those areas in which they are weakest.

Once selected, project managers must use a variety of techniques to alleviate implementation problems. The effective manager develops a strategy that draws on a number of these techniques to suit the particular project circumstances, including those discussed below.

Involvement. Lower-level project staff have the potential to make a far greater contribution to project success than they have been allowed to make:

> One of the most dehumanizing assumptions ever made is that workers work and managers do not think. When we give shopfloor workers control over their work, they are enormously thoughtful.[15]

This statement emphasizes the advantages of drawing on a valuable information source. There is a

concomitant benefit that is perhaps more relevant:
involving workers in this manner can affect their
agendas; it can lead them to take a proprietary
interest in the project outcome.[16]

There is also evidence that involving development
staff in project decision making can pay other
dividends. In the Gros Morne Rural Development
Project in Haiti, for example, the result was
better-informed decisions and increased dedication and
responsibility on the part of the staff.[17]   In
contrast, the lack of staff involvement in the Tonosi
project in Panama contributed to disruptions that
included physical violence.[18]

Some techniques may be employed to generate a
sense of involvement in development projects.[19]
Members of the project team, for example, might be
convened to acknowledge their differing agendas and
discuss how those agendas relate to project
objectives. The discussions should include the
agendas of the team members as well as of all key
institutional and individual players in the project.
Efforts to coordinate individual aspirations with
those of the project may well result in a positive
outcome for all involved. At the least, this kind of
meeting should generate mutual respect and understanding among team members; it may also lead to the
development of new approaches to tasks that give
workers more satisfaction and fulfillment.

Creating New Incentives. Discussing the problems
of existing agendas can have salutory effects, but
more concrete measures can also be taken. In most
situations, it is possible to specify objectives and
provide rewards for realizing them.[20] Admittedly,
techniques that involve management by objectives must
be applied with discretion: the pursuit of inter-
mediary targets can sometimes become a goal in itself.
Effective use of these techniques, however, could
benefit development projects.

The following actions are useful in restructuring
incentives:

- Provide information on progress toward goals;

- Arrange periodic meetings for open discussion;

- Show subordinates what other employees can do
  and are doing;

- Delegate responsibility early and encourage
  rapid promotion;

- Show personal interest in workers' knowledge,
  skill, and progress;

- Provide informal coaching and teaching on the reasons behind the job;

- Allow some freedom for individual judgment in assigning work;

- Involve workers in broad-range goal-setting for the project;

- Provide access to information as related to job requirements and needs; and

- Create an atmosphere of positive attitude and approval.[21]

Table 8.3 uses a broader frame of reference, providing a useful taxonomy for the initiation of organizational change.

Improving Institutional Linkages. It is also possible to improve cooperation between institutions involved in project implementation. Representatives of supporting institutions can be invited to team meetings. A project newsletter might include information not only on project activities but also on topics of interest to other organizations working in the project area. The newsletter might even praise the activities of cooperating organizations. This approach was taken in the Bicol Integrated Rural Development Program in the Philippines. In addition, the project provided several valuable information services to agencies whose cooperation was needed.[22]

The Use of Outsiders. It is sometimes useful to have outsiders critique project activities as they progress. Outsiders can often identify issues that project staff do not recognize or on which they cannot comment; on occasion, they can also intercede at higher levels on behalf of the project.[23] In situations in which conflicts might arise, it is sometimes useful to provide the outsiders with an element of autonomy that a subcontractor would not have. For example, the Dutch aid organization has contracted directly with research institutes to provide independent critiques of some projects that Dutch engineering firms are implementing. These critiques can provide a useful supplement to periodic project evaluations.

CONCLUSION

Individuals and institutions have agendas that differ considerably from those of the projects they

TABLE 8.3
Comparison of Three General Approaches for Initiating Organizational Changes

Approaches for Initiating Change	Typical Intervention Techniques	Intended Immediate Outcomes	Assumptions about the Major Causes of Behavior in Organizations
Individuals	Education, training, socialization, attitude change	Improvements in skill levels, attitudes, and motivation of people	Behavior in organizations is largely determined by the characteristics of the people who compose the organization
Organizational structure and systems	Modification of actual organizational practices, procedures, and policies that affect what people do at work	Creation of conditions to elicit and reward member behaviors that facilitate organizational goal achievement	Behavior in organizations is largely determined by the characteristics of the organizational situation in which people work
Organizational climate and interpersonal style	Experiential techniques aimed at increasing members' awareness of the social determinants of their behavior and helping them learn new ways of relating to one another within the organizational context	Creation of a system-wide climate that is characterized by high interpersonal trust and openness; reduction of dysfunctional consequences of excessive social conflict and competitiveness	Behavior in organizations is largely determined by the emotional and social processes that characterize the relations among organization members

Source: L. W. Porter, E.E. Lawler III, and J.R. Hackman, Behavior in Organizations (New York: McGraw-Hill), 1975, p. 440.

implement. These agendas may be too powerful to be
overcome. However, explicit attention to the
differences before and during project design and
implementation usually can improve the implementation
record.

One recommendation is that donors and host
countries place more emphasis on the effective
implementation of existing projects than on the design
of new ones. More attention also should be given to
the selection of project managers. If additional
training cannot build needed expertise, new managers
should be recruited for the project team. Finally,
the project staff can be better motivated to make the
project succeed through various techniques, which
should be part of an overall project implementation
strategy.

NOTES

1. William J. Siffin, <u>Administrative Problems and
Integrated Rural Development</u> (Bloomington, Ind.:
Indiana University, Program of Advanced Studies in
Institution Building and Technical Assistance
Methodology, 1979); Jeffery L. Pressman and Aaron B.
Wildavsky, <u>Implementation: How Great Expectations in
Washington are Dashed in Oakland</u> (Berkeley:
University of California Press, 1973); Elliott R.
Morss and Victoria A. Morss, <u>U.S. Foreign Aid: An
Assessment of New and Traditional Strategies</u> (Boulder,
Co.: Westview Press, 1982); L.W. Porter, Edward E.
Lawler III, and J. Richard Hackman, <u>Behavior in
Organizations</u> (New York: McGraw Hill Book Company,
1975); Elliott R. Morss and Robert F. Rich, <u>Government
Information Management: Counter Report to the
Commission on Federal Paperwork</u> (Boulder, Co.:
Westview Press, 1980); Anil Bhatt, "Bureaucracy and
Development" (Ahmadabad, India: Indian Institute of
Management, 1981); Stanley Heginbotham, <u>Cultures in
Conflict: The Four Faces of Indian Bureaucracy</u> (New
York: Columbia University Press, 1975); E. Bardach,
<u>The Implementation Game</u> (Cambridge, Mass.:
Massachusetts Institute of Technology Press, 1977);
Anthony Downs, <u>Inside Bureaucracy</u> (Boston: Little,
Brown and Company, 1967).

2. Siffin, <u>Administrative Problems</u>, p. 11.
3. Albert O. Hirschman, <u>Development Projects
Observed</u> (Washington, D.C.: The Brookings
Institution, 1967), p. 1.
4. Siffin, <u>Administrative Problems</u>, p. 2.
5. A. H. Barclay et al., <u>Evaluation of the Abyei
Development Project, Sudan: Final Report</u> (Washington,
D.C.: Development Alternatives, Inc., 1981).
6. Soesiladi, <u>Technical Assistance for IRD: A
Counterpart's Perspective</u>, IRD Working Paper no. 5

(Washington, D.C.: Development Alternatives, Inc.,
June 1981).
    7. For further documentation of this point, see
Donald R. Mickelwait et al., New Directions in
Development: A Study of USAID (Boulder, Co.:
Westview Press, 1979), pp. 225-231.
    8. David D. Gow et. al., Differing Agendas: The
Politics of IRD Project Design in Panama, IRD Field
Report no. 17 (Washington, D.C.: Development
Alternatives, Inc., June 1981) pp. 1-5.
    9. Morss and Rich, Government Information, chapter
2.
    10. Such pressures can lead to serious
misunderstandings as they did in the Abyei Development
Project and the Maasai Range Management Project. See
George H. Honadle and Richard McGarr, Organizing and
Managing Technical Assistance: Lessons from the
Maasai Range Management Project (Washington, D.C.:
Development Alternatives, Inc., 1979) p. 28; and
Barclay et al., Evaluation of the Abyei Development
Project.
    11. George H. Honadle, The Art of Fishing Is Not
Enough: An Examination of Capacity Building for Rural
Development, (Washington, D.C.: Development
Alternatives, Inc., April 1981), pp. 20-21.
    12. Vernon W. Ruttan, "Integrated Rural
Development: A Skeptical Perspective," International
Development Review 17:4 (1975).
    13. Anil Bhatt, "Bureaucracy and Development," p.
12.
    14. Csand Toth and James T. Cotter, "Learning from
Failure," Focus 3(1978): 27-31.
    15. "The Built-In Obsolescence in Today's System,"
Special Report, Business Week (May 11, 1981), p. 87.
    16. Porter et al., Behavior, pp. 120-128.
    17. "Project Evaluation Summary (80-81)," Gros
Morne Rural Development Project (Washington, D.C.:
Agency for International Development, 1980) pp. 3,
37-38.
    18. David D. Gow et al., Differing Agendas.
    19. Frances J. Korten, "Community Participation:
A Management Perspective on Obstacles and Options,"
Bureaucracy and the Poor: Closing the Gap, eds. David
C. Korten and Felipe B. Alfonso (Singapore: McGraw-
Hill, 1981) pp. 181-200. This topic is dealt with
more fully in Chapter 5.
    20. Paul Mali, Managing By Objectives (New York:
John Wiley and Sons, 1976).
    21. Ibid. p. 190.
    22. Herbert Rubin, "Integrating Rural Development:
The Problems and a Solution" (Bloomington, Ind.:
Indiana University, Program of Advanced Studies in
Institution Building and Technical Assistance
Methodology, 1980), pp. 10-14.
    23. Bhatt, Bureaucracy and Development, p. 27,
ftn. 20.

9
Sustaining Project Benefits

Elliott R. Morss, David D. Gow, and Christopher W. Nordlinger

INTRODUCTION

The principal objective of development initiatives is to generate self-sustaining improvements in
human well-being. In attempting to realize this
objective, project designers and implementers must
confront all of the problems discussed in earlier
chapters.

PROBLEM DEFINITION

Many donor projects are based on the assumption
that the efforts that the donor initiates will take on
a momentum of their own, or at least that the host
government will continue to be support them. Unfortunately, the development landscape is littered with
the remains of projects that died when donor funding
ended. Although the projects were intended to foster
a process of self-sustaining development, they
provided little more than a temporary infusion of
assets, personnel, and services.
Such a case is reported from Kenya, where U.S.
scientists were engaged for almost 15 years in trying
to develop improved varieties of maize. They achieved
some notable successes; but when the last of a series
of American technicians left in the mid-1970s, the
research necessary for further varietal development
came to a halt. No institutional capacity had been
developed to promote and carry out future maize
research. As a result, indigenous maize-breeding
programs remain limited in Kenya, as elsewhere in East
Africa.[1]
One response to the sustainability problem has
been to focus on a project's recurrent costs,
specifically, the potential for the host country
government to assume these costs once donor financing
ends.[2] This attention to recurrent costs is
appropriate, but lack of financing is only one factor

in the disappearance of project benefits once foreign
assistance terminates. Often the magnitude of
recurrent costs reflects a previous decision to base
project activities on public sector mechanisms, rather
than exploring opportunities for private sector
entities to implement the same activities. Large-
scale projects involving salaried government personnel, office facilities, and vehicles carry a heavy
cost burden, and they are difficult to dismantle or
streamline once they are under way.

But there are other dimensions to the sustainability issue besides cost. These include the
political and economic climate in which project
activities take place and the viability and maturity
of the institutions responsible for managing the
activities. Temporary interventions can compensate
for weaknesses in either of these areas--for example,
input subsidies or high-level political sponsorship
may be applied, or external technical assistance may
be supplied to fill a personnel gap--with a positive
but short-lived effect on project implementation.
These measures do not necessarily solve the sustainability problem, however. They may in fact exacerbate
it, by concealing the seriousness of constraints that
must be eventually dealt with and that will be less
tractable once external resources are no longer
available.

REASONS FOR THE PROBLEM

The reasons why benefits are not sustained are
complicated and interwoven. The dearth of good
studies on impact indicates that the problem has not
been well documented. Until recently, sustainability
was not a major consideration in project design, and
the factors that could affect it were rarely examined
in the planning process. These factors fall under
three broad headings:

- Financial factors, including the use of
  excessively costly technologies and service
  delivery systems in a setting in which
  revenues are insufficient to cover future
  financial needs;

- Political and economic factors, including the
  macroeconomic policy environment in which the
  project is set and the degree of political
  support that the project receives; and

- Institutional factors, including inadequate
  organizational and individual capacity to
  carry on project activities without outside
  assistance, lack of incentives to produce

sustainable project benefits, and insufficient project duration.

Financial Factors

Revenue Generation. Financial sustainability is most obviously an issue when revenues are insufficient to cover the costs of project activities. Revenue collection is not a function of most development projects, although many of them are intended to increase beneficiaries' incomes. Even when this objective is met, the net increase may be too small to provide a margin for covering the costs of project services; and even when a sufficient margin exists, there may be serious political and administrative obstacles to recapturing costs. As a result, self-financing activities are more the exception than the rule.

Profitable activities are rarely identified and implemented with public sector financial support. One can argue that public monies should not be committed to activities that might be sustained by private sector interests. But there is no reason why public projects, once established, could not be handed over to private sector firms for continuation. Unfortunately, most project designers do not have the incentive or the vision to plan projects that make money.

In addition, projects are frequently designed in areas in which there is no immediate prospect for financial viability. In these cases, a component analysis, as described below, could help determine long-run prospects for sustainability.

Excessive Costs. In both public and private sector projects, the delivery of goods and services is usually required for benefits to be sustained. Yet often these goods and services are more expensive than they should be, given the availability of local resources. These high costs reduce the possibility that the goods and services will continue to be provided after outside funding stops.

Several factors combine to create this high-cost bias in development projects. Project planners sometimes design projects as though donor funds and host country resources were unlimited. There are other causes as well: domestic political pressure in donor countries to use foreign assistance to promote exports may result in capital-intensive designs; [3] developing country officials frequently express a preference for sophisticated capital goods; [4] and technicians trained in the developed countries are likely to select familiar methods and equipment. Often these technicians prefer to experiment with

state-of-the-art technologies rather than use mundane,
yet proven, methods. One AID evaluation, for example,
observed that a rural roads project in the Philippines
emphasized engineering that required capital-intensive
construction and excluded community participation.
The availability of excess U.S. equipment at
artificially low prices reinforced this bias.[5]

Excessive project costs have stemmed from this
failure to tailor delivery systems to local conditions, and from trying to do too much too soon. Sometimes projects are launched on a larger scale than is
justified, given the level of technological understanding that exists.[6]

There is abundant evidence that donor agencies
give greater attention to the short-term task of
transferring resources than to the long-term one of
reducing dependency on outside funding. A review of
project documentation suggests that this dependency
either is overlooked or is addressed in an unrealistic
fashion. For example, a team reviewing a feeder roads
project in Jamaica concluded:

> . . . There is no evidence to indicate that the
> [USAID] Mission either called for a sufficient
> maintenance plan to start with or that it
> followed the issue sufficiently in recent
> years.[7]

In a similar vein, a review of an integrated rural
development project in Jamaica found:

> The Project Paper thus failed to address the
> question of sustainability . . . . No thought has
> been given to making the transition from being a
> resource-intensive project to one dependent
> solely on normal government input and local
> organizational capacity . . . .[8]

A study of recurrent cost financing in the Sahel
concluded pessimistically:

> It is, of course, unrealistic to hope these pro-
> jects could finance such activities out of
> commodity sales proceeds after the donors have
> left. Nor is it any more realistic to believe
> that the government will agree to allocate
> sufficient funds to maintain such activities at a
> level superior to the average level of service
> available in the country as a whole.[9]

Similar sentiments are offered in an AID country
development strategy statement for one Sahelian
country in fiscal year 1983:

. . . We can estimate . . . that the potential
total recurrent cost burden on the Government of
Upper Volta (GOUV) budget (of USAID-sponsored
projects) will easily surpass 70 million 1980
dollars . . . by 1987, or almost a quarter of the
projected national budget. The GOUV will clearly
not be able to finance all of these costs.[10]

Why were these obvious dependency problems
ignored? First, little was known about how to deal
with them. Second, donor agencies have traditionally
rewarded staff for programming monies. Only in the
last few years have comprehensive studies shown the
contradiction between short-run disbursement goals and
incentives and long-run considerations of financial
self-sufficiency at the project level.

Recent analyses of the recurrent budget implications of development support are a step in the right
direction. A tendency exists, however, to view the
recurrent expenditure obligations as a fixed
proportion of development expenditures. Table 9.1
summarizes indicative measures of the recurrent
expenditure implications of various development
outlays. These coefficients can be useful for
predicting recurrent costs; also actions can be taken
to reduce the recurrent budgets associated with
development outlays. One recommendation, reflected in
several of the essays in this volume, is for larger
investments in capacity building--both institutional
and individual--at the opening stage of projects,
along with longer time frames for the projects
themselves. Over time, this appears to offer the
prospect of reducing the need for recurrent budget
support.

Political and Economic Factors

Political Factors. Political support for a
project at various levels of government is necessary
for the continuation of benefits. In the absence of
this support, a project can be undermined by changing
objectives or diversion of resources to other activities. When broad political support does not exist,
host country officials who favor the project may be
unwilling or unable to commit themselves to it.

Even when the government is committed to a
project, political pressure may still undermine long-
term success. For example, the need for quick,
visible results may cause the introduction of
expensive service delivery systems or technologies
that cannot be sustained in the long run. Strong
political support and publicity in the early stages
may delude project staff into thinking that this

TABLE 9.1
Illustrative Summary of the Recurrent Expenditure
Implications of Projects as a Proportion of Investment

Activity	Annual Recurrent Expenditures Required As Percent of Investment Outlay
Forestry	0.04
General Agriculture	0.10
Livestock	0.14
Rural Development	0.08 - 0.43
Agricultural Colleges	0.17
Polytechnics	0.17
Primary Schools	0.06 - 7.00
Secondary Schools	0.08 - 0.72
Universities	0.02 - 0.22
District Hospital	0.11 - 0.30
General Hospital	0.183
Rural Health Centers	0.27 - 0.71
Urban Health Centers	0.17
Housing	0.03
Manufacturing	0.01
Feeder Roads	0.06 - 0.14
Trunk Roads	0.03

Source: Peter Heller, "The Underfinancing of
Recurrent Development Costs" Finance and Development,
March 1979.

backing will always exist. in contrast, political
pressure may promote the continuation of a project
that is not achieving its stated objectives or
providing benefits to its target population.

The political environment influences all aspects
of project design and implementation: choice of
technology, time allowed for implementation, structure
of recurrent cost financing (including the willingness
to institute user fees or increase local government
revenues), and related macroeconomic policies.
Political considerations may also favor introduction
of a government subsidy program that takes on a life
of its own and cannot be terminated.

Often, apparent political support for a project
veils the basic motive of obtaining the maximum amount
of foreign assistance. An Indonesian official, for
example, notes that national-level officials who are
responsible for negotiating project agreements with
donors are primarily interested in the amount of
foreign aid that will be provided. Lower-level
government officials, who have had little or no
involvement in the design process, are then made
responsible for implementing the projects.[11]

Various forms of political conflict also affect
the shape of development efforts. In some cases, the
ruling powers discriminate against geographic areas or
groups. Sometimes, a general tendency toward exploi-
tative policies within a country dims prospects for
the sustainability of any project initiative that
favors the poor.[12]

Bureaucratic lethargy may also pose a passive
threat to projects spanning several levels of government. In the case of one Indonesian project, a
management analyst observed:

> The political support for the Provincial Area
> Development Project (PDP) is strong at higher
> levels (provincial leadership), but diminishes as
> one moves down the administrative chain through
> district, subdistrict, and village levels. The
> understanding of and commitment to capacity-
> building objectives weakens while, at the same
> time, dependence on special PDP-supported
> personnel increases.[13]

Yet there are examples of benefits being sustained when active political support is forthcoming.
The evaluation of a successful rural roads project in
Thailand indicates the importance of political
commitment:

> There seem to be three major reasons for this
> success. First, the commitment to the principles
> of the Accelerated Rural Development (ARD)

program of Prasong Sukhum and the serendipity of
his dual foothold in the Thai civil service as
deputy director of the budget and as secretary
general of ARD during its formative years.
Second, massive AID grants provided all the
equipment for the provincial construction
programs under authority delegated to the
governors and funded the training of the required
technical staff at all levels, from engineers to
mechanics, site foremen, and machine operators.
Third, and perhaps most significantly in the long
run, the project was from the very beginning a
Thai undertaking, heavily dependent on AID
technical and financial assistance, rather than
an AID project supported with interest, good
wishes, and some counterparts by the Thai
government.[14]

Economic Factors. Developing countries typically
suffer from such economic problems as lack of domestic
savings, internal demand and supply imbalances, and
hard currency shortages. In turn, these difficulties
have led to slow growth, unemployment, and high rates
of inflation.[15] In many cases, governments choose
to, or are forced to, address these problems in ways
that inadvertently hamper project implementation and
thus reduce impact.
Macroeconomic policies can impede project
implementation in many ways. Domestic price ceilings
that are designed to promote exports and maintain low
food prices in urban areas often lower or eliminate
the incentives for farmers to increase production or
adopt agricultural innovations. Artificially low
producer prices can also inhibit investments in the
agricultural sector and discourage middlemen from
delivering critical services. This was observed in
the case of a Sahelian country:

. . . It lacks individuals ready to exploit
opportunity for profit, particularly in the
sphere of commercial activity. The discussion
thus comes back to the issue of producer price
policy: an inadequate producer price does not
leave room for a sufficient margin to convince
traders to participate on a regular basis in the
distribution and demonstration of new inputs.[16]

A flourishing parallel market for agricultural
products can be another consequence of these policies.
In the Niger Cereals Production Project, a seed multiplication effort was failing because of the low
official price and high parallel market price for
grain. Rather than deliver the new seed to the
project, the farmers who contracted to mass produce

the seed sold it for twice the official price to
buyers smuggling it into Nigeria, where it was
consumed rather than planted.[17]

Import tariffs or quotas to foster domestic
production of agricultural inputs also may increase
production costs and lower incentives to produce.
Foreign exchange controls may restrict the importation
of critical inputs such as fuel. In the North Shaba
Rural Development Project in Zaire, for example,
rehabilitation of the roads has been delayed on
several occasions for precisely this reason.

Government monetary policies can also have a
constraining effect on activities at the project
level, especially with regard to credit availability
in rural areas. Similarly, budgetary commitments from
the central government that are made early in the life
of a project may later be cut back as a result of
macroeconomic problems. The effects on project
implementation, in terms of funding for host country
personnel, administrative support, and transport, may
be severe.

National policies often favor the public sector
and parastatal bodies over private sector initiatives.
Public sector entities often become overextended and
perform poorly. Moreover, they frequently lack the
incentives to ensure the cost-effective provision of
services. Thus, where profitable investment opportunities exist, the encouragement of private sector
initiatives may more effectively ensure benefit
sustainability.

Institutional Factors

A third set of sustainability issues exists at
the institutional level. Three critical factors
influencing the prospects for long-term success are
the capacity of organizations and individuals charged
with major roles in a project, the incentive structure
in which those organizations and individuals operate,
and the amount of time allowed for strengthening
capacity and improving incentives.

Inadequate Capacity. Few project ideas are so
compelling that they will perpetuate benefits without
institutions equipped to carry them forward. Usually
these institutions, either public or private, will
have to be created or strengthened during the implementation process. When external assistance ends, the
institutions must be able to continue certain activities, often with fewer resources than before. Institutional capacity, therefore, is a key element in
project sustainability.

While increased attention has been paid to the
financial prerequisites for sustaining project bene-

fits, relatively little emphasis has been placed on the organizational and individual prerequisites to sustainability.

These issues are rarely raised in the design process. For example, an evaluation of the Haitian-American Community Health Organization (HACHO) Project concluded:

- No provision was made for HACHO to be transformed from a private agency with foreign donors and local government support to an autonomous government agency coordinating regional services. The government's policy has been to treat HACHO as a device for ensuring foreign donations, rather than trying to transform it into a regional development agency;

- No linkages were developed with any government departments. As a result, there was no government of Haiti commitment to the idea of HACHO as a regional coordinator of either governmental services or non-governmental programs; and

- HACHO staffers regarded it as an American agency and, as a result, were demoralized by the funding cutoff.[18]

Institution building was popular in the early days of U.S. bilateral foreign assistance. However, by the mid-1960s, the boom had subsided, owing largely to the belief that institution building had become an end in itself, rather than a means to achieve observable development benefits. This disillusionment contributed to the dramatic change in development strategies adopted in the early 1970s by both AID and the World Bank. The new strategies focused on providing direct assistance to the poor populations of developing countries through area-specific projects.

However, these projects have underemphasized the need for institutionalization, institution building, and training. For example, the creation of special project management units, divorced from the regular host government bureaucracies, has been a favored implementation approach of the World Bank. This bypass technique is often justified on the grounds that existing institutions are too weak to implement planned activities within the required life of the project.

Autonomy avoids many of the bureaucratic constraints that can hinder a project, and it can ensure the donor greater accountability over the resources and funds spent. Moreover, project management units, because they are independent of the

country's civil service system, can pay higher
salaries and attract more capable staff than would
otherwise be possible. Often, however, these
individuals come from regular ministerial positions
where they are also needed. Thus, a temporary device
initially created to bypass institutional weaknesses
may actually exacerbate them. Moreover, because the
management of these projects is bureaucratically
isolated, they have little effect on the performance
of permanent institutions.[19]

A case in point is provided by the North Shaba
Rural Develoment Project, a maize production effort in
Zaire. Because Zaire's Department of Agriculture
(DOA) lacked the institutional capacity to implement
the project, a separate management unit was created.
After five years of implementation, and despite
success in raising agricultural production, an
evaluation concluded there were few indications that
the project had strengthened DOA's capacity. The
government had failed to meet many of its commitments
to the project, as demonstrated by:

- The continuing cash flow problem--without U.S.
  counterpart funding, the project would have
  ended long ago;

- DOA's inability to recruit personnel for key
  slots; and

- The project's inability to incorporate
  existing DOA personnel in North Shaba into the
  project.[20]

Even when institutionalization is a stated objective, the desire for short-term results often
overrides efforts to build capacity. This problem was
apparent in the early stages of the Indonesia
Provincial Area Development Program (PDP) in the
province of Nusa Tenggara Timur.[21] At each
successive level below the provincial leadership,
dependence on special PDP-supported personnel
increased. Below the district level, there were few
institution-building activities. At the village
level, project personnel made little effort to work
with or through existing local organizations,
primarily because they are seen as weak and peripheral
to the financed activities.

A project may emphasize training individuals at
U.S. universities, even though it is less expensive
and more effective to bring technicians to the
developing country to provide applied training based
on local conditions. Moreover, when efforts focus
entirely on individuals, rather than on organizations,
there is less chance that performance will improve.

Providing on-the-job training to counterparts offers no guarantee of dramatic results. Part of the problem is the scarcity of qualified host country staff to serve as counterparts to technical assistance personnel. Also, it is easier to measure impact by counting kilometers of road built than by assessing changes in organizational behavior. As a result, technical assistance staff tend to focus on producing immediate results rather than on building capacity.

It is legitimate to ask whether the virtual cessation of institution-building grants was not a serious mistake, particularly when comparing development progress in Asia (the recipient of many earlier institution-building grants) with that of Africa.[22] The reconsideration now being given to institutional capacity building is reflected in statements by AID Administrator Peter McPherson, and in a recent AID policy paper on institutional development.[23]

Inappropriate Incentives. For project benefits to be sustainable, incentives are necessary to elicit the support of both individuals and organizations. These incentives were conspicuously lacking in Lesotho, where the Thaba Bosiu Rural Development Project was handicapped by farmers' failure to increase agricultural production beyond subsistence levels. Many of these farmers worked in South African mines, where in a few days they could earn as much as in an entire year of farming. Most of them farmed only the minimum amount necessary to maintain their landholding rights. The project's efforts to have farmers invest more time and resources to increase production were ineffectual.[24]

The presence of incentives for other groups of potential beneficiaries may be even more crucial. Local merchants, for example, may see a project-supported cooperative as a threat. When these merchants are the major providers of rural banking services, they often have the leverage to undermine the development of the cooperative. In this situation, the merchants are unlikely to support either the implementation efforts or the post-project cooperative activities.

In contrast, local merchants played a crucial marketing role in the North Shaba project in Zaire. Many perceived long-term benefits from an expansion of maize production and took advantage of the incentives offered, such as storage of marketing materials, truck rental, and provision of fuel. One particular merchant, who also happened to be a prominent national politician, consistently attempted to exploit his position for short-term gains. The project resisted his pressure to acquire privileges and services not available to his competitors.

Incentives also must influence host institutions to do what is necessary to deliver benefits. Otherwise, bureaucratic opposition to project activities may develop. This was the case with an AID-funded agricultural research project in Thailand. The Ministry of Agriculture and Cooperatives initially supported the creation of a regional agricultural research center, even though it was to be housed in another agency. But when ministry officials began to view the center as a competitor for resources (budgets, personnel, and external aid), their initial enthusiasm for the project waned. As long as AID controlled funds for training, research equipment, and commodities, open political maneuvering against the project was restrained. Once AID's involvement ended, the opponents of the center moved openly against its budget and mandate, and it was subsequently stripped of most of its resources and authority.[25]

Insufficient Duration and Inadequate Phasing. Timing problems interfere with the implementation and sustainability of development projects. Project designers and managers can address some of these problems more readily than others. More realistic project planning, for example, can improve the time phasing of project inputs and activities. In contrast, development planners have less influence over the political and administrative realities of the project approval process.

In practice, project designers often underestimate the amount of time necessary to initiate sustainable development processes, even without procedural delays. Expatriate technicians need time to develop working relationships with their counterparts, if their aim is to transfer problem-solving capabilities. It is not easy to generate and introduce ideas to increase income and productivity, and it frequently takes many years to create local institutions capable of sustaining development activities.

ALLEVIATING THE PROBLEM

Dealing with Financial Factors

If project benefits are to be sustained, some substitute will normally have to be found for the finances provided by foreign aid. The alternatives should be considered during project design, and a strategy to develop local funding should be part of the implementation process. The alternatives to external financing are considered below.

Limiting Costs. In recent years, much research has been done on low-cost delivery systems for developing countries.[26] These studies give a general picture of how to structure these systems.

Involving the beneficiary population in project design and implementation also produces cost savings. Frequently, the population's knowledge of the local situation will permit cutting corners with resultant direct savings. And, if the beneficiary population is interested enough in the service to make a direct commitment to it, cost problems can be alleviated.

Central Government Funding. Central governments clearly have a role to play by assuming some share of responsibility for funding local development, but central funding for development should always be weighed against the value of local initiative and control.

An initial assessment should be made to gauge the willingness and ability of an institution to shoulder the financial burden of project activities. In the North Shaba project in Zaire, for example, the national agency responsible for construction and maintenance of primary roads was put in charge of maintaining the secondary roads constructed by the project. Yet that agency had neither the mandate nor the resources to maintain secondary roads. Because its weaknesses were not scrutinized at an early stage, it was assigned a role it could not fulfill.

User Charges. User charges are based on the premise that persons benefiting from a service should pay at least a portion of the cost. The objection to this premise is that it leads to withholding benefits from those who need them most but are the least able to pay. One response may be to structure charges to allow for differing payment abilities. An example, notable for user participation in setting the rate structure, is described in an evaluation of a Tunisian water project:

> Of the five project sites visited in Kairouan, we found three in which the users had taken collective action to establish variable rates to pay diesel fuel costs. Fees were assessed by household on a monthly basis ranging from 500 millimes ($1.25) per month to nothing for those too poor to pay. In one community a local organization grew out of an existing series of quarterly clan meetings and provided basic types of assessment, collection, and accounting of water use fees.[27]

Although good arguments can be made for introducing user charges to cover project operation and
maintenance costs, the difficulties should also be
recognized. In the short run, beneficiaries may be
unwilling to cover the costs of the activity. Often,
this is because it is too early for them to perceive
the long-term benefits. When free services have
traditionally been provided, introducing user fees may
be extremely difficult. Or, if the service is one of
several self-help endeavors, the very poor beneficiaries may be unable to contribute to it. Even though
the individual projects may not charge excessive
rates, their collective effect will strain limited
resources.

Failure to introduce user charges is an important
policy decision in itself. Without them, the entire
financial burden of the service will eventually fall
on the government. Thus, the burden will be borne by
all taxpayers, whether or not they benefit from the
service.

Local Government Funding. Inputs from lower-
level governments can also help plug a revenue gap.
Frequently, project services are provided within a
limited area and local government revenue collections
are a more appropriate source of financing than the
central government budget. A local tax or fee may be
fashioned to provide the needed funds.

Yet local government revenue-generating
opportunities are limited in many rural areas of the
developing world, often because local jurisdictions do
not make full use of their taxing authority. Even
when they do, the taxes generated are more likely to
go to administrative costs than to development
activities. More common are various revenue-sharing
agreements in which decentralized control of rural
development is still dependent on national grants. In
these cases, decision making may reside closer to the
ultimate beneficiaries, but many of the constraints
and limitations of central funding remain.

Funds that are raised locally are usually a more
reliable source of support than those allocated (but
not always disbursed on time, or in the full amount)
by central treasuries. Nepal, for example, replaced a
traditional national land tax with a panchayat
development and land tax. Arrangements called for 55
percent of the proceeds to be retained and controlled
by the village panchayat, 10 percent by the district
panchayat, and 35 percent by the national government.
The result has been greater self-reliance on the part
of the villagers in development matters, a "significant increase" in revenues, and a closer feeling of
partnership between people and government.[28]

Local Participation. The importance of using beneficiary resources such as voluntary labor has been well documented.[29] The use of available local resources is one way to reduce the costs of delivering goods and services. Beneficiary involvement in planning and implementation may produce additional cost savings. Frequently, their knowledge of the local situation will prevent wasteful and inappropriate schemes designed by outsiders. Also, when the beneficiary population is interested enough in the project activities to make direct commitments to them, cost burdens are shared and sustainability enhanced.

Private Sector. In some cases, private sector involvement has advantages similar to those of local participation. Some project activities may be turned over to the private sector, perhaps a private firm or a group of small-scale farmer beneficiaries, when the activities reach a certain point. Many agricultural production projects, for example, are designed to provide a series of services to farmers, such as the supply of improved seed, fertilizer, and credit, followed by the purchase and marketing of cash crops. There are many opportunities to help local entities build their capacity to perform these functions, although this potential is often not tapped.

Planners should consider a basic issue before turning to the private sector for project support: would a private firm use project resources to serve the same set of beneficiaries and to the same extent? In some cases, private profit-making firms are more efficient than public concerns, but they seldom have the same objectives. In the end, the revenue source selected to cover the recurrent project costs will depend on the characteristics and environment of the individual project.[30]

Dealing with Political and Economic Factors

Political and economic policy constraints are extremely difficult for project managers to alleviate, especially when the managers are outsiders. Project managers have three options when facing these constraints. First, they may decide to do nothing about them. This is a logical decision when the costs involved in attempting to alleviate the constraints outweigh those entailed in working within them.

Second, project managers may decide to expend project resources to overcome the problems. This could involve, for example, allocating staff time to expedite delivery of commodities or to influence policy decisions, establishing closer relationships with key decision makers, or taking on additional

responsibilities that were not part of the project
design.

Third, project managers may change the project's
basic implementation strategy to circumvent the
constraints. This may involve changes in target
groups, geographic areas of concentration, project
components, and outputs. These changes are most
effective when project staff, government officials,
and community leaders are all involved in the process.
Similarly, it may be effective for project staff to
document the deleterious impact of political and
economic policies on project implementation. Staff
could, for example, offer seminars to government
officials and local community leaders dealing with
issues such as where the project is going and what is
needed to get there.

Staff members in the North Shaba project in Zaire
combined some of these strategies to introduce an
element of economic rationality into the regional
government's pricing policies. Each year, project
representatives participated in meetings with the
regional governor, merchants, and other interested
parties to establish the official price for maize. As
the project matured, they were able to present
increasingly solid economic data to justify increases
in the farm-gate price. For several years in
succession, however, their recommendations were
dropped in favor of a lower, more politically
acceptable price level, intended to limit escalation
of food costs in the urban areas. As a result of this
experience, the staff spent a considerable amount of
time lobbying with the governor, the heads of the
parastatals, the U.S. consul, and other groups in the
region. A major breakthrough took place in 1983, when
the Zairian government abandoned price controls on
maize produced in Shaba.

Dealing with Institutional Factors

Organizational and Individual Capacity. Points
to consider when examining the capacity of organizations and individuals to sustain project benefits are:

- The history of the organization in building
  its stock of resources;

- The organization's performance in managing the
  human and material resources at its disposal;

- The technical skills of its staff members and
  their ability to keep abreast of new devel-
  opments; and

- The problem-solving practices of the staff.[31]

Indicators of the first point include the number of staff members available to perform critical functions, the budget and growth of an organization over recent years, the amount and type of equipment it possesses, and the quality of its facilities. An organization's ability to attract resources is also judged by staff members' ongoing efforts to identify and tap alternative sources of funds. These include revenue-raising activities to obtain supplementary funding.

The second point addresses the ways in which the stock of resources is used to achieve the organization's goals. The size of the administrative staff relative to the task at hand is one indicator of the capacity for management. In some cases, a project may suffer from a bloated, top-level management structure. In other cases, inefficient use of resources, past or present, may indicate potential problems. For example, the amount of slack time in the use of equipment or vehicles or idle staff time may be symptomatic of underlying procedural, incentive, or leadership problems.

A third aspect of institutional capacity is the technical competence of the personnel within the organization. One element of this is the current level of expertise. A second is the ongoing preparation for future needs, such as the percentage of personnel being trained to fulfill future project needs and the amount of on-the-job training being provided by technical assistance personnel.

The fourth component, which is harder to measure, is the ability of the staff and the organization as a whole to anticipate and solve problems. One indicator is the ability of staff to assess objectively the strengths and weaknesses of their program and its performance. That is, do they admit error and learn from it, or do they hide failure and repeat mistakes? Another indicator is the amount of attention project personnel have given to sustaining benefits after the project ends.

Lessons have emerged from attempts to develop local capabilities. A recent study of experiences in five Asian countries suggests that organizations go through a three-phase learning process. First, they learn to be effective in their internal tasks and in their interactions with the environment. Second, they learn to be more efficient in those activities. Third, they expand their capabilities either by entering new geographic areas or by engaging in new functions.[32]

Another study in Latin America concluded that successful organizational strengthening invariably originates with a single function requiring cooperation and using skills already possessed by organization members.[33] And a study of 36 development projects in Africa and Latin America found that risk sharing was an important factor contributing to self-sustaining development.[34]

Experiences such as these suggest that the process of organizational capacity building includes the following components:

● Risk sharing;

● Involvement of multiple organizational levels;

● Collaborative implementation styles;

● Demonstration of success; and

● Emphasis on learning.[35]

This process of capacity building can be facilitated by careful decentralization. In many countries in which it has been implemented, decentralization is seen as a way to improve the efficiency of planning and management within the central bureaucracy.[36] The evidence indicates that controlled decentralization, which strikes a viable balance between the center and the periphery, can stimulate the local capacity to plan, implement, evaluate, and sustain development activities.

Incentives. Although the provision of resources is necessary to sustain project benefits, it is not alone sufficient. Incentives are also necessary to ensure that the organizations and individuals play their roles in delivering benefits. Incentives affect the potential for sustainability at three levels: organizational, staff, and beneficiary.

At the organizational level, the importance of adequate, timely support (such as the number of personnel and the amount of resources allocated to the project) cannot be overemphasized.

At the individual level, project staff rarely stay with a given project or activity for long. Frequently, staff members are transferred by their agencies to other areas or regions, to meet changing government priorities and commitments (such as staffing new donor-funded projects). From the perspective of the individuals, the benefits of being assigned to an agency's national headquarters or to a major urban center are greater than those gained from working in a remote rural area. Moreover, the incentives to continue in a job (such as the support received and the possibility of promotion) usually decrease once the project officially ends.

Finally, the project beneficiaries themselves must also have incentives to continue the activities that benefit them. Ultimately, they have a larger stake in sustainability than anyone else.

Incentives should be structured to support sustainability objectives. Agricultural extension agents involved in organizing farmers' groups, for example, might be judged on the capacity of those groups rather than on such mechanistic measures as the number of groups formed or how often they meet. Moreover, evaluation standards should allow for differences in the agents' operating circumstances. For some agents, working with existing groups may be more appropriate than forming new ones. Whatever incentive system is established, the agents must understand it if they are to respond to its intent. That is, the staff must have verifiable tasks to perform with specific targets, dates, and standards of performance. And these criteria must be effectively communicated so that supervisor and staff expectations are consistent. Communication will often be enhanced if performance standards are set jointly in light of shared commitment to a goal such as sustainability.

Particular attention should be given to improving the procedures for project evaluations. For most donors and host governments, the horizons of evaluation are narrowed by the need to monitor funds expended and physical construction completed, usually according to centrally defined criteria. Two negative consequences result. First, the measurement of staff performance is linked to short-term production targets, no matter what institution-building rhetoric may surround the project. Second, evaluation becomes an end-of-project control exercise rather than an ongoing part of the development planning process.

When careers, budgets, and donor reimbursements are keyed to these monitoring exercises, little incentive exists for project staff to invest time and money in the slow, experimental process of building capacity in local administrative systems or among beneficiaries.

Timing and Phasing. Achieving sustainability will take much longer than expected. Three procedures can make timing and phasing to achieve sustainability more realistic:

- A larger up-front investment, particularly for training;

- The development of reasonable implementation plans that are regularly and systematically updated; and

- The monitoring and evaluation of project activities against these plans and the incorporation of the results into the updated implementation plans.

Project benefits will not be sustained unless local organizations and individuals have the capacity to manage project activities. A consistent finding is that more time and training are needed to accomplish this transfer than are usually allowed. Also, allowing adequate time and training in the beginning can help reduce future recurrent budget requirements. There are thus reasonable grounds for claiming that a larger up-front investment may help to achieve sustainability.

Every planning decision should be made in light of the need to achieve sustainability. Among the questions that should guide project planning are:

- What benefits are to be sustained?

- What resources will be required to fund long-term benefits?

- If external resources will be required, what will be their source?

- Do benefits justify external investment in light of realistic constraints and opportunity costs?

- Is there existing administrative capacity to maintain essential systems?

- Are permanent aspects of service delivery being institutionalized in the government structure?

- How much of the requirement for both financial and administrative inputs can be met locally?

The answers affect the selection of activities for a development project and the manner in which those activities are organized.

Finally, periodic evaluations are usually scheduled throughout the life of a project and beyond. If those evaluating a project for benefit sustainability want their recommendations to be followed, they must accomplish three tasks:

- Make project staff and decision makers sensitive to the importance of benefit sustainability and aware of limitations in their
  current approach;

- Obtain some consensus among the principals,
  such as project administrators, host
  government staff, and donors, concerning an
  adequate approach to improving benefit
  sustainability; and

- Develop a revised implementation plan with a
  detailed strategy for overcoming those
  specific impediments to benefit sustainability
  that were identified.

In undertaking these tasks, evaluators have three
major tools: written reports, discussions with key
decision makers, and workshops.[37]

CONCLUSION

    This final chapter has summarized the most
crucial problem looming over the implementation of
most rural development projects. Sustainability is
the bottom line for measuring implementation efforts.
The link between the two can easily be obscured by
short-run considerations, particularly the desire of
project managers to achieve visible results, both in
terms of financial disbursements and meeting specified
targets. The project design process tends to
exacerbate the problem; it is rare that the
continuation of benefits in the post-project period is
seriously examined as an issue during design.
    Although sustainability is a multifaceted issue,
some guidelines for addressing it can be identified.
These points, which have been explored in greater
depth in the preceding chapters, provide a framework
for more realistic planning:

- Begin by considering what ought to be
  sustained. Activities are not the same as
  benefits, although some activities may have to
  continue to support benefits. A careful distinction should also be made between temporary
  project-related outputs and intended long-term
  benefits.

- Plan projects in light of sustainability
  criteria. What resources will be required
  when external funding ends? Will project
  systems be self-supporting, or will a
  permanent subsidy be required? If external

resources will be required, what will be their
source? This source should be identified
before the subsidized activity begins.

- Ask whether project benefits justify the
  investment of external resources in light of
  realistic constraints and opportunity costs.
  Projects often represent funds in search of
  activities. Continuation, in contrast, repre-
  sents activities in competition for funds. A
  host government may see many activities, for
  good reason, as a poor investment, even though
  they were once approved for donor funding.

- Pay particular attention to recurrent cost
  obligations. These costs lack glamor but are
  essential to maintain benefits. A common
  error is to ignore depreciation of initial
  capital facilities such as buildings and
  equipment.

- Identify needs for organizational and administrative infrastructure. Does the administrative capacity exist (or is it being developed)
  to maintain essential systems to continue
  benefits? Training, capacity building, and
  resource control are key elements.

- Emphasize local resources and management
  inputs. Local control reduces dependency and
  increases predictability of inputs, especially
  if local inputs are used. Local government
  revenues, user charges, or direct beneficiary
  investment are possibilities.

- Create incentives for staff to focus on
  capacity building. Pressure for short-term,
  visible results should be balanced by recognition for efforts that build sustainable
  systems.

- Use evaluation as a planning tool. Link
  criteria to sustainability objectives and use
  evaluation as an ongoing information source to
  support redesign and other adjustments.
  Involve local staff and beneficiaries in the
  information system.

- Remember that a central aspect of development
  is to increase the capacity of people to solve
  problems for themselves. Judge development
  initiatives accordingly.[38]

Project planning and implementation are more art than science. Although empirical knowledge can improve the planning and implementation process, the ability to be creative with that knowledge is crucial. The viewpoint expressed throughout this book is that development is a gradual, evolutionary process that assumes considerable uncertainty. This approach is characterized by continual openness to redesign and changing circumstances.[39] Without this openness and flexibility, the attainment of sustainability will remain as elusive as ever.

NOTES

1. Kitale Maize: The Limits of Success, Project Impact Evaluation Report no. 2 (Washington, D.C.: Agency for International Develpment, May 1980).

2. Jerome Wolgin, "AID Policy Towards the Recurrent Cost Problem in Less Developed Countries," draft (Washington, D.C.: Agency for International Development, July 1981); Clive Gray and Andre Martens, "Recurrent Costs of Development Programs in the Countries of the Sahel: Analysis and Recommendations" (Report prepared for the Working Group on Recurrent Costs of the Comite Permanent Inter-Etats de Lutte Contre La Secheresse Dans Le Sahel Club du Sahel, Washington, D.C., August 1980).

3. Gray and Martens, "Recurrent Costs," p. 288.

4. Daniel Dworkin, Rural Water Projects in Tanzania: Technical, Social and Administrative Issues, Office of Evaluation, Special Study no. 3 (Washington, D.C.: Agency for International Development, November 1980), p. 12.

5. Irwin Levy et al., The Philippines: Rural Roads I and II, Project Impact Evaluation Report no. 18 (Washington, D.C.: Agency for International Development, 1981), p. 15.

6. Gray and Martens, "Recurrent Costs," pp. 11-12.

7. Robert J. Berg et al., Jamaica Feeder Roads: An Evaluation, Project Impact Evaluation Report no. 11 (Washington, D.C.: Agency for International Development, November 1981), p. 12.

8. Paul R. Crawford, Implementation Issues in Integrated Rural Development: A Review of 21 USAID Projects, IRD Research Note no. 2 (Washington, D.C.: Development Alternatives, Inc., May 1981), p. 120.

9. Gray and Martens, "Recurrent Costs," p. 79.

10. Upper Volta Country Development Strategy Statement 1983 (Washington, D.C.: Agency for International Development, 1981).

11. Soesiladi, Technical Assistance for Integrated Rural Development: A Counterpart's Perspective, IRD

Working Paper no. 5 (Washington, D.C.: Development Alternatives, Inc., June 1981).

12. AID Auditor General, "Problems in Implementing the Integrated Development Project in Liberia," Audit Report no. 80-82 (Washington, D.C.: Agency for International Development, July 16, 1980), pp. 3-5.

13. Jerry Van Sant et al., Supporting Capacity-Building in the Indonesia Provincial Area Development Program, IRD Field Report no. 12 (Washington, D.C.: Development Alternatives, Inc., February 1981), pp. A15-16.

14. Frank J. Moore et al., Rural Roads in Thailand, Project Impact Evaluation Report no. 13 (Washington, D.C.: Agency for International Development, December 1980), p. 6.

15. For a good discussion of the reasons for these policies, see Robert H. Bates, Markets and States in Tropical Africa: The Political Basis of Agricultural Policies (Berkeley: University of California Press, 1981); Accelerated Development in Sub-Saharan Africa: An Agenda for Action (Washington, D.C., The World Bank, 1981).

16. Gray and Martens, "Recurrent Costs," p. 77.

17. Marvin P. Miracle, "Evaluation of Some Aspects of Niger's Cereal Project," Project Evaluation Summary, Annex VI (Washington, D.C.: Agency for International Development, 1979), p. 5.

18. Glenn R. Smucker and Jacqueline N. Smucker, "HACHO and The Community Council Movement," Project Evaluation Summary 30-2 (Washington, D.C.: Agency for International Development, January 1980).

19. Annual Review of Project Performance Audit Results (Washington, D.C., The World Bank, 1980), p. 46.

20. Five Years Later: Progress and Sustainability in Project North Shaba (Washington, D.C.: Development Alternatives, Inc., March 1982), pp. 11-12.

21. Jerry Van Sant et al., Supporting Capacity-Building, pp. A15-16, 21-22.

22. Uma Lele reported to the 1981 International Development Conference her feeling that institution-building efforts in India seem to be paying off. Dr. Lele points to both production gains and, perhaps of even greater interest, the important lobbying role for agriculture that the strengthened institutions play.

23. "Institutional Development," Policy Paper (Washington, D.C.: Agency for International Development, March 1983).

24. "Project Evaluation Summary--Thaba Bosiu Rural Development Project (80-4)" (Washington, D.C.: Agency for International Development, 1980).

25. "Asia Bureau Agriculture and Rural Development Conference: Summary of Proceedings and

Recommendations" (Washington, D.C.: Agency for International Development, 1981).

26. For example, The World Bank and AID have completed studies on what the per unit costs of different low-cost delivery systems should be.

27. Ross E. Bigelow and Lisa Charles, Tunisia: CARE Water Project, Project Impact Evaluation Report no. 10 (Washington, D.C.: Agency for International Development, October 1980), p. 9.

28. Bruns Knoll, "Popular Participation in Nepal" (Paper prepared for the U.N. meeting for Experts on Popular Participation, 1978), p. 10.

29. Elliott R. Morss et al., Strategies for Small Farmer Development, 2 vols. (Boulder, Colo.: Westview Press, 1975), 1:36-100.

30. Elliott R. Morss, Paul R. Crawford, and George H. Honadle, Toward Self-Reliant Development: A Guide for Evaluating the Sustainability of Project Benefits (Washington, D.C.: Development Alternatives, Inc., May 1982), pp. 1-31.

31. For a further discussion of capacity-building definitions, see Beth W. Honadle, "A Capacity Building Framework: A Search for Concept and Purpose," Public Administration Review 41:5 (September/October 1981): 575-580.

32. David Korten, "Community Organization and Rural Development: A Learning Process Approach," Public Administration Review 40:5 (1980): 480-511.

33. Judith Tendler, Evaluation of Small Farmer Organizations: Ecuador and Honduras (Washington, D.C.: Agency for International Development, 1976).

34. Elliott Morss et al., Strategies, vol. 1, pp. 36-100.

35. George H. Honadle, Fishing for Sustainability: The Role of Capacity-Building in Development Administration, IRD Working Paper no. 8 (Washington, D.C.: Development Alternatives, Inc., June 1981).

36. G. S. Cheema and D.A. Rondinelli, "Decentralization and Development: Conclusions and Directions," Decentralization and Development: Policy Implementation in Developing Countries, eds. G.S. Cheema and D.A. Rondinelli (Beverly Hills: Sage Publications, 1983) pp. 271-315.

37. For further elaboration see Morss, Crawford, and Honadle, Toward Self-Reliant Development, pp. 33-38. See also J.P. Hannah et.al., Sustaining Rural Development: A Guide for Project Planners, Managers, Evaluators, and Trainers (Washington, D.C.: Development Alternatives, Inc., 1984).

38. George H. Honadle and Jerry Van Sant, Implementation and Sustainability: Lessons from Integrated Rural Development (West Hartford: Kumarian Press, forthcoming).

39. C.F. Sweet and P.F. Weisel, "Process Versus Bluepoint Models for Designing Rural Development Projects," <u>International Analysis for Development Projects</u>, eds. G. Honadle and R. Klauss (New York: Praeger, 1979), pp. 127-145.